NINETY SECONDS AT
ZEEBRUGGE

NINETY SECONDS AT ZEEBRUGGE

ZEEBRUGGE

The Herald of Free Enterprise Story

IAIN YARDLEY

Dedicated to the memory of my mum, Barbara, my
dad, Joseph, my cousin Lee, friends Natalie and Neil,
and all those who are gone long before their time.

First published 2014

The History Press
The Mill, Brimscombe Port
Stroud, Gloucestershire, GL5 2QG
www.thehistorypress.co.uk

© Iain Yardley, 2014

The right of Iain Yardley to be identified as the Author
of this work has been asserted in accordance with the
Copyright, Designs and Patents Act 1988.

British Library Cataloguing in Publication Data.
A catalogue record for this book is available from the British Library.

ISBN 978 0 7524 9783 9

Typesetting and origination by The History Press and Printed in Malta by Melita Press
Production managed by Jellyfish

CONTENTS

ACKNOWLEDGEMENTS

There are a great many people who have contributed to the book in one way or another. I am extremely grateful to them all. This is by no means an exhaustive list, but I would particularly like to thank the following.

All the survivors, relatives and people who participated in the rescue and care in the aftermath, and who contributed to this book.

Pascale Bernard for French translations, and Christine Geyer for German translations; Inge Desmedt for being a better Belgian detective than Hercule Poirot ever could be (sorry for the chair); Jackie Badger and Paul Wightman for turning a blind eye when I should have been working; Nicola Dobson for proofreading; Eamonn Farrell for saving my laptop from the bin; Rebecca Sawbridge, Janet Johnson and Peter Southcombe for filling in the blanks; Patrick Mylon for his encouragement; Gary and Tracy Sexty, Steve and Jan Booth, Caroline Mylon, Mike Peach, Chris Mooney, Eric Sauder, Brian Hawley, Lynne Hawkins, Paul Rogers and Katie Beresford for their support and enthusiasm; and to Mick Goddard for his day-to-day support, reading, driving me around and putting up with my many tantrums.

Finally, I would like to thank Chrissy McMorris and Amy Rigg at The History Press for having enough faith in me to make this book a reality.

1

BEGINNINGS

Players

Former artillery officer Captain Stuart Townsend was fed up with being charged exorbitant fees to transport his car across the English Channel by steam packet boats. He decided to start his own shipping line and, after talks with the Automobile Association (AA) and Royal Automobile Club (RAC), Townsend Brothers Ferries Ltd was in business by 1928. The coal ship *Artificer*, capacity fifteen cars and twelve passengers, was chartered, and a shipping link between Dover and Calais was established in June of that year. The service became so popular that it became permanent in 1929. Owing to the demand, the *Artificer* was replaced by the *Royal Firth*, followed by a former minesweeper, renamed the *Forde*, in April 1930.

The *Forde* could carry thirty cars and 168 passengers. For six years, cars were lifted by mobile ramp onto the *Forde*, until a strike by Calais dockers and crane operators in 1936. For the duration of the strike, the *Forde*'s stern rails were removed and cars driven onto the ship via makeshift platforms. Although strictly a 'one-off' temporary arrangement, it undoubtedly gave Townsend the idea for roll-on/roll-off (RORO) ferries for the future. It wasn't until fifteen years later, in 1951, that drivers were allowed to drive their own cars onto a ferry, when the *Forde* was replaced by a converted frigate.

The first RORO berths in Dover and Calais were installed in 1959. Then, in 1962 the frigate was superseded with the introduction of Townsend's first purpose-built car ferry, *Free Enterprise I*, on the Dover–Calais route; so named because Townsend were celebrating their private sector status and breaking away from a state-run service.

The second purpose-built ferry, the *Free Enterprise II*, became the first British registered, seagoing, drive-through ferry with bow and stern doors, upon its introduction in 1965. A year later, *Free Enterprise III* was introduced onto Townsend's second route, Dover–Zeebrugge.

Frank Bustard was an apprentice and friend of fellow Liverpudlian, J. Bruce Ismay, who was chairman of the White Star Line (WSL). Ismay survived the sinking of the *Titanic* in 1912. Bustard was awarded an OBE for services during the First World War, after which he became the passenger traffic manager for the WSL. In 1934 – the same year that the WSL merged with Cunard – Bustard set up the Atlantic Steam Navigation Company Ltd.

Bustard wanted to set up a line offering a moderately priced transatlantic passenger service between Europe and the United States. He was unsuccessful in acquiring surplus Red Funnel Line vessels and, despite approaching Vickers Armstrong for two new ships, the government was reluctant to see a new company operating in competition to Cunard White Star. The Bank of England refused him a loan.

The looming Second World War put paid to his intentions – Bustard was called up to the army reserve. During the war, he was present at the trials of landing craft loading and unloading vehicles on the beach at New Brighton, and after the war, in 1946, Bustard concentrated on vehicle-carrying ferries to operate on the short sea routes across the North Sea.

Atlantic used chartered converted tank carriers, *3519*, *3534* and *3512*, to start a service from Tilbury to Hamburg, predominantly for freight. Twelve years after being founded, Atlantic sailed its maiden voyage in 1946, using the converted *3519*, now renamed *Empire Baltic*. Two years later, the world's first commercial RORO service was established by Atlantic when the *Empire Doric* sailed between Preston, Lancashire and Larne.

A service to Rotterdam was established in 1960, also mainly for freight, and this lasted for six years. Atlantic's Felixstowe–Rotterdam services, developed in 1964, and Felixstowe–Antwerp service in 1965, had led to the demise of the Tilbury operations. All services from Tilbury ended in 1968 as they became uneconomical. In 1968, Atlantic became part of the National Freight Corporation. The seven ships which had been its fleet all gave a nod to ships of the White Star Line.

Southampton based Otto Thoresen Shipping Company was set up in 1964 by a group of Norwegian investors. The Norwegian registered company operated RORO Services between Southampton and Cherbourg and Southampton and Le Havre. Thoresen Car Ferries, a wholly British-owned subsidiary company, was formed as an agent for these RORO services in the UK. Services began that same year with the ferries *Viking I* and *Viking II*. A year later these two ferries were joined by *Viking III* and *Viking IV*. The ferries were so named to reflect the company's Scandinavian origins.

These three major players eventually became the same group in 1971 after a series of acquisitions by George Nott Industries, formerly Monument Securities, incorporated in 1935. Monument acquired all the capital of Townsend in 1959. It then acquired Otto Thoresen in 1968, liquidating the company but retaining its subsidiary Thoresen Car Ferries. With the merging of the two major ferry companies, George Nott changed its name to European Ferries Ltd (EFL). With the takeovers of the

Stanhope Steamship Company Ltd, Monarch Steamship Company Ltd and Atlantic in 1971, the company used the name Townsend Thoresen to market their combined ferry services.

There were two types of traffic carried by EFL – freight and tourist. Freight comprised commercial road haulage vehicles and the importing and exporting of new cars. The vessels assigned to carry predominantly freight were mostly multi-purpose RORO ferries or purpose-built ferries. Tourist traffic was classified as foot passengers, cyclists and accompanied vehicle traffic, including the drivers and passengers of cars, coaches and caravans. Tourist traffic also included both pleasure and business travellers. These journeys were mostly undertaken by multi-purpose RORO or passenger and vehicle ferries.

The decline of cross-Channel overall profits in 1980 was blamed on the fall in freight due to the recession, competition and a blockade by French fishermen. EFL, on the other hand, enjoyed a 50 per cent rise in tourist traffic in 1980 compared to the previous year, with the Dover routes accounting for almost all shipping profits that year.

In the late 1970s the competition for cross-Channel passenger and cargo traffic in the Dover Straits was fierce. Most of the British short sea routes were still under the control of Sealink, the state-owned railway fleet. Freight completion had become crucial as firstly railway-owned hovercraft had grabbed a large share of the passenger market. Although a joint UK–French Government-backed scheme to build a channel tunnel between the two countries had been cancelled in January 1975, it was still anticipated that a tunnel would eventually be built, which would take an even bigger part of the passenger market. In answer to this, Sealink had planned to monopolise the market by building new ferries with double-decker vehicle decks, primarily for the Dover–Calais route, the shortest crossing between the United Kingdom and the European continent, and also the most profitable. By operating vehicles on one ferry at a time, it would ensure a high freight capacity, which was vital for business. When it learned of Sealink's plans, the Townsend Thoresen response was immediate.

Debut

Traffic figures for Dover–Zeebrugge in 1980 showed that 1,560,881 passengers had utilised the service, whilst vessels had carried 291,683 accompanied and 158,368 freight vehicles. Clearly, the Dover–Zeebrugge run was becoming very popular.

It soon became clear that the four vessels on the Dover–Calais service would need to be replaced due to the increasingly high tourist demand. EFL introduced the '*Spirit* Class', three brand new, state-of-the-art ferries that would offer their passengers higher speed, greater passenger and vehicle capacity, increased catering facilities and a faster turnaround. The three new ships would sail under the orange livery of Townsend Thoresen. The '*Spirit*' vessels were designed to compete against the higher operation speeds and fast loading and unloading hovercraft capabilities. Plans for the new ships showed that up to 1,325 passengers and 350 cars could be carried, with the car capacity reduced according to the number of freight vehicles, coaches or caravans taking their place.

To finance the three ships, EFL undertook additional borrowing, an investment of £51 million, which was planned to cover anticipated traffic levels throughout the 1980s. EFL claimed no more shipbuilding commitments would begin until the future of the short sea shipping market could be ascertained. Although they didn't know it, the *Spirit* vessels would become the last ever commissioned by EFL.

Townsend Thoresen's in-house naval architect, Wallace Ayres, designed three ferries that would be faster and more spacious, capable of making five return trips per day each, and outperforming any rivals. Ayres' ideas were unlike anything ever constructed. Ship design is usually governed by national and international regulations, with new ships making only small changes to existing designs. Ayres aimed to design ferries that would be capable of making Dover–Calais journeys of just seventy-five minutes, compared to Sealink's one-and-a-half-hour crossings, with the emphasis on carrying freight.

Townsend Thoresen placed orders for three new ferries with their favoured shipbuilders, Schichau Unterweser AG, in Bremerhaven, West Germany. To power these faster ferries, each would be propelled by three 8,000bhp, 12ZV 40/48 internal combustion diesel engines, supplied by Sulzer Bros of Winterthur, enabling a speed of 24 knots. The three engines and propellers would provide excess power to make up time for any delays. Electrical power was provided by three internal combustion driven alternators with a capacity of 1,063Kva. Emergency power was provided by diesel driven alternators with a 515Kva capacity.

The triple screw RORO passenger/vehicle ferries would weigh 7,951 tonnes gross. They were 131.9m (433ft) long, 121m (397ft) between perpendiculars and 22.7m (74ft) wide. Each of the ferries would have a capacity of 1,325 passengers and 350 cars.

The centre of gravity was kept low to enhance stability, by reducing the distance from the waterline to the lower vehicle deck on G-deck amidships. The superstructure was narrowed, with the eight lifeboats stowed in recesses on either side of the upper vehicle deck on E-deck. On C-deck, which was primarily passenger accommodation, the superstructure sloped up and outwards to maximise the space inside, then sloped back inwards again on B-deck, where the crew accommodation was situated. This gave the ferries a dynamic, modern and angular appearance.

Further innovation was in the design of the bow and stern doors, which opened up 'clam shell' style, the doors not protruding beyond the ship itself, offering both operational and safety enhancements. It appeared that Ayres achieved his vision of making these new-design ferries much different from Sealink's ferries.

For the purposes of nautical terms, 'weathertight' applies to doors and bulkheads (walls) that are only required to prevent the ingress of water from the side exposed to the weather. 'Watertight' refers to doors and bulkheads that are to keep in or keep out water. Of an all-welded steel construction, the ferries each had eight decks, above the tank top level and double bottom:

H-deck (below waterline) – sub-divided by thirteen watertight bulkheads and nine watertight doors for access between compartments. Four watertight flats were devoted to passenger accommodation (drivers' cabins) and store spaces. The compartments between the watertight bulkheads were devoted to the steering gears (bow and stern), main and auxiliary machinery, fuel and fresh water storage, sewage plant, ballast tanks and voids.

G-deck (main deck) – a through-vehicle deck enclosed by a full superstructure. There was a single watertight door at the stern with a clear opening of 8.5m x 4.73m (28ft x 15ft) and double watertight doors at the bow with a clear opening of 6m x 4.9m (20ft x 16ft).

F-deck – mezzanine level car deck with ramps leading down to each side of G-deck. An emergency generator was situated starboard side of F-deck. The remaining space on the port and starboard side was crew accommodation.

E-deck – upper vehicle deck, through-deck enclosed by side houses with weathertight doors at both ends, and a clear opening of 6m x 4.9m (20ft x 16ft).

D-deck – suspended vehicle platform on a mezzanine level with ramps leading down to E-deck.

C-deck – main passenger accommodation with cafeteria, drivers' restaurant, bar, duty-free and perfume shops, observation lounge, bureau de change and information office and galley.

B-deck – passenger lounge, Blue Riband restaurant, Salad Bowl cafeteria, bar, TV lounge, crew and officer mess rooms on port side, ratings mess room and crew accommodation on starboard.

A-deck – officers' accommodation and radio room.

Wheelhouse – on mezzanine level between decks A and B.

The access between A and G-decks was by means of staircases at the port and starboard sides at the aft end, midships and forward. The staircase at the forward went all the way from top to bottom down to H-deck.

There was more than enough lifesaving equipment for everyone on board. Eight lifeboats, four of them motorised, were stowed in the external recesses of E-deck. They could carry 630 people. Sixteen inflatable life rafts with Marine Escape Systems (MES) were installed on each side of D-deck. An inflatable slide or chute, similar to those used when evacuating aircraft, enabled passengers to slide straight into waiting life rafts. These rafts could hold a total of 672 people. Other lifesaving devices aboard included seven 'throw over' life rafts (175 people), five buoyant apparatus (70 people), twenty lifebuoys and 1,525 lifejackets (including 139 for people weighing under 32kg).

In Bremerhaven, Schichau Unterweser was able to construct each ferry in only one year. The first completed was the *Spirit of Free Enterprise*, launched on 21 July 1979 (Yard No. 2279) and entered into service in January 1980, nine months before Sealink's *St Anselm* was completed at Belfast's Harland And Wolff shipyard. The *Spirit of Free Enterprise* became the first passenger carrying ferry with a double vehicle deck with simultaneous double loading on the Dover Strait. Townsend Thoresen marketed the route as their 'Blue Riband Service' after the ferry claimed the record for the fastest Dover–Calais crossing by conventional ferry.

On 12 December 1979, the *Herald of Free Enterprise* was launched (Yard No. 2280) and the *Pride of Free Enterprise* on 31 May 1980 (Yard No. 2281). The *Pride* was launched in a publicity stunt for BBC television's *Jim'll Fix It* programme.

The *Herald* was delivered to Townsend Car Ferries Ltd in Dover in May 1980, its official number 379260. The International Maritime Organisation (IMO) gave it the new ship number 7820405. Its call sign was GBJV. Apart from the name on her side, the *Herald* could be distinguished from her two sister ships by the paintwork. The bridge roof was white, along with the vents and lift housing and there were black surrounds to the bridge windows. On 29 May, the maiden voyage of the *Herald* took place between Dover and Calais.

In September 1980, John Hendy wrote in *Sea Breezes* (Vol. 54, No. 417) about a record-breaking crossing of the *Herald* on 10 July, during a Force 8 gale. The new ferry had beat by one minute the personal best record held by the *Spirit*, making it from Dover to Calais in fifty-four minutes and fifty-three seconds.

In early December 1982, the *Herald* suffered damage in a collision with a pier. It necessitated a visit to her builders in Bremerhaven at the end of January 1983 to replace plating on the starboard side and to straighten out deck plating. Two years later she went for refit. In February 1987, it was announced that during the refit planned for early March, a dedicated video lounge and additional passenger cabins would be fitted in the area of the present B-deck bar. The refit was scheduled to take place after completing her Zeebrugge–Dover voyage on 6 March.

The lower vehicle deck bow doors of the '*Spirit* Class' sister ships were built by Cargospeed on Clydeside, Scotland, which ceased trading in the 1980s. They were designed to swing horizontally on vertical axes on radius arms. They were stowed against the ship's sides when open, and when closing, the doors would meet at the centre point.

On a normal crossing, once all the vehicles had been loaded and the car ramp raised, the deck officer placed a chain across the width of the lower vehicle entrance, between the inner and outer doors. He then used a walkie-talkie to communicate to the bridge that vehicle loading was complete. Called 'Neatstow', the sets of two doors, internal and external, were set 12ft apart, on the vehicle deck of the ferries. Both of the doors were fitted with bells and flashing red warning lights.

The doors did not swing freely; they were held in place by a pneumatic power system run by two power packs. When the power packs were activated, the doors were operated from a horizontal control panel. A lever would be inserted. The external doors were slid shut first in a 'clam-shell' fashion, followed by the internal doors, which were watertight. The door control was moved to the 'open' position, raising the door clear of the latches. Then the latch control was moved to 'off' and the locking pin control moved to 'out', then it was held. The door control was then moved to 'close' and held again until the doors were fully closed. The warning bell was then cancelled.

Closing both sets of doors took around four minutes. The red warning light then turned green to indicate the doors were in place and secure. Additional lights indicated that the locking pins were locked vertically into the deck in the 'in' position. All the controls were then returned to the neutral position. Finally the telephone to the left of the control panel was used by the assistant bosun to report to the bridge that the bow loading doors were locked.

This four-minute door-closing procedure did not happen on the night of 6 March 1987.

Takeover

In December 1982, the EFL vehicle ferry *European Gateway*, sailing in Townsend Thoresen livery, collided with Sealink's *Speedlink Vanguard* off Felixstowe. Consequently, the ship flooded and capsized, with the loss of six lives. This would not be the last time a Townsend Thoresen ferry would end up on its side in the North Sea.

The chairman of the EFL board was MP for Dorking, Keith Wickenden. In July 1983, whilst piloting a reconditioned Mark XIV Supermarine Spitfire aircraft, Wickenden was killed when the plane he and his brother Allen had lovingly rebuilt over the previous three and a half years crashed after taking off from Cranfield, Bedfordshire. Wickenden had often been described as the 'guiding star' of European Ferries. His successor was EFL Managing Director Ken Siddle.

After the death of Wickenden, two Canadian shareholders of Noramco, a company involved in EFL's property interests, were appointed to the board of EFL that same month. In 1985, P&O Group sold their cross-Channel interests to EFL. By 1985, over 2.5 million vehicles per year were passing through Dover's nine berths. The operating income of EFL that same year was £45.5 million.

A year later, in January 1986, P&O struck a deal with the board of EFH (European Financial Holdings: a company owned by Noramco) obtaining all of Noramco's interests in European Ferries (EF). P&O purchased 50.01 per cent of EFH from Noramco for £35,920,549. Noramco retained 49.99 per cent. Effectively, P&O were now the major owners of European Ferries.

The P&O chairman since 1983, Sir Jeffrey Sterling, was appointed to the board of European Ferries with Managing Director Mr Bruce MacPhail as his alternative. A P&O representative was appointed to the board of EF International, EF's property holding company in the US. The appointment of P&O's chairman to the board had been a precondition of its purchase of Noramco's interests.

July 1986 saw the resignation of Ken Siddle as chairman of the EF board. He had always been uncomfortable as the public face of EF. Siddle's successor was Geoffrey Parker. Siddle remained with EF as its managing director until September 1986, when he resigned from the company, along with another executive director, Mr J.R. Parsons.

The resignation of Siddle and Parsons on 10 September 1986, happened at the same board meeting in which EF had to face the reality that P&O considered itself able to influence the policy of European Ferries. Takeover of the EF group was now inevitable, and Sir Jeffrey Sterling was instrumental in putting forward the action.

Other ferry operators using British ports had concerns over a P&O–European Ferries merger. Sealink and Brittany Ferries were worried that it would lose P&O's Ferrymasters contract if P&O decided to keep the lucrative business 'in-house'. Societe Nationale des Chemins de fer Francais (SNCF) expected to have to 'rationalise' its workforce.

Port operators were also expressing concerns. Harwich Harbour Board believed that a merger was likely to produce a decline in the port industry. Ipswich Port Authority thought that North Sea Ferries would transfer its services to Felixstowe, forcing the closure of its RORO terminal with the immediate loss of 100 jobs from a workforce of 430. Ken Weetch, MP for Ipswich, considered that a merger would have an adverse effect on employment in the area due to anticipated rationalisation.

The Road Haulage Association (RHA) feared that a merger would limit the choice of sea carriers, again down to probable rationalisation. The Automobile Association (AA) thought that there would be a possible reduction in competition.

The Transport and General Workers' Union (TGWU) were convinced that a merger would have serious adverse effects on its members' employment in P&O ports, particularly at Ipswich, Tilbury and Southampton. The TGWU agreed with Ipswich Port Authority, that relocation by North Sea Ferries to Felixstowe would result in job losses. The Transport Salaried Staff's Association (TSSA) also expressed concerns that rationalisation would lead to job cuts at Southampton and Felixstowe, where P&O and European Ferries were in direct competition. The Department of Transport noted that a merged company would not only be a large ferry network, but also a large deep-sea-liner trading fleet, thus making it dominant in the UK shipping industry and swallowing up a large proportion of the profits earned by the industry. The Ministry of Defence said that rationalisation would lead to fewer ferries, and pointed out that there would be some loss of flexibility to meet its defence needs.

The concerns of other ferry operators, ports and their staff were at their height when P&O Group took over Townsend Thoresen European Ferries on 5 December 1986.

Notoriety

The White Star liner *Titanic* sank in 1912, with the loss of almost 1,500 lives. The disaster raised numerous questions about maritime safety, prompting the British Government to host the International Convention of Safety of Life At Sea (SOLAS), adopted in January 1914 but not enforced until July 1915 due to the outbreak of the First World War. Lessons learned from the disaster and incorporated into the regulations included the provision of lifeboats for every person on board. It does seem incredible that, at the time, people were willing to travel on a ship knowing that in the event of an emergency, there was no way to escape.

After the United Nations was formed in 1948, it was realised that an international treaty was essential to promote maritime safety. The Intergovernmental Maritime Consultative Organisation (IMCO) was established at a conference in Geneva. The IMCO changed its name to the simpler 'International Maritime Organisation' (IMO) in 1982.

There had been concern expressed about the safety of RORO ferries ever since they were introduced. ROROs are unique in design. On conventional ships, transverse bulkheads — many watertight — create a series of separate holds within the hull. If the hull is breached in any way, these bulkheads will control or delay the inrush of water, enabling the ship to stay afloat long enough for the evacuation of everyone on board or to stop it sinking at all.

In 1977, the 'free liquid surface effect' became a major concern at the Subcommittee on Subdivision, Stability and Land Lines. The effect of loose water due to leakage, fire extinguishing water and such, in enclosed spaces — such as a vehicle deck of a RORO ship extending the ship's full length with no internal bulkheads — could lead to serious consequences. Internal drainage was offered as an answer to this problem. Adopted by the IMO in 1983, it was incorporated into the 1989 SOLAS amendments.

The whole point of a RORO ship is to be able to drive onto the ship at one end and off again at the other. To install transverse bulkheads or walls on these 'through' decks would be a major obstacle to vehicles. Even though ROROs are fitted with watertight collision subdivision, along with bulkheads in the engine room below the freeboard (uppermost watertight) deck, as prescribed by SOLAS, water can still rapidly enter the huge vehicle decks.

Fire can spread quickly in the same manner. Potential risks on ROROs include the cargo access doors at the stern and bow, and side doors, equipped on some ROROs. On older ferries, these access doors can become misaligned or damaged over time, particularly when the doors also double as access ramps.

The shifting of cargo on vehicle decks can affect the stability of a RORO ferry, causing it to list. A sudden inrush of water due to hull damage or watertight door failure can be even more rapid, endangering a ship. Stability can also be affected when the ferry has a very large superstructure which can be prone to buffeting by wind and bad weather.

Cargo-only ROROs often have cargo access doors very close to the water-line. A sudden list caused by the movement of cargo, for example, could push the entrance to the vehicle deck below the waterline. A sudden inrush of water would follow, resulting in an increased list, leading to possible capsize. Listing can cause cargo to break loose, if not stowed or secured correctly, and the crew of the ship are not usually aware of how individual lorry trailers are packed, which may worsen the problem. A heavy load breaking loose could cause others to follow suit, resulting in an increased list, or the spilling of dangerous substances as well as hull and structure damage.

There are several ways in which cargo can prove dangerous on board a RORO ferry. Designed for the road, every vehicle is packed differently, with no universal method in place. Different forces are present, and the lorries often lack securing points; a lorry's suspension system could cause lashings to disengage and a toppling trailer could dislodge nearby units, causing a domino effect. Loading conditions cannot be arranged properly, since lorries and trailers arrive for the journey in random order. A spot check of loaded vehicles leaving RORO terminals in Sweden showed that 45 per cent of the cargo on trailers was partly or completely unsecured.

The first RORO ship lost at sea was the *Princess Victoria*, which sank with the loss of 133 lives on a 1953 voyage from Belfast. Heavy seas had battered in the stern door, exposing the vehicle deck to the open water.

In 1966, the Greek ferry *Heraklion* was lost off Piraeus after heavy seas caused it to sink, with 264 fatalities. The *Heraklion* was not strictly a RORO, but it did have a large car deck with transverse bulkheads. The deck flooded when a vehicle deck broke loose and smashed the loading hatch.

The *Wahine* capsized at the entrance to Wellington harbour, New Zealand, in 1968, after water flooded the vehicle deck when the ship grounded in a storm. Fifty-three people died.

The cargo RORO, *Hero*, was lost partly due to a leaking stern door in 1977 in the North Sea, with one crewman dying of injuries while being rescued by helicopter.

The *Princess Victoria*, *Heraklion* and *Hero* were all lost in heavy seas; other ROROs have been lost in port or sheltered waters.

The *Straitsman* sank in Melbourne in 1974, with two deaths, after the crew, una-ware that the stern door was still below the waterline, opened the door as the ship approached land.

In 1977, the *Seaspeed Dora* listed and capsized while berthed at Jeddah, after cargo shifted and water seeped through an open bunker door.

The problematic design features of RORO ferries were still being mulled over by international maritime safety bosses when the *Herald of Free Enterprise* began its fateful journey in March 1987.

2

DISASTER

Departure

The *Herald of Free Enterprise*'s normal route was between Dover and Calais, which was the shortest and most profitable sea crossing between the UK and continental Europe. Vehicles could normally be loaded onto the three ferries in the *Spirit* class simultaneously through G-deck (the main vehicle deck) and E-deck (the upper vehicle deck) using double deck link-spans (ramps) in use at both ports.

However, there was no double deck link-span at Zeebrugge, and all vehicles had to be loaded one deck at a time. Also, the ramp at Zeebrugge did not extend to the higher E-deck, due to the high spring tides. This was common knowledge to the *Herald*'s crew and was overcome by 'trimming' the ferry, on this occasion filling the ferry's forward ballast tanks to allow it to sit deeper in the harbour, bringing the E-deck in line with Zeebrugge's single deck link-span. This allowed both vehicle decks to be loaded, albeit one after the other, and therefore taking longer than it would have on the *Herald*'s normal run. To prepare for this, ballast tank No. 14 (deep tank, capacity 268m³) began to fill about two hours before the *Herald* was due to arrive in Zeebrugge. This added an additional 268 tonnes. This was followed by the filling of No. 3 (port double-bottom ballast tank, capacity 42m³ – an additional 42 tonnes).

Officially 8,874 tonnes, it was estimated that an additional 250–270 tonnes in modifications, as well as overweight vehicles, made the *Herald*'s displacement 9,250 tonnes, 3ft lower in the water and 'significantly overloaded' at departure, for the conditions in which she set sail.

The *Herald* was designed for the Dover–Calais run, with the intention of rapidly disembarking passengers and vehicles, and embarking the same without delay for the return journey. Because of the fast turnaround to keep within tight schedules, the ships on this run were manned by a complement of a master, two chief officers and a second officer. However, this was reduced by management for the Zeebrugge run as it was believed that, because the journey time was four and a half hours, there was more time for the officers to relax. Therefore, for this journey, there was only one chief officer, Leslie Sabel, aged 40. Sabel's duty on this trip was to oversee the loading of the vehicle decks, to ensure that Assistant Bosun Mark Stanley closed the doors and to be on the bridge at departure. It seemed that as soon as the last vehicle was aboard, Chief Officer Sabel would have to leave the vehicle deck. He would not be there to see if the doors were closed. Sabel couldn't be in two places at once.

E-deck, the upper vehicle deck, was loaded first, using the single ramp. Then G-deck, the main vehicle deck, began to load.

The timings hereon use the twelve-hour clock for the UK (e.g. 1 p.m. or 1 a.m.) and the twenty-four-hour clock (e.g. 1300hrs or 0100hrs) for Continental Europe. Western Europe is generally one hour ahead of UK time, known as GMT+1. For example, if an event occurred in Belgium at 1400hrs, it would be 2 p.m. in the afternoon in Belgium, but 1 p.m. in the UK.

There were three shift patterns in operation aboard the *Herald*. On this sailing, the eighty-strong crew belonged to 'C' Watch. Their working day had begun at 11.30 a.m. when they joined the ship at Dover. The ship sailed at 12.30 p.m. for Zeebrugge, and the crew would leave the ship when it arrived back in Dover at 10.30 p.m. that same night.

Lorries (commercial transport) were the first vehicles to drive onto the *Herald*, followed by coaches, cars and foot passengers. That evening, for the return journey, lorry driver Paul Roberts, driving for Interox of Warrington, Cheshire, had actually driven onto the *Herald*, but was told to reverse off because the vehicle deck was full – they could not squeeze him on. One who did get on, was 39-year-old lorry driver Brian Gibbons, originally from Birmingham. He was returning to his wife and six children in Melton Mowbray, Leicestershire, after delivering a consignment of carpets to Belgium. His was the fourth lorry aboard the ferry, and so he had plenty of time to prepare for the four-and-a-half-hour journey back to Dover. He went straight to the drivers' restaurant and was served his meal by Henry Graham, before going below to occupy one of the drivers' cabins.

Non-commercial passengers had begun to embark the *Herald* for the return journey at 1830hrs, half an hour before the scheduled departure time. Assistant Purser Stephen Homewood was lying on his bunk listening to a tape of classical music when his walkie-talkie burst into life, signalling that the first passengers were coming aboard. He went to his post in the information office and made a tannoy announcement for the staff: 'Attention catering department and catering personnel, open all services. Passengers on board.' He then chatted briefly with fellow Assistant Purser, David Didsbury, who was in charge of the bonded stores and retail outlets on this trip. Didsbury was to have his meal first and then come back to take over from Homewood.

At 1840hrs local time, No. 14 ballast tank began to empty – its job done – to prepare for the journey home. Tank No. 3 would empty later. It was estimated that 50 tonnes had been emptied by the time of departure.

Assistant Bosun Mark Stanley (28) had finished tying down the last of the lorry trailers on G-deck and, at 1850hrs, had returned to his cabin for a short rest. He drank a cup of tea and sat on his bunk, intending to read for a few minutes before the call to report to harbour stations. He was due to return to G-deck to close the bow doors before the ferry got under way – that is if someone hadn't done the job already, as was often the case. The warmth of the cabin and the welcome rest after a long and dreary shift overwhelmed him and he fell asleep. Stanley missed the call to report to harbour stations.

Lorry driver Ian 'Jock' Calderwood (44), originally from Stranraer, was almost the last to be loaded and had to walk round the front of his truck to get off the vehicle deck. Jock was returning home to his wife, Wendy, and four children in Dagenham, Essex. He estimated that he left his cab about six or seven minutes after the *Herald* had left the berth. 'The doors were wide open. The ship was reversing out and I could see the whole of the harbour through the doors.' He didn't think it unusual, as experience told him that the freight deck doors were often left open until the ship reached the open sea, for fumes to clear. 'I saw two crewmen banging furiously at the hydraulic mechanism with a hammer or spanner as I went up. I left the freight deck and didn't think anything of it. I've seen the doors open like that umpteen times'.

Once Chief Officer Sabel had overseen the loading of the vehicle decks, he later testified that he thought he saw Assistant Bosun Stanley return to G-deck to close the bow doors. He saw a man dressed in orange overalls about 20ft from the bow door controls. Assuming that the crewman responsible for closing the bow doors was at his post, Sabel left for the bridge.

Bosun Terry Ayling (39) was the last man to leave the vehicle deck on G-deck and, as far as he was aware, there was no one there to close the doors. After the last vehicle was loaded, he merely put the chain across. Harbour stations had already been called, and he was in his cabin. When asked later why he had not ensured the doors were shut, he replied, 'It has never been part of my duties to close the doors or make sure anybody is there to close the doors.'

Sean Trower (27) missed the ferry after being arrested following a row in a restaurant in Zeebrugge. He was locked up in a police cell.

Billy Schmidt (34) and Brenda Lamb (31) had reluctantly left their six children with relatives in Reynes Park, south London, to take a romantic break. Sammy (13) and Angie (12) were Billy's daughters by his first marriage. John (15), Neil (13) and Lee (11) were Brenda's sons by her previous marriage. Robyn (5) was both of theirs but all the children lived together with the couple. They had been together for ten years.

Brian Smith (29) had planned to leave the Royal Corps of Transport to be a lorry driver. He was taking his family – wife Donna-Marie (27), daughter Kerry (5) and son Sean (21 months) – back to their native Manchester for a last holiday before returning to Germany for his final three months of service.

Andrew Parker (33) of Herne Hill, south London, stopped by the information office to enquire if there were any spare cabins for his Filipino-born wife, Eleanor, and daughter Janice (12). Also travelling with them was family friend Oriana Gomez and her 12-year-old son, Jonathan. Stephen Homewood told them to come back after the ferry had departed, because the cabins and their forty-four bunks were automatically allocated to lorry drivers first and it was not yet known if there would be any left. (Pink tickets were issued to lorry drivers, which were included in the price of the freight ticket. A certain amount of time was given for drivers to take up a bunk if they wanted. Any tickets left over were then taken to the information office for resale to the rest of the passengers at a cost of £4.50 for a single bunk, or £9.00 for the whole two-berth cabin. There was usually a fairly long queue for these cabins, particularly for people who had driven through the night across Europe to join early morning ferries.)

Henry Graham (24) was supervising the commercial drivers' restaurant on C-deck as a steward. The restaurant was situated next to the self-service cafeteria, between the servery and the eating area, in an area described as 'like a greenhouse', with a separate entrance on the starboard side. A port-side doorway led to the galley, feeding both restaurant and cafeteria. Henry was officially listed on the crew list as a kiosk steward (leading hand) but had been training to become a purser as part of a promotion. The training had taken him to every part of the ship except the engine room. The thirty-two-seat restaurant had begun to fill half an hour before sailing and with thirty-six trucks aboard and usually two drivers per truck, Henry was going to be busy. The normal routine was for drivers to eat first and then retire to their cabins on H-deck, below the waterline, for the rest of the journey.

Chief Cook Paul White then approached Assistant Purser Homewood about supplies. Homewood made two unsuccessful attempts to contact the radio operator, Robert Mantle, about having the additional supplies ready for loading at Dover. Whilst the ferry was still at berth stations, steward Paul Cormack handed Homewood the ship's bag, holding the captain's cargo, passenger and freight manifest. These figures would need to be radioed through to Dover for the port authorities to make proper arrangements for the *Herald*'s arrival.

The workers in Dover would need to know how many semi-trailers (detached rear half of an articulated lorry) there were, in order to allocate the same number of cabs to take them off the ferry. They would also need to know the number of foot passengers on board so that they could organise enough coaches to transport them to the terminal, as well as providing enough baggage trolleys. In addition, they would need to know if any animals would need to be quarantined. On this trip, there were none. Again, Homewood attempted to contact the radio operator but still could not get through. He never did speak to Robert Mantle.

By this time, many of the passengers had started to crowd into the bars in the public areas and it was getting quite noisy and rowdy. Clearly, people were determined to make the most of their day out.

Jan Willis was a 'very lowly' bank clerk at the NatWest Bank at Finsbury Circus in the City of London. 'I hated the job, pushing pieces of paper around a desk and to be honest I did it very badly.' Realising that she had achieved very little at school, and no one having any expectations or hopes for her, she had enrolled for a BTEC evening class in business and banking at Barking College of Technology, near her home in Essex.

The *Sun* national newspaper had been offering a Channel crossing aboard Townsend Thoresen ships to its readers for just £1, as part of a promotional campaign. In her second year at college, when Jan was 19, she and a group of six fellow students had decided to go on a day trip, using the *Sun*'s £1 tokens. Her friend, Karen Watson (18), organised it. With them were Karen's boyfriend Tony Curley, two boys (both named Vijay) and two girls who Jan didn't really know. After their 'pretty uneventful' day out in Belgium, the group had hoped to catch an earlier ferry but they had missed it.

Whilst waiting for the 1900hrs sailing in the ferry terminal building, Jan found herself chatting to a woman in a wheelchair who was from Dagenham, close to where she lived. Nora Woodhouse (54) was travelling with her husband and son.

Once aboard, Jan and four of the others made their way to the cafeteria, while two of the girls minded the group's bags. Jan ordered chicken burger and chips at the counter but had to wait for it to cook. While she waited, she noticed the large deep fat fryers behind the counter. The others went to find a table.

Mrs Sheila McKenny (54) of Hastings, East Sussex, had been collecting the *Sun* tokens for her whole family to partake in a daytrip. Despite the uninviting weather, with drizzle and early morning fog, the family had been determined to enjoy their day out. Husband Richard (64) drove their car onto the ferry with Sheila, their son Wayne (15), Sheila's daughter Lynette Carvley (37), of St Leonard's, and Lynette's 18-year-old daughter, Rebecca. Despite spending only four or five hours in Zeebrugge, and the poor weather, the trip to the continent had been a success. Lynette was enjoying a day off from her job at the Inland Revenue. Richard recalled:

> My wife befriended a lady in a wheelchair as we waited to board. The lady became quite friendly with Sheila as it turned out they were from the same area, Lancashire, and they chatted, as women do, for quite some time … the lady in the wheelchair asked if she could sit with us [in the cafeteria], at the end of the table, but in her chair in the alley way, so that she and my wife could carry on chatting to each other.

The woman in the wheelchair was Nora Woodhouse, whom student Jan Willis had chatted to in the terminal building before boarding.

Also on a day trip, from Hastings, were five members of the Perkins family. Mother, Sheila (42), and her three sons Darren (21), Simon (18) and Anthony, and Darren's fiancée, Nicola Payne (20). They had spent a great time in Zeebrugge and were 'happy all day, laughing and joking about incidents that had happened during the day'.

A group of four friends from Kent had enjoyed a day out on the continent, and were now relaxing in the lounge on C-deck. Colin (44) and Jackie Virtue (46), of Bromley, were with Steven (38) and Janet Turner (30), of Meopham.

Bombardier John Gaylard (36), serving in the Royal Artillery, had left his base in Dortmund, Germany, intending to catch an early ferry to meet his brother at home that evening in St Albans, Hertfordshire.

Lance Corporal Gary Thomas (24) of the Royal Electrical and Mechanical Engineers, was returning home to Liverpool to marry airport shop supervisor, Susan Lambert (22) of Feltham, Middlesex. Their wedding was scheduled for the following Saturday, 14 March. They had met after becoming penfriends.

Warehouse manager Rosina Summerfield (24) had taken a large amount of cash with her to Eindhoven, Netherlands. She hadn't planned to blow it all on a spending spree – Rosina was convinced that something bad was going to happen and that they would need the money to get them out of trouble. She thought there may be a problem with their car at the very least. She had been on a road trip to Eindhoven to visit her future mother-in-law, with her boyfriend Kevin Batten, their 4-year-old son Ryan and 20-year-old Julie Clark, who lived with them in Park Royal, west London. Julie had decided to go with the family at the last minute after Rosina's friend Kim had to drop out. Julie worked as a receptionist at the local Asda superstore and had called in sick. 'Little did she know that she would be splattered all over every newspaper in England a week later', Rosina said.

> The week went fine and nothing had happened to the car or anything so I started to relax. We got to the ferry early and were one of the first cars to load. We had time to park up and go out on the deck which is where I first noticed the name of the ship on a life ring. I remember thinking that you never really know the name of the ferries on which you travel.

School pals Cheryl Taylor and Nicola Simpson should have been in lessons at Monk's Walk School, Welwyn Garden City, in Hertfordshire. Instead, the 14-year-olds had been to Belgium for the day with Nicola's parents, Tony (41) and Patricia (39). Tony worked for British Aerospace as an engineer, while Patricia was a dental nurse. As a family, the Simpsons, including Nicola's brother Darren (16) and sister Linda (17), had travelled all over Europe, having camped in Yugoslavia, Spain, Switzerland and Germany. They were no strangers to ferry travel. They had boarded the midnight ferry the night before in order to have a full day out.

Captain Brian Bunker (28) of the 1st British Corps, British Army of the Rhine (BAOR), had met Diane when they were both 16, at a Catholic social dance in Enfield, Middlesex. Brian was commissioned from the Royal Military Academy at Sandhurst before being posted abroad, including four years with the Gurkhas in Hong Kong, South Korea and Nepal. Brian and Diane were posted to Bielefeld, West Germany in 1984.

He had received a phone call from his father the day before to say that Brian's grandfather was seriously ill and was not expected to live much longer. Urgent arrangements were made at Brian's base in Bielefeld, Germany, for Brian and his family to return to Enfield, to support the family. Brian, his wife Diane (29) and their 9-month-old daughter, Nadine, arrived at Zeebrugge in time for the 1900hrs sailing to Dover – the route they had used so many times before. After parking up, the Bunker family made their way to the lounge on C-deck, opposite the duty-free shop. Settling them down in a corner of the lounge on the starboard side, Brian left his wife and daughter briefly to fetch some hot drinks and snacks. The cafeteria on C-deck was very busy so Brian made his way to the deck above, where he knew there was another cafeteria called the Salad Bowl.

A group of four, associated with Lancing College, West Sussex, were also on board. College marshal Peter Martin (53), his wife Kay (also 53), and their friends, grounds-man Richard Davies and his wife Georgina, made their way to the lounge on C-deck.

The Rogers family from Cheltenham, Gloucestershire, had settled down to watch a cartoon on the lounge's TV, after having a meal of chips in the cafeteria. Successful self-employed builder Alan Rogers (36) had been working flat out, and the trip was just what the family needed. He and his 27-year-old wife, Susan, had spent a happy day in Belgium and were now heading home with their children, 'very happy-go-lucky' twins William and Emma (3), and their 18-month-old brother Adrian, laden with shopping and early presents for the twins' upcoming birthday.

Lorry driver Barry Ducker, of Narborough near Swaffham, Norfolk, had been reluctant to take the trip abroad for work as his wife was recovering in hospital from a cancer operation. He was desperate to get home.

A group of seven young friends from the Black Country in the West Midlands were having a great day out. They had started out from Dover at 5.30 a.m. when they had crossed to Zeebrugge on Townsend Thoresen's smaller ferry *Free Enterprise VI*, using the *Sun*'s £1 tokens. Brothers Ian (21) and Nicholas Wood (18), of Lye; and their pals Ian Moore (18) of Netherton; Alan Cartwright (21), a labourer of Quarry Bank; Andrew Bridge (19) of Clent; Andrew Dingley (18) of Hagley; and Lawson Fisher (18) of Stourbridge, had all spent the day in Zeebrugge, mainly drinking in the bars. They had found the town itself a bit boring. Now, the seven friends were aboard the *Herald of Free Enterprise* for the long journey home to the Midlands. 'We weren't drunk, like, but we were a bit merry.' Lawson said.

Lance Corporal Conrad Wilson (24) was taking his family home to Bury St Edmunds, Suffolk, for his parents' twenty-fifth wedding anniversary celebrations. His wife, Angela, and their two children, Rebecca (4) and 6-year-old Steven, had left family quarters at their British Army base in Germany earlier that day. Steven was celebrating his sixth birthday that day.

A party of six were on their way back to Cotmanhay, Derbyshire, and had set-tled down in the bar, before the drive back to the East Midlands. Richard (31) and

Hazel Hartley (38) had spent the day with Richard's parents Joseph and Elsie (both 65), son Martin (8) and family friend Patricia Hawley (40) known to Martin as 'auntie'. Hazel was using a wheelchair due to her severe arthritis, which made mobility very difficult. Martin's stepbrother, Lance, and his girlfriend, Lesley, should have been on the trip but had to cancel after putting down a £2 deposit – 'We were just flat broke', he said.

Petar Zutic (22), a Lance Corporal in the British Army, was taking his wife Julie (also 22), and their 9-week-old daughter, Carly, to Halifax, West Yorkshire, where Carly was due to be christened. The Zutics lived on base at Sennelager, Germany, but when they were in the UK they called Dumfries, Scotland, home. Unable to book a cabin for the trip across the Channel, they made their way to the cafeteria. They were on two weeks' leave, and it would be the first time that either set of grandparents would see their new granddaughter.

Cecil Naftel had hitched a ride with a lorry driver back to the UK after popping into the EastEnders bar in Zeebrugge for a pint and a chat with his friend, landlord Dave West. At least that's what Dave knew him as – it later transpired that 'Cecil' was carrying a false passport and birth certificate.

Michael and Maureen Bennett, both 41, of Crawley, West Sussex, had never been to Belgium before and so had taken advantage of the *Sun's* £1 offer, along with their daughter, Theresa Gander (20), and her fiancé Mark Webb (24). The Bennetts were being treated to the day out for their ninth wedding anniversary by Theresa, who worked as a secretary. They opted not to go to Bruges, like so many of their fellow day trippers, but instead had spent the day on the coast tram, visiting Ostend and Blankenberge.

Five members of the Drury family from Henlow, Bedfordshire, had settled themselves down in the ship's cinema, a lounge on B-deck with a television showing videos. Parents, Graham and Julie, daughters Emma (4) and Margaret (6), and 1-year-old son Michael, hoped for a rest before the drive back home.

Devoted Polish couple Pitek Swietochowski, a 33-year-old civil engineer, and 22-year-old fourth-year medical student Malogosia Wieliczko, were returning home to London. They were known to friends as Peter and Margaret. Peter lived in Ealing, whilst Margaret was from Sydenham. They planned to marry in 1988.

Peter Hilling (47) and his fiancée Beverley Taylor (26) lived on an army base in Germany. They were going to Wiltshire to finalise plans for their wedding on 18 April.

Army captain Andrew Teare (25) of the Royal Electrical and Mechanical Engineers, and fiancée Susan Jacobs (28) were also on their way home from Germany.

Long lost brothers Christopher Moy (29), of Cheriton, Folkestone, and London fireman Stephen Smith (33), of Herne Bay, had been on a day trip with Stephen's wife, Julie, a senior travel consultant. Chris's wife, Janet, had been unable to go. They went to the Blue Riband restaurant.

A group from Somerset had also taken advantage of the *Sun*'s £1 offer and had enjoyed the day out, but faced a long drive back to Yeovil in the West Country. Paddy and Carole Buckley and 13-year-old daughter, Nicola, had invited their next door neighbour, Stuart Hurley (17), along for the ride. The Buckley's' 20-year-old son Ian awaited their return after being unable to go.

Keith Baddeley (53) of Wallasey, Merseyside and his wife, Eileen (41), were aboard with Eileen's daughter, Gillian (16), and her two stepbrothers, Colin (14) and Mark (18). Their uncle, Eileen's brother David Whitworth (38), was accompanying them. Once aboard, the family went their separate ways – Keith went to duty-free and the two boys went to the cinema room, while Eileen and her brother went to relax in the lounge. Gillian's mother gave her some money for something to eat and she left them to take some air on the open deck, with the words 'I'll see you in a minute'.

Karen Ray (22) was on board with her fiancé Alan Woodall (24), of Luton, and her two brothers, Anthony (20) and Peter, with whom she lived at the family home in Wembley Park. Karen and Alan had recently made plans to buy a house together.

Brian Delafield (47) of Maidstone, and his wife Carol (44) were aboard with Brian's daughter, Sharon (17), and Carol's 11-year-old son, Andrew Fox. They were returning from a family outing.

The Lamy family of Bow, east London, had shared a meal and birthday cake the night before. They spent the day on the continent for George Lamy's 54th birthday. Having taken a day off from the post office, he was taking his mother Victoria (75), wife Frances (42), daughter Kim (20) and 11-month-old grandson, Stevie, out for the day, using the *Sun*'s £1 foot passenger tokens.

George had booked his car on board with as many passengers as he could fit into it. Having spent the day in Bruges, they had bought toys for Stevie and some sweets for their other grandchild, 5-month-old Sarah, who should have been on the trip with the Lamys' other daughter, Tracy Edwards. Tracy had decided to stay behind as there wasn't enough room for two baby seats in the car, and it was the law in Europe for babies to be strapped in. She had suggested that her nan go with the family instead. They laughed at themselves for taking a picnic of cold chicken and salad on a freezing cold day like this. George drove the car and four generations of his family up the ferry ramp onto the *Herald*'s vehicle deck at 1846hrs.

Now on board, they made their way up to the lounge where it was warm. Just as the women decided to freshen up, George sneezed. Frances turned to him and said, 'Before you catch your death of cold, I'm going to get some hot drinks'. His daughter Kim added, 'We won't be long', as she took Stevie to the ladies with her mother and grandmother to change the baby's nappy.

John Bray (32) had met Jenny Pierce (24) at the twenty-fifth anniversary celebrations of the Teynham and Lynsted Cricket Club, where he played cricket. He worked for Gillingham football boss, Ray Wood, as a fitter at R.J. Wood Distribution. 'They met and fell in love at the dance, and they found they also needed one another because of the children', said a family friend. John's wife, Margaret, had died, tragically young, from a brain haemorrhage, leaving John to bring up their two sons Mark (12) and Jody (7). The boys' grandmother, Eileen Bray, had helped care for them and they were living with her in Teynham.

Jenny Pierce's marriage had broken up. She was now looking after her 4-year-old daughter, Emily, helped by Jenny's parents, Vic and Edna Coleman. Carol Drury, who had been Margaret's best friend before she died, said, 'I was very pleased when he met Jenny – she was such a lovely girl. Her little girl was truly beautiful. Her mother was fair but Emily had long red hair. Everyone was struck by how pretty she was.'

Now John Bray and Jenny Pierce were together, they had taken their three children on a day trip to the Continent. Twelve-year-old Mark left his family behind to explore the *Herald*, 'I went off alone to look at the amusements'. Jenny said, 'We were in the bar area. We had only been sitting down a couple of minutes. We wanted to settle the kids down a bit.'

Passenger Simon Osborne (23) of Hinckley, Leicestershire, excused himself from the company of his six friends and went to the duty-free shop where he hoped he would be able to buy his girlfriend a decent bottle of perfume as a present.

Lance Corporal Philip Wilson (33) was returning to his home town of Grange-over-Sands, Cumbria, to start a new life in 'Civvy Street' with his wife, Christina, and two baby daughters, Angelina (18 months) and 6-month-old Sabrina. All day Philip had endured a feeling of dread that he could not comprehend. It had manifested itself into a splitting headache by the time they were on the road to Zeebrugge. Christina had urged him to get to the port in time for the 1900hrs sailing, otherwise they would have to wait until the next crossing, hours later. All Philip wanted to do was pull over and stop driving for a few minutes but, as they were running late, he decided to carry on. They arrived at the port and joined the standby queue, where they were the last but one vehicle aboard. Philip recalled that, as they were heading up the stairways to the upper decks, the whole ship vibrated as the engines started for their journey. The family headed towards the cafeteria for something to eat before doing anything else.

Terence Maloney (55) of Hitchin, Hertfordshire, had sold a house in the Dutch town of Eindhoven, and had asked his sister, 58-year-old Margaret Pelling, of Beckenham, Kent, to help him pack the house up. He thought that the trip would be a nice break for her too. Margaret had asked her daughter, Jane (20), to go along with them but Jane was working and couldn't afford to lose out on the commission, so older sister, Shirley Lopez (40) of Caterham, Surrey, had gone instead. The three had not originally been due to return from Zeebrugge at all but found themselves ahead of schedule and had decided to try and get on board an earlier ferry from Zeebrugge. Now on board, they settled themselves down near the duty-free shop.

Irish lorry driver Larry O'Brien (33) of New Ross, County Wexford, had just finished a five-week stint on the Continent when he got a last-minute call from his bosses – there was a load stuck in Holland and his help was needed to get it home. He arrived in Holland from Rosslare on the morning of 6 March. He had secured his load of medical supplies for transportation back to Ireland when he received another call. His company had another truck in England which had been involved in an accident. They were looking for a back panel for a Mercedes lorry. This held Larry up for three hours, and he found himself arriving in Zeebrugge for the 1900hrs crossing. He made his way to the cafeteria.

The Johnson and Bushaway families from Milton Keynes, Buckinghamshire, had been enjoying a day out together. Now they were on their way home. Thomas and Kathleen Johnson and their two sons, Edward (17) and Thomas Jr (12), went to the cafeteria with Ronald Bushaway (63), wife Rosina (59) and their 12-year-old daughter Laura. After a while, Thomas Jr said he wanted to watch videos in the TV lounge, so he and his father made their way there, leaving the five others from their group to finish their meal.

A group of friends from Borehamwood, Hertfordshire, had paid £1 per head and £5 for their car, an Austin Maxi, using the tokens from the *Sun*. Miles Southgate (30) and 'Big Martin' Spooner (31) had lived within just 50yds of each other throughout their youth. Their other friend Stuart Orpwood (30), and Miles' girlfriend, Cath, were with them for the day out to Bruges. After a successful day sightseeing and visiting bars, Miles suggested that they have a drive around Bruges, but he was berated by his friends – 'We'll miss the ferry!'

Being a 'devil for attention' in all things mechanical, Miles had paid particular attention to the bow doors as they drove up the ramp to board the *Herald*. They had been loaded onto the lower car deck and he knew that, judging the distance between the car deck and the sea, water could easily come above the ledge. They then made their way to the passenger areas above via the stairway, and stopped off at the bureau de change on C-deck to change their unused Belgian francs back into British pounds. Seeing that the bar and lounges on C-deck were quite crowded, the group of friends decided to go one deck above to B-deck. Martin wanted to do some last-minute shopping in the duty-free shop across the corridor from the money exchange, so they planned to meet in the B-deck lounge later for a few drinks and a game of cards. His three friends went up to the open deck to watch their departure from Zeebrugge harbour. The air temperature was −5°C, so they went back inside where it was warm.

Miles, Cath and Stuart settled themselves in the B-deck lounge near to the exit on the port side. There were plenty of seats to choose from as there weren't that many passengers who had ventured this far yet. They found themselves next to an open wrought iron 'gate' serving as a room divider, which ran the length of the lounge. Next to the port side of the lounge was the Blue Riband restaurant, and across the corridor from that was another lounge given over to a 'TV, or video lounge' – on this particular journey showing cartoons and children's films. On the starboard side of the lounge was the B-deck bar, which had remained closed for this crossing, as was the Salad Bowl cafeteria further forward.

Four young army pals were going home on leave from their base at RAF Gütersloh in Germany. Julian 'Jules' Pratt (18) from Bradford was on his way to see his fiancée, Louise James, of the Women's Royal Army Corps (WRAC), who was based at Donnington, near Telford. Lee Williams (21) was from Telford, and was going home to his parents in Stirchley Park. With them were Derek Laing and Bill Waller. They had been booked on a later crossing but arrived early and paid extra to travel aboard the *Herald*. Lee had not told his family he was coming home on leave and so they were not expecting him. The four went to the cafeteria for a meal.

Professional cyclist, Richard Smith (28) of Hove, West Sussex, had competed in Belgium earlier that day. He was the 1975 national junior 3,000m pursuit champion, and had made a professional comeback in 1985 after nine years out of the sport. Today, he had retired on the fourteenth lap of a sixteen-lap criterium at Blankenberge, just along the coast from Zeebrugge. He had decided to return to England that night on the 1900hrs sailing.

And so the list of passengers went on – families, groups of friends, young couples, soldiers, lorry drivers, and neighbours from every corner of Britain joined the *Herald*; some returning to the UK for the first time in months, others transporting goods bound for their employers, but mostly people returning from holidays and day trips. As they settled in the bars, cafeteria, restaurant, cinema and lounges, or took a stroll on deck, they contemplated the journey ahead, and the long drive back home for some. To most, the Channel crossing represented a four-and-a-half-hour uneventful journey, whilst to others, particularly the children and teenagers on board, it was an opportunity to explore – part of a big adventure.

On the bridge, Chief Officer Leslie Sabel reported that the shore ramp was being lifted. Another message from the port control station at Zeebrugge informed the *Herald* that the harbour channel was now clear of traffic and that they could depart.

In 1987, Captain David Lewry, aged 46, lived at St John's Green, Sandwich, Kent, with his wife and three sons. He had served at sea for thirty years, held a Master's Certificate of Competency (Foreign Going) for twenty-one years, had been with Townsend Thoresen for sixteen years and had served as one of five masters of the *Herald of Free Enterprise* since 13 March 1980, continuously for seven years, since it first went into service. As master, he was responsible for the safety of his ship and every person on board. Townsend Thoresen's set of standing orders included:

> Heads of department are to report to the master immediately they are aware of any deficiency which is likely to cause their departments to be unready for sea in any respect at the due sailing time … in the absence of any such report, the master will assume, at the due sailing time, that the vessel is ready for sea in all respects.

Captain Lewry issued orders to his crew on the bridge – Second Officer Paul Morter, Quartermaster Tom Wilson (37) and Seaman Richard Hobbs (23). On this voyage, Hobbs had several responsibilities, including steering, lookout and navigation, and was, in effect, a petty officer.

The *Herald of Free Enterprise* backed out of Berth 12 at 1905hrs – five minutes late. Lewry went outside to the wing of the bridge and watched the stern of the ferry as she departed. Had he turned to look at the dock, he would not have known that the bow doors were still gaping open as they were blocked from his view. There were no indicator lights installed on the bridge to alert the crew that the doors were open.

With the aid of a harbour tug, *Herald* turned around within Zeebrugge's inner harbour. She then glided out amongst the pleasure craft and fishing boats at 5 knots. At the end of the Kennedy Quay she turned to starboard. Reaching the dredged channel at Zeebrugge's Outer Mole at 1924hrs, the *Herald* prepared to take to the open sea.

On board were approximately 473 passengers, eighty crew members, eighty-four cars, thirty-six lorries, four vans, one motorcycle and one trailer. The four-and-a-half-hour journey was expected to be incident free – after all, the weather was good, with a light south-easterly breeze and very little or no swell.

A young couple from London, Gary and Joan, were holding hands as they looked through the windows at the lights of Zeebrugge. The sun had set an hour before. Like many of their fellow passengers, they had taken the opportunity of the *Sun's* £1 offer, having collected the tokens for four days. Another young couple nearby were reminiscing about their day out. The man worked in a library while his girlfriend was an art student. They had hung around the port for most of their trip, eating crab sandwiches and looking at the seagulls diving into the sea off the beach. They had been daydreaming when the tannoy announced that the duty-free shop was now open. Gary and Joan joined the other passengers on the way to duty-free. They had just opened up the steel shutters ready for a busy night's shopping.

Some passengers had opted to watch the ship's departure from the open deck, among them people who were afraid of getting seasick. Most of the passengers were inside the warm ferry. Military personnel, some with their families, made up around 100 of the passengers. Some of them were in the bar with thoughts of going home on leave. They were being served by waiters pulling pints. Others had settled in lounges or the cafeteria, while those that could afford it chose to eat in the waiter-service Blue Riband restaurant. The majority were carrying bags of food, drinks, clothes and presents from Belgium.

Upstairs in the bars and lounges, the atmosphere was hotting up. Bottles of duty-free were opened and there was a lot of noise, laughter and joviality.

Unlike his fellow lorry drivers in their adjacent cabins, Jock Calderwood didn't feel like sleeping and he looked for a steward. He found Martin Barnes (18), who happened to have a bottle of whisky handy for his thirsty lorry drivers. Whisky in hand, Jock made his way back to his cabin.

Eight crew members were in the crew's mess preparing for their meal after their duties to make the ferry ready. Brian Kendal (19) was the first in the 'mad dash' to get to the mess room and had just finished his chicken tandoori and recommended it to Mark Squire, who had just walked in.

The *Herald* manoeuvred on combinators (engine controls on the bridge). Lewry and the bridge officers testified that, when entering or leaving Zeebrugge with the ship trimmed at the bow, they would restrict speed to avoid water coming over the bow spade, the lip separating the sea from the entrance to the car deck.

Rosina Summerfield, her boyfriend, son and friend had settled themselves down in one of the lounges as the cafeteria was packed:

> Julie and I went to the purser and asked if we could go down to the car to get some things for the journey. He said that we could, but they would be locking it up soon and we should hurry. We went to the car, which was near to the ferry doors. I remember being fascinated by the fact that the water was the same level as the floor and it was like a massive infinity pool. There was a guy whacking the hydraulic mechanism with the biggest spanner I'd ever seen, which looked like a novelty one because of its size.

Lewry stated that at Combinator 4, the speed is 10–12 knots, and at Combinator 6 is 15–16 knots. The *Pride of Free Enterprise* experimental tests held in June 1987 for the formal investigation showed that Combinator 4 was capable of 14 knots, and Combinator 6 managed 17½–18 knots. Lewry recalled the events of that day as the *Herald* passed the Outer Mole at 1924hrs, repeating that 'It was such a normal day.'

He had set Combinator 6 on all three engines, accelerating rapidly from 14 knots to a possible speed of 18 knots. The subsequent increase in the bow wave height, along with the ballast tanks dragging the bow deeper in the water than its natural trim, caused water to be scooped up over the spade and flow freely onto G-deck. The *Pride of Free Enterprise* tests indicated that, at Combinator 6, the bow wave would have been well up above the floor level of G-deck, maybe as much as 2m above the top of the spade. A large amount of water entered G-deck and soon there was enough water on the deck to cause a 'free liquid surface effect'. It was at this point that water began to pour down the stairs to H-deck.

Rosina Summerfield and Julie Clark had just returned to the vehicle deck:

> We took some things from the car and made our way to the heavy metal sliding door. Julie went through first and I just made it through as it started to shut. I laughed with Julie, saying it would be just my luck had I been stuck the whole journey in the car. Little did I know that was going to be the difference between me surviving or not.

Most people throughout the ferry heard the following tannoy announcement: 'Ship's carpenter contact the information office immediately.' Contrary to media reports, this was not a coded message but Assistant Purser Stephen Homewood added the word 'immediately' because he had just had a worrying message from a colleague. Homewood had just spoken to steward John Butler who was looking after the freight drivers on H-deck, one deck below the main vehicle deck, and below the waterline – 'There's water coming down the stairs'. Homewood immediately put the call out for ship's carpenter Mick Tracy, who would investigate what he thought may have been a burst pipe or a leak, but something in Butler's voice told him this was no ordinary leaking tap or toilet. Tracy was in his cabin on F-deck when he heard the Tannoy announcement. He had been chatting to Bosun Terry Ayling and stewardess Gail Cook.

Nearby, Rosina and Julie were on their way back upstairs from the vehicle deck, 'As we walked up the stairs, we heard an announcement on the ship's speaker system "Ship's carpenter to the bridge". I jokingly said to Julie "What's the use of a ship's carpenter on a metal ship?"'

Meanwhile, soldier Robert Smith (29), his German wife Emmi (28), and their 4-year-old son Mike, had just left their car. They lived in army quarters in Menden near Dortmund with their older children Sven (10) and Jane (6). They were going on an extended weekend trip, and so had left their two other children in the care of their aunt.

In the case of the *Herald*, the centre of gravity inside the hull of the ferry was moved when the large amount of flooded water on the car deck began to slosh around – much like trying to carry a tray full of water without spilling any. Called the 'free liquid surface effect', the mass of water shifted with the ship's natural heave, pitch and sway and caused an initial lurch to port, reaching as much as 30°, and taking approximately six or seven seconds.

The journey out of Zeebrugge that night had promised nothing more than a normal typical ferry crossing the English Channel. As the *Herald* passed the Outer Mole and began to gather speed, the sea water, now seeping across the ship's open vehicle deck, began to cause the ferry to lose its balance. Firstly, the *Herald* swayed a few degrees over to port. The passengers in the public areas were mildly concerned, but a sway in the opposite direction, to starboard, sent a cheer up in the bar, with some nervous laughter. Then a shift back to port but this time there was no steadying the *Herald*.

Lewry said:

I was looking in the radar when Hobbs shouted back, 'I've got a port helm on but she's going to starboard'. I looked up from the radar and the obvious thing was that the ship was starting to list then and listing to port very quickly. I realised that something abnormal was happening, pulled the combinatory handles back to zero and then full astern. The ship began to list quickly. I ordered watertight doors to be closed.

With the angle of loll, the port screw propeller was still deeply immersed and doing its job but the starboard propeller and rudder were now out of the water, and were now powerless to stop the *Herald* from turning towards starboard.

Henry Graham, the steward looking after the lorry drivers in the commercial restaurant, thought it was 'just one of those things' as the ship swayed. 'You get to know a ship's movements, noises, like your second life, at sea.' With the increasing list, he began to think, 'this isn't right', and in the next few seconds, Henry knew that the ship was going to capsize.

After water had collected in the port wing of G-deck, and with another loll in the ship's movements as the ferry's centre of gravity was re-established, the *Herald* briefly became stable again. Water continued to pour in through the open bow doors at the rate of approximately 200 tonnes per minute until the centre of gravity was completely shifted to the port side, with the weight of the flooding water and overturning vehicles. The *Herald* performed a full half circle turn to starboard, with her port side dragging through the sea. The ferry then capsized slowly to port and floated on her side, more or less on her beam ends for about one minute. The tide then pushed the ferry a little way to the east before it struck a sandbank on the seabed and came to rest at an angle of 100°, less than 7 cables (approximately 0.7 nautical miles) from the harbour entrance. She settled on the seabed on a heading of 136° at position, latitude 51° 22' 28.5" N, longitude 3° 11' 26" E. The *Herald* was facing back towards the direction from which she had sailed, over half-filled with water that was barely above freezing.

Capsize

There had been five men on the bridge when the *Herald* capsized. As a fire alarm sounded, signalling the first seconds of disaster, Captain Lewry shouted out, 'What's happening here?' and immediately tried to execute an emergency stop, badly hurting his hand on the power handles. Lewry then plunged 40ft from the starboard side of the bridge to the port side, hitting fixtures and instruments on the way down, before ending up in the water. Lewry later testified:

> I tried to get back to the VHF [Very High Frequency] radio but I was unable to. I was thrown across the bridge and I must have blacked out. The next thing I knew I was floating. I was held up by my bridge coat. It was getting dark. The first and second officers and the chief officer were there.

Quartermaster Tom Wilson (37) of Deal, witnessed the whole scene. 'I saw the captain lose his grip and fall heavily. There had been no bumps, crash or explosion. No warning about the open bow doors.' Grabbing a handrail near the wheel, Wilson was the only man present not to plunge into the water below.

George Lamy (survivor), wife Frances, daughter Kim and grandson Stevie (all victims).

Margaret Pelling, brother Terence Maloney and Margaret's daughter Shirley Lopez (all victims).

Heidi Pinnells (victim) died with her sister and future brother-in-law; Richard McKenny (survivor) whose wife died; Ann English (victim) with son David (not on board).

Steward Henry Graham (survivor).

Ship's cook Steve Helkvist (victim) with sister Sara's son, Michael.

The inside of the cafeteria of the *Herald* while still capsized. On the night of the disaster, there were dozens of people fighting for their lives in the water in complete darkness. (Courtesy of Fred Vandenbussche)

The *Herald of Free Enterprise* lying on its side after capsizing, the morning after the disaster. (Courtesy of Fred Vandenbussche)

The half-submerged observation lounge of the *Herald*, looking forward. On the night of the disaster, the only lights visible would have been those of the rescue ships shining through the windows. (Courtesy of Fred Vandenbussche)

The *Herald of Free Enterprise* lies at the entrance to Zeebrugge harbour, with more than 120 victims still aboard. (Courtesy of Fred Vandenbussche)

In the lowest passenger deck of the ferry, H-deck, where the lorry drivers' cabins were situated, lorry driver Brian Gibbons had undressed and settled in bed before the ferry left port. He was just about to go to sleep when the ferry began lurching 'a little bit rocky to begin with' from side to side. The ferry appeared to right itself before it began its final slide to port. He was thrown out of his bunk onto the floor. He suddenly became aware that the sea water was rushing in from below, along with the smell of sewerage from the ferry's toilets and petrol fumes from the vehicle deck. Suddenly the lights went out as the water drowned the ferry's engines.

On the vehicle deck, Joe Kay (46) was still in the cab of his refrigerated lorry. Another lorry parked alongside slid into his and Joe climbed out. Seeing his only way out above him, he cried out to God for help and leapt a 'superhuman' 12ft across a gap and grabbed for the walkway above.

Truck driver Barry Ducker had been resting in his cab, preparing for the drive home to Norfolk. He was eager to get back to his wife, who was in hospital recovering after having had a cancer operation three days earlier:

> Before I knew it, the cab was upside down. I had time to pull my trousers on and then I slipped out into the water. I bobbed up and down in the water and tried to reach for a chain. I missed but finally hauled myself on to a tyre and just held on.

He escaped with his life by using a floating car as a life raft. Barry eventually got out of the *Herald* and dropped into the sea where he was rescued by Andre Vermoote and Aime Moens.

Thomas Everard (24), a lorry driver from Ratoath, County Meath, Ireland, is also thought to have been sleeping in his cab. He was employed by a local haulage contractor. Thomas had three brothers and three sisters.

Rosina Summerfield and her friend Julie Clark were in the stairwell, making their way back from the vehicle deck to Rosina's son and boyfriend in a lounge:

> We started up the stairs and the ship started to tilt. All of a sudden we were walking on the glass panels between the banisters. For a while it did not cross my mind that anything was wrong. The ship was on its side and I thought, 'That's fine. They will right it soon and we will be on our way.' We climbed up higher and I dropped my keys down the well. The lights went off but our space was illuminated by a window, not a skylight. I scrabbled to get the keys and managed to get them, thinking Kevin would kill me if I couldn't drive the car off! Then the water burst in and I could see what I thought was a body in the water. Julie was hysterical, which was good because it didn't give me time to join her. I shouted at her and I think that she was then just in shock. I always remember the ship's booming distress call while we sat. It drowned out to a whisper and stopped so we thought no one would come and get us. We sat terrified in the small confined space which was full of petrol fumes

and humid. The windows above gave us light as I think it must have been a full moon. We waited, sitting on that ledge for what seemed an eternity listening to all the people screaming and crying through the wall. That was probably the worst part. We called out and I am sure I heard Kevin saying they were OK but he was nowhere near us so I obviously imagined it.

Soldier Robert Smith and his German wife Emmi had just been leaving the vehicle deck with 4-year-old son Mike, when the ferry tipped over. 'We were pressed against the outer wall as if drawn by a magnet. Then came the water.' Mike, who had been holding his dad's hand, screamed. 'A young man grabbed me, pushed me against the stairs and shoved me up, using the last of his strength. Then – while the water rose within seconds – I could only see his hands. He drowned. He saved my life and died himself.'

In the bosun's cabin, Bosun Terry Ayling, ship's carpenter, Mick Tracy, and stewardess, Gail Cook, had been chatting before going up for a meal. Tracy heard the tannoy announcement for him to contact the bridge. It sounded urgent. He heard the crashing of lorries and cars falling into each other as the ferry heeled over. Ayling had just taken off his coat after his vehicle-loading duties when the ferry began to turn over.

Everything started sliding off the table. Ayling fell against a locker and out of the cabin into the corridor. 'Stop being silly', Gail said to Ayling, thinking he was messing about. 'No, we're going over!' Within seconds she was looking down at him. Gail fell out of the cabin too and slammed her shoulder into the corridor wall, breaking her collarbone.

Assistant Bosun Mark Stanley later told the inquiry his account of the night of the disaster:

> I thought I was dreaming. I never fell off my bunk – I leaped, because I knew something was not right. My thought then, was, 'The doors … the doors.' The doors had not been shut. I knew I hadn't checked them. I was just hoping someone else had done it.

Mark stumbled across his cabin and out into the corridor, where he met Ayling and Gail. The ship was still capsizing. Stanley blurted out, 'The doors, Terry!'

Ayling replied 'Don't worry about that now, we've got this to sort out.'

Tony Simpson had been sitting opposite his wife, Pat, in the cafeteria, with daughter Nicola next to her mum, opposite school friend, Cheryl Taylor, happily chatting away. Suddenly, all the trays started sliding off the tables and plates crashed to the floor. Initially, people were laughing, 'It's tipping up more than usual tonight'. Then the ferry lurched violently and mother and daughter were pitched backwards over their seats.

Cheryl tried to stop Nicola from falling. Holding onto her arms across the table, Nicola slipped further and further back, while trying to climb back up. Suddenly

Nicola was knocked from Cheryl's grasp as people falling past hit her on the way down. Nicola and her mum were thrown against a wall and the inrush of seawater swept them both along. They grabbed each other and Pat kept telling her to 'hold on'. Nicola was screaming and was up to her shoulders in freezing water. She kicked her boots off when she realised they were dragging her down. All around her people were screaming. She couldn't see them as the lights were out. She grabbed onto a man's arm. Someone in the water nearby was shouting, 'I'm drowning! I love you!'

In the cafeteria, Richard McKenny and his family had been enjoying their meal when the ferry tilted suddenly, spilling food and cutlery into their laps. 'That was when the screaming and sounds of fear started to erupt.' His step-daughter, Lynette Carvley, saw her mother Sheila McKenny vanish into the night:

> The ferry listed suddenly and very briefly and everything fell off the tables and wheelchairs began to move. There was this poor old lady hurtling down the aisle in her wheelchair. My mum got up and put out her arm to try to stop her but the force just carried both of them down through a glass wall where the water was gushing in. She was whisked away. She disappeared in this great mass of water.

Sheila and Nora Woodhouse were gone. Before Lynnette could comprehend what was happening she found herself fighting for survival:

> I remember holding onto the table; it took every ounce of strength and more, as things were being sucked out and flying through the air at a speed of what seemed to be hundreds of miles an hour. We were trapped under the glass partitioning, which then became the roof of the cafeteria. The water was filling up, I can't swim but I didn't start to panic. I was trying to hold on to some thin metal at the side of me, and push myself out of the rising water. I went under the water for what seemed ages, but my daughter Rebecca pulled me up, as she was a good swimmer.

Richard found himself standing on the edge of the table and with one arm supported himself against the glass partitioning above while up to his waist in seawater. Lynette's daughter, Rebecca, found herself up to her neck in water and unable to find a foothold under water. 'It was so cold', she said, 'I was totally numb and I blacked out. Then I realised my mother was pulling me up and somehow we managed to get out to an open part of the ship.'

Raymond Cook, of London, was in the cafeteria, whilst his wife Kitty Hirst was in the duty-free shop. Immediately after the capsize, he tried to make his way to the shop to find her but couldn't get through, 'We were trying to get to the women but there were men fighting to get out.'

Irish lorry driver Larry O'Brien was also in the cafeteria. He spoke of seeing people being sucked through portholes. 'All around there was panic. While I was sitting there, I was trying to hold onto the table. Water burst through the portholes and people were sucked out like you see in films about air disasters. The people who went that way had no chance.'

Jan Wallis, on a day trip with a group of students from Barking College, Essex, had just sat down in the cafeteria when her plate slid forward. They started to laugh but the ferry kept going over. Jan said:

I went forward, somehow grabbing a table. I recall the white foam of the water flooding in and the pitch blackness. The screams. I was too frightened to scream. The water was rising and I remember Karen [Watson] said we had to move because the water was rising. It is hard to say how I got there but I moved to hold onto a window panel and stood on something hard. Below me in the darkness there was a boy at my feet. He was in a state but I was very calm, probably frozen with fear. I remember trying to keep him calm. His name was Wayne and we talked about his dinner – steak and kidney pie. I said to him I would buy him the biggest pie ever when we got out of this.

American-born Richard 'Dick' Maitland (46), originally from Greensburg, Pennsylvania, had been working in the UK as a trucker for sixteen years. He was in the cafeteria when the ferry capsized. 'These kids climbed like monkeys up the chairs … they dropped down ropes with loops on them. Someone pushed me ahead, because I'm big and could give them a hand hauling. Then we got the women and children out.'

The Bennetts and their daughter, Theresa Gander, were in different parts of the ship when it went over. Theresa was sitting with her boyfriend, Mark Webb, near the duty-free shop whilst her parents were enjoying an anniversary meal in the cafeteria. After ordering something to eat and coffees, they found a free seat and settled down, talking about the nice day they had spent on the Continent. 'We hadn't even noticed that the boat had left until the ferry suddenly began to lean over to one side', said Maureen. Her husband Michael instinctively grabbed her hand, as all around them everything that was not bolted down began to fall towards them – plates, cutlery and people. There was a cracking noise as the ferry heeled over, there was breaking glass, screaming and shouting. Then suddenly, all the lights went out.

In complete darkness, Michael and Maureen managed to stay upright, standing on an unseen object which was underwater, with the water rising rapidly. They were convinced that this was the end. When the water reached Michael's armpits, it stopped rising. It was only then that Michael began to hope again and he attempted to lift Maureen's spirits, whose hand he was still holding. As he stood there, chest deep in water, they listened to the people around them, unseen in the darkness. Children were screaming, others were crying out for help, injured or trapped or drowning. Maureen became aware of an English woman nearby. She told Maureen she was a nurse and tried to calm people down.

Conrad Wilson, heading for Suffolk to spend time with his mother, found himself saving his family twice as the ship began to fill with water:

It was like a scene from 'The Poseidon Adventure' … there were about fifty of us in the cafeteria trying to keep our heads above water. There were a few who couldn't make it. There were people pinned underneath the cafeteria tables.

Conrad finally managed to get his family out of the water and to the relative safety of a ledge but disaster struck again:

I tried to escape along a glass partition. I was holding my wife and son in my arms. I told Rebecca 'hang on to my neck, love'. Suddenly the partition broke and we fell into the water … there was blood everywhere and I remember thinking that my strength was going and that if we didn't get out soon that would be it.

Twenty-four-year-old soldier Jim Garvey, from Coventry, was with his girlfriend, Manuela Meltschack, a 20-year-old German citizen. They were returning to Coventry from their base at Bielefeld. The couple were in the cafeteria when disaster struck and the ship began to tip over:

It started very slowly. Plates started to slip across the tables. Everyone began to joke about it and waited for the plates to slide back. Then suddenly there was an almighty crash as a pile of plates fell to the floor in the kitchen. Some thought it was a big wave and some people clapped. The ship rolled back and then rolled over to the opposite side, slow at first, then it suddenly accelerated like a wire had been cut. Flickering lights went out and there was a huge screeching noise. No one had a chance. We were plunged into darkness. It was now a race against time.

Jim immediately leapt into action and began climbing up the fixed tables and chairs, urging his girlfriend along with him:

People moved fast despite the fear and chaos. People were climbing over each other and holding onto others to keep afloat. I am convinced we only survived because we were in the cafeteria and the furniture was so close together and fixed to the ground we could keep climbing to safety.

Had they not been near the doors, about 10ft away, Jim is certain they would have died. Jim and Manuela watched in amazement as the water came crashing through the windows and kept on rising. 'That was probably the worst part, not knowing when the water was going to stop. If it didn't stop, we had nowhere to go. We would have died like half the people on board. We were very lucky.'

At one point, Jim and Manuela believed the ship was sinking as they saw the waves lapping against the windows at the lower end of the ship. They stripped off the sodden clothes that were weighing them down. Others did the same. 'People threw off jumpers, sweaters, jackets, anything that was getting too heavy as they tried to escape.' They could only watch from where they were perched as the carnage unfolded below them. 'There were people screaming and crying everywhere. It was a bizarre sight – people climbing over tables and chairs just in their underwear.' He helped a young girl aged about 10 or 11 to safety. She was alone and crying. 'She said her name was Amanda and I remembered that because I told her my sister was named Amanda too. After we were rescued we never saw her again.' Once safe, they were given borrowed orange overalls. 'We arrived on deck virtually naked.'

The couple later thought about the people they had seen around them in the cafeteria before the capsize – the elderly couple alongside them; the young couple and their baby. They were saddened to think that all of them were most probably lost.

Steward John Jackson (41) described how a fridge fell and trapped him during the capsize. 'As the water rose, the fridge floated off me. I floated up too. I grabbed hold of a girl aged about 2.' He placed her on a partition but the glass broke and they both fell back into the water. He could only hold onto her for a short while because his strength was failing him in the cold so handed her to another man who put her in a drier position.

Cyclist Richard Smith, returning from his race in Belgium, had been in the lounge next to the cafeteria. He slid down the glass wall separating the two rooms, before getting up. Hammering on the windows with his bare fists, he fell down again, got to the stairs and climbed up to the ceiling. Again he fell down along the corridor wall, surrounded by darkness and the screams of terrified passengers.

In the lorry drivers' restaurant, enclosed by the main cafeteria on C-deck, Steward Henry Graham knew exactly what was happening. He had been serving drivers in their restaurant. Remaining calm, he realised he had to get everyone out. The drivers were in total disbelief and had no time to react. Cups, plates and cutlery began to slide off tables. A lorry driver stood up and immediately fell over, slipped down the deck past Henry and straight through a glass partition. Through the broken glass, Henry could see seawater rushing in. He clambered up the fixed tables and chairs, using them like a ladder, trying to get to the starboard door to get away from the freezing cold water. Concentrating on the here and now, one step at a time, he knew he had to stay out of the water where there was air. His training in difficult scenarios had kicked in and he was helping other drivers pull themselves up.

Lorry driver Arthur Edwards (45) of Gnosall, Stafford, was in the drivers' restaurant. He told of the moment of capsize, 'It all happened so fast. It took several seconds for people to realise it was going over. There were just one or two squeals from where I was and that was it.' Within seconds the warm and comfortable surroundings suddenly became a death trap. Hundreds of terrified people began falling into freezing cold water, crashing into walls, through windows and into each other on the way down. Some passengers, who realised what was happening, tried desperately to cling on to whatever they could, but many who had been injured by flying bottles, glasses, furniture and people simply did not have the strength and began landing on top of those unfortunate enough to be piling up at the bottom of the abyss.

Chief Cook Paul White had just stepped out on his way to place an order for supplies with the purser. He had left nine colleagues behind when the ship went over. As he could not get back to the galley to check on them, he had no idea of their fate but feared the worst. 'I left my nine cooks in the galley. They were working with boiling fat. I dread to think what happened to them.'

Stephen Homewood, who had just made a tannoy announcement for the ship's carpenter, later testified, 'Within seconds the ship started to list. Then she wobbled a bit, then she went over. There was no bang or explosion.' He likened the ferry going over to 'a submarine going down, ploughing into the water. As the ship went over, I told Paul [White] to hold on. The furniture started to move and we just held on.'

Holding onto a partition in the information office, pens were rolling and trays slid off the desk. Next, chairs began flying past the office. People who had been in front of the office began shrieking and screaming. Homewood managed to hold on and he glanced towards the duty-free shop and bar at the far end. The bar was packed two deep and almost all of the seats had been taken. He saw people being thrown 30–40ft 'like rag dolls' against the side. 'I remember all the people on the starboard side flying through the air and hitting windows on the port side. There was no time to phone the bridge. It was actually a relief when the lights packed up.'

Chief Cook White had been in the office talking to Homewood. He grabbed Homewood and pulled him out of the debris up into the main lounge. Believing that the ship was about to sink, Homewood's life flashed before him.

White, who had stepped out of the galley just seconds before to order supplies with Homewood, said people struggled to put on lifejackets as they were the only things that could be seen in the darkness. The jackets' fluorescent strips would be picked out in torchlight as the ship's lights had gone out and the emergency lighting had only kicked in for a few seconds before that too was extinguished. Passengers were stumbling in the dark using cigarette lighters to find their way.

Homewood stood up. Having lost contact with Paul, he made his way towards No. 3 stairway. In the dark, he almost fell through the open door of the ladies' toilets, now beneath his feet.

London couple, Gary and Joan, had been sitting in the bar area on C-deck. Their duty-free shopping began sliding downwards along the floor. Gary jumped up to catch it but the momentum of the ship capsizing threw him back into his seat. Before the lights went out, he saw a cupboard burst open and lifejackets spill out. He was ejected from his seat and thrown into the darkness, landing heavily. Objects fell on top of him. He called for Joan just as a bag hit him in the face, and broken glass fell on his chest. The room was full of horror, then silence, then the noise of people moaning. 'Gary! Gary! I'm here!' Joan suddenly cried out.

'You OK?' he answered.

A man with a cigarette lighter guided Gary and Joan towards each other. The few seconds of calm were not going to last. There was a thunderous crash as an immense wave crashed through the bar, filling the room with broken glass, tables, chairs, freezing water and bodies.

Lorry driver Graham Green (22) said a big cheer went up, people thinking that they had hit a big wave. Then the cheers turned to screams. He started climbing up the floor, which was fast becoming the wall, as water rushed in, but when he got to the top he couldn't smash though a window. Realising he was about to be engulfed by the rising water, Graham accepted that he was about to die, but wasn't really frightened. He just wondered what it was going to feel like.

Jenny Pierce and John Bray had only been sitting down in the bar area for a couple of minutes, with Jenny's daughter, Emily (4), and John's son, Jody (7). John's oldest son, Mark (12), had gone off to play on the amusements. Jenny later told the inquest:

> The boat began to tip over. People were screaming and panicking and being thrown out of their seats and sucked out of the windows. We were still hanging onto one another and the furniture. I had wrapped my body around the table and had a hold of Emily. John was below me, holding onto Emily's waist. Jody was hanging onto his legs. Suddenly a girl appeared from nowhere and she grabbed John's legs. John said he could not hang on any longer. He managed to get Emily wedged between two chairs.

Then John lost his grip and both father and son fell. 'John and Jody disappeared under the water and that was the last I saw of them.'

Eight-year-old Martin Hartley had been in the bar with his parents, grandparents and 'auntie'. Martin saw what happened to his mum and dad. He remembered his mother rolling away in her wheelchair and his dad going after her, getting further away in the water. Martin's dad shouted for him to swim towards him but, only being able to do the backstroke, Martin lost sight of him. Then he saw his dad being pushed into the water by someone else as panicked people scrambled over others in a frantic bid for survival. Then Martin was pushed under water and he was trodden on. Someone in a wheelchair – not his mum – hurtled towards him and he was bowled through a broken window. The next thing Martin knew he was waking up in hospital.

Sonia Saunders of Gillingham, Kent, was celebrating her 48th birthday by taking a trip to the continent with her husband Mick:

> We always went over on my birthday, 6 March. He did not want to go because we were saving for our summer holidays. One minute we were sitting together in the C-deck bar and laughing and joking. Next, he slid to his death in the icy water.

I grabbed hold of a chair but had to let go because I was in mid-air. I fell straight in the water – so cold. I tried to stay up but the lifejacket kept pushing me under.

Alan Cartwright, travelling with six of his pals, found himself crawling his way up the tray slide in the cafeteria, first feeling water that was 'really hot from the tea urn and then went icy cold in seconds'. His friends, Ian Woods and Lawson Fisher (18), of Stourbridge, were together in the bar having just bought more pints of lager. As the ferry capsized, Lawson saw a baby fly past him 'like a javelin'. He couldn't stop what happened next. 'I made a desperate leap to grab it but missed it and had to grab a chair. Just behind the baby came a woman in a wheelchair. I never sobered up so fast in my life.' The two friends became momentarily trapped under glass screens that were preventing them from climbing up.

Stephen Thirkettle (24) of Enfield, north London, on board with his wife, Debra, and 59-year-old father, Donald, witnessed the carnage in the bar, 'Several young lads and some adults came literally whizzing past me – then there were dull thuds as they hit the side, 30–40ft below.'

Martin Jones (20), an accounts clerk of Carshalton, Surrey, was in the bar with four friends, all of them on the *Sun*'s £1 promotional offer. 'I can't swim. I really thought I was going to die … it was horrific. I was thrown all over the place and kept smashing against the windows.'

Nine members of a village social club were returning home to Newdigate near Dorking, Surrey. Among them were gas inspector John Ede, his wife Ann and their friend Alan Roberts, a lorry driver. All three had been drinking in the bar when they were thrown through a plate glass window. Their friends, builder Ray Armstrong and his wife, Jackie, were also thrown into the water. Jackie began to float away so Ray took off his jumper and threw it to her, between them, like a life line. She clung to it.

Philip Wilson and his family were in the lounge across from the duty-free shop when the ship started to go over. As it began to tilt, he heard pots and pans break loose and fall on to the floor of the galley between them and the cafeteria serving area. A great cheer went up 'like it does when there are a load of soldiers aboard.' Philip was facing the port side and saw a wave of water lapping against the lower half of the lounge windows. When the next swell of seawater completely covered the windows he knew they were sinking. A man who had been walking up the aisle past their table suddenly went hurtling back downwards straight into a window separating them from the sea. 'The water began to slowly creep in through the spider-effect cracks that his body had punched into the window and then suddenly the whole thing gave way and the water came crashing in.' The man was shot back upwards past their table by the torrent of water. Philip knew he had to act immediately if he and his family had any chance of avoiding getting hurt. To save Angelina, and keep them both clear of the rising waters, Philip wrapped her baby reins around his neck leaving his hands free to climb to safety. Little Sabrina went under the water twice and almost drowned, only surviving because her mother Christina resuscitated her.

The Wilson family were now above the water, which had stopped rising just 2½ft below them. But they were still trapped below a glass partition. Seeing movement above, he tried to get their attention by banging his fists on the glass and then tried punching his way out, thinking the glass was breakable. 'I managed to dislocate all the fingers in my right hand.'

In the perfume shop adjacent to the duty-free shop, a mother had placed her baby on the counter for a moment while she was being served by Jennifer Leslie (34). As the ferry began to capsize, the mother slipped away and Jennifer grabbed the baby. Mother of four Jenny ended up in the freezing water still holding the baby. Gradually the cold numbed her muscles and she lost hold of the baby. Jenny found a chair to hold onto, numbed with cold and fear. It was down to a fellow crew member, who was outside the ship, who shouted down to her and swore at her to get herself out. She was smacked on the head with a rope, which seemed to bring her around and she managed to climb out. Later, another crew member told her that the baby had been saved.

In the duty-free shop, Senior Duty-free Officer Dave Hawken had been serving customers when the ferry began to capsize. He began to duck bottles as they flew from the shelves. Suddenly he was catapulted from the shop, across the corridor, and smashed into the locked door of the bureau de change, bursting it open and breaking a bone in his shoulder. He ended up at the other end of the cashier's office. The lights went out and came back on briefly before going out forever. That's when the water came crashing in. 'The bank started to fill up and we started to float up to the ceiling. But the water kept rising and when we could float up no further, it went over our heads. I thought "this is it!" I had no illusions, I thought I was going to die.'

David Matthews (57) had been serving customers at the counter of the bureau de change when the ferry capsized. 'I was buried beneath debris with at least one man [who turned out to be Dave Hawken] on top of me. I felt the water rising beneath me and this eventually released me and we floated into the duty-free shop.'

Just then the pressure of the water blew out the bulkhead, and they floated upwards back towards the duty-free shop. Hawken managed to get out of the water by grabbing onto some shelving, and hung onto it awaiting rescue.

Assistant Purser Charles Smith (57) was just inside the entrance to the duty-free shop. He was hanging onto a door frame there. Reassuring people that the ferry would 'come back' from its list – it didn't. 'A passenger asked me to move over. He pushed me out of the door and I fell into the water.'

As he surfaced, a dead body landed on his shoulders, pushing him under again. He fought to get the body off. Then survival instinct kicked in. Charlie knew that if he kept still, he was bound to come up again. When he did, he was surrounded by floating bodies. Most appeared to be unconscious and were making no attempt to swim. He grabbed onto a post, which promptly broke away on top of him and he went under for a third time. By this time he had swallowed so much water he thought it was the end. His feet never touched the bottom. He saw Steward Ken 'Kiki' Hollingsbee clambering halfway up the floor, which was now the wall because of the capsize. Kiki shouted to Charlie to pull himself up.

Paul Fisher (28) was on board with his wife Barbara (26), their four-year-old daughter Lisa and family friends Nick and Caroline Harley, all of Northamptonshire. They had taken advantage of the *Sun's* £1 offer and had missed the return ferry home and so were forced to take the *Herald*. Leaving their daughter in the care of Caroline, Mr and Mrs Fisher had gone to the duty-free shop to pick up some last-minute bargains. 'We felt the boat tip', said Paul, 'then it got sharper and the floor dropped to the right. The next thing we knew it was on its side. It happened in seconds.'

Paul grabbed hold of the duty-free counter, now above him, while Barbara hung on to his legs. Then the ferry began to flood with sea water 'at an alarming rate'. They realised there was no way out. Below them was freezing water and above them were the sealed windows of the duty-free shop. Paul thought 'the speed the water's coming up, we haven't got long left.' Suddenly Barbara lost her grip and fell into the water. Paul was convinced that would be the last time he would see his wife.

Mark Webb (24), on board with his girlfriend, Theresa Gander, and her parents, Michael and Maureen Bennett, had been minding the group's bags in a lounge. Theresa recalled:

> The ship suddenly appeared to turn heavily and people began to laugh and joke about rough weather. The glasses just shot off the table. I looked at Mark and I saw him flying across the room and smashing into a window. I managed to hold onto a table. I thought I'd never see him again. But then it was on its side and the width of the ferry became a deep shaft filling with water. People were treading on each other, screaming and shouting and a memory I will never forget is what appeared to be a forest of hands clutching at the air. I grabbed someone round the neck and he shouted 'Let me go! You're strangling me!' I was answering that I had no intention of letting go because I would drown if I did, when I realised it was Mark.

Suddenly, a locker burst open spilling dozens of lifejackets onto the people struggling in the water below. Installed in the ferry to help save lives, they instead caused people to become trapped by them. Theresa said:

> The lifejackets came down from above us as if a cupboard or something had opened suddenly. Ironically there were so many lifejackets that many people were having even more difficulty trying to find space to move. It does seem that the lifejackets in these circumstances gave added difficulties. Everyone was tangled up in the straps.

Mark panicked when water rose to his head. He was pushed further under water by lifejackets, which tumbled onto him from a cupboard above. In the water next to him was a woman holding a girl aged about 12. She was keeping her chin above water but Mark could tell the child was already dead, her body limp and her eyes closed. The woman did not let her go.

Lorry driver William Cardwell (42) from Scarva, County Armagh, confirmed their observations, 'The worst part was the lifejackets that floated up from under the seats and got tangled round people, tying them up so they couldn't help themselves. That was scandalous – those lifejackets were there to save lives but they were one of the biggest problems.'

After finding each other again in the freezing water, Mark and Theresa were struggling for space below the ruins of the duty-free shop. They were growing increasingly weak and numb with cold. Nearby was a man who told them his name was Robert O'Neill. 'He kept our spirits up when we were ready to give up and die. I'm alive now thanks to the bravery of that bloke.' Robert kept telling them to keep calm and even shared his Toblerone with them.

Caroline Harley (20), of Northampton, was minding her friend's four-year-old daughter, Lisa Fisher. They had just returned from the ladies' to the lounge outside the duty-free shop. 'I saw people being thrown around in the *Herald* as the ship capsized. When the boat tipped over, someone shot out of the duty-free shop backwards through the window. I never saw her again.'

Lisa-Jo Cain (11), from Feltham, Middlesex, was on board with her parents, Bob and Janice, and grandmother, Astrid. 'They had all gone up to the duty-free shop and had left me in charge of the luggage. When the boat began to tip, a lady grabbed me and stopped me falling through a window. I never found out who she was and I never saw her again.' (Lisa-Jo was later reunited with Joan Davis, her rescuer.)

Lifeguard Clifford Byrne (22) of Tooting, London, and motor mechanic Andrew Simons (30) of Bushey, Hertfordshire, had been sitting in the lounge when the ferry went over. Andy was thrown about 20ft. As they struggled in the freezing water, the two pals vowed that if they were going to die, they would die in each other's arms. Cliff said, 'It was terrifying. People were hurtling into each other and were trying to grab anything they could get hold of. Then we saw a woman screaming for help and pleading with us to get her baby girl.' Cliff leaned over to catch the baby and fell back into the water but still managed to pass the baby girl to Andy. The baby was screaming so they passed her to another woman.

Army nurse Shirley Laverick (29), stationed in west Berlin, was on her way back to Newcastle to see her boyfriend, Les. She had been sitting in an area outside the duty-free shop when it literally exploded during the capsize. Everyone around her was thrown, and bottles began raining down on their heads. Shirley wedged herself as near to the wall as she could but continued to be hit by full, litre bottles of whisky and vodka. Already covered in cuts and bruises, another shelf was about to come down on them.

Stan Mason, a 26-year-old Lance Corporal with the 1st Battalion of the Queen's Lancashire Regiment based in Germany, was taking his wife Catherine (25) and their four-month-old daughter, Kerry, back home to Golborne, near Wigan, Lancashire, where the couple had grown up. They were going to get Kerry christened there, amongst their families. That day, there was a special parade at their base in Paderborn near Osnabrück, which Stan didn't want to miss.

They had stopped for a meal at the last services on the German autobahn, and to fill up with petrol. 'Cath was so excited about the weekend. She was nattering away about Kerry's christening dress, whether it would be OK, looking forward to seeing her dad and all our friends.' They were not worried about the ferry journey; it was as routine as 'taking a bus to the supermarket'. They'd arrived at the docks early but settled down in the middle of one of the lounges. While Stan gave Kerry her bottle, Cath went off to look round the shops. She returned with some newspapers and a little rag doll for Kerry, who was now being winded by her dad.

The ferry began to roll, held for a few seconds and then went over, as if someone had cut a wire. The Masons were thrown out of their seats and downwards, tumbling like snowballs. 'I remember hitting a table on the way down, but because I was holding on to Kerry, I just clasped her tightly to me instinctively', said Stan. When they hit the bottom, water poured in and they were plunged into darkness when the lights failed. The lighting came on briefly for a few more seconds and then went out for good. Cath screamed, 'My baby!' – the last time Stan ever heard his wife's voice.

The water continued to pour in and rise rapidly. Everyone was screaming, amongst them was Stan calling out for Cath, but he never saw or heard her again. Stan turned his attention to getting Kerry away from the freezing water. He knew the only way out was upwards, using the tables and chairs bolted to the floor. Grasping Kerry's romper suit in his teeth, he used both free hands to climb. Pulling them clear of the water, he made his way to where he could hear other people. He realised the water level had stopped rising, but there was still a lot of screaming and shouting. All the time he was thinking about Cath and hoping she was safe somewhere, but he couldn't go back and search for her because he had to get Kerry to safety. Had he not been holding Kerry during the capsize, he would have been looking for them both.

Stan, carrying his baby daughter Kerry, her romper suit in his teeth, came across a group of people, perched on a ledge above the water and shivering from the cold. An elderly man had taken charge, busy telling people to calm down, that the boat was no longer sinking and must have hit the bottom. There were lifejackets everywhere, so it was difficult to move. One of the passengers on the ledge was Irish lorry driver William Cardwell. He had seen Stan with his daughter, 'I saw this chap climbing over the tables and chairs holding the child in his clenched teeth. It was unbelievable'.

William Cardwell had been having a flutter on a one-armed bandit and was spared the fate of dozens of fellow passengers in the nearby lounge. The bank of gambling machines lined a corridor of what had become the roof of the bar and stores area and hadn't fallen very far. The Irishman had helped save the lives of two girls in the water below but a third girl had lost consciousness:

> We were all in the water, fighting for our lives and there were two girls aged about 20 near me. One of them slipped under, came back, then slipped under again and was floating face downwards; she was just lying in the water and couldn't understand my instructions. I tried my best to reach her but it was impossible. We couldn't do anything for her. She was quickly gone. The other girl went hysterical when she saw she'd gone but we managed to grab her and push her out into an alleyway near the purser's office … it was a horrible black freezing nightmare. We could see a woman in the middle, a way off, and we all saw her just sink and drown. There was nothing we could do about it. We felt so helpless.

One deck above, on B-deck, more than fifty people were dining in the waiter-service Blue Riband restaurant. Irene Blanchard, her husband Norman (49), their daughter Sharon Horton (27) and 25-day-old granddaughter Rebecca were at their table. Sharon's husband, taxi driver Maurice (30) was on his way to try and book a cabin for his family. Irene recalled, 'I remember the boat tilted and the sweet trolley went flying and the gateaux went all over the floor. The water had come right up to the windows and my daughter said "if that glass breaks we will be under water." Then within seconds it happened.' A man fell across their table, dying in front of them. His wife fell on the floor between their tables. Irene was sucked into a whirlpool after her husband fell down:

> A chair came past and I hung onto it. A man then told me to hold onto him and said we could swim to a wall. I think it was the ceiling of the ship. But then I had to let go of the man as he wasn't speaking and I thought he was dead and was pulling me down. I reached the wall and I put my foot in something. I think it was a light socket and I shouted out and a young boy named Gary helped me and put me on some tables.

Frankfurt-based auditor Sue Hames (33) was on board with her boyfriend Rob Heard (40), returning to Binley Woods, Coventry. Rob had only meant to be with Sue in Germany for two days, but ended up staying for a week. His parents didn't even know that he wasn't back in Coventry. It was 'pure chance' that they secured a place aboard the *Herald*, having arrived in Zeebrugge expecting a long wait for the later Felixstowe sailing. The waiter had just taken their order. Sue likened the ferry capsizing to a car taking a corner too fast. They held onto each other. Suddenly she felt as if she was in mid-air and grabbed onto a door frame, while Rob clung to a table. They yelled to one another 'Are you all right?' As the ferry heeled over further, Rob lost his grip and disappeared, the water sweeping them apart. She never saw him again.

Sue was then pitched into the water and was swept through a doorway into a corridor, with the door shutting behind her. She was sucked into the freezing cold water but, despite the numbing cold and pitch dark, she managed to pull herself onto a ledge. There were other people already there, exhausted from their escape through the water:

> There was one man near to me. I know now he was called John, he was bleeding very badly. His daughter Claire was hanging round his neck and his wife was above him, holding a baby. The girl Claire was in the water and with her father's help and permission, I was able to haul Claire up and put her in a position where she was out of the water.

The terrified 9-year-old thought she was going to die, and Sue pulled her towards her to comfort her. She kept saying, 'I've been such a good girl. I've never told any lies.' Their wait for rescue seemed like an eternity. Clare's 11-month-old brother, Christopher, was being comforted by their mother. Sue fell into the water again but she was hauled back up.

Alan Cross (41) of Windsor and his wife Margaret, also 41, had spent the day with neighbours Alan and Molly Waters. Now all four were heading home. Alan Cross had just managed to kiss his wife when the sea came crashing through the restaurant windows. 'We were totally separated and I thought I'd had it. But I reached up and found myself in a pocket of air. I looked around but there was no sign of Margaret.'

Another soldier, Martin Norton of Kent, was travelling home on leave. He had just ordered his meal with the waiter when he found himself tumbling through space. He ended up in the water, struggling to keep his head above the surface. 'I ordered the fish', he recalls, 'but I wouldn't have bothered had I known I was expected to catch my own.' Martin was comforting a girl from the Dartford area, above the water line and although his brand new jacket was soaking wet, he wrapped it around her to offer some sort of warmth against the freezing cold.

Industrial chemist Terry Meade (34) of Sittingbourne, Kent, was having a meal with his girlfriend of three years, Christine Young (32). As the ferry went over, Terry waited for it to right itself, but it carried on. 'I was frightened by now. We were having to hold onto a table to stop ourselves from falling. I used one hand to steady myself at first, and one to hold Christine across the table. The crew were going around telling people there was nothing wrong and not to worry.' Terry thought for a moment that the list was caused by the ferry turning to avoid something.

By the time the restaurant's windows were under water, Terry was holding onto Christine's wrists with both hands. 'Then the windows blew out and the water flooded in.' Christine was torn from his grasp by the force of the water and he lost her forever. 'There was a lot of shouting, mothers screaming for their children and even I was calling for Christine.' Christine vanished as the lights went out and everything was under water. Turning a somersault under water and kicking through one of the glass partitions, Terry found himself facing the ceiling of the TV lounge. Now alone, he feared the worst for Christine, simply because of the struggle he'd had.

Terry was now in the lounge that was being used to show cartoons and videos during the crossing. A corridor had separated the restaurant from the TV lounge. 'Then a couple of people who must have been crew, told everyone to shut up. A couple of others climbed onto the television cabinet and then we could start getting people out.'

In the TV lounge, Alan Rogers and his wife, Sue, grabbed hold of their three children as the water rose outside the windows facing the Blue Riband restaurant. The ship's siren was wailing as the ferry turned over. There were screams as people flew through the air. Someone went through one of the glass windows and was cut to shreds. 'We've had it!' Alan cried out. Three-year-old William fell underneath the table where they had been seated and Alan, still holding his arm, couldn't pull him back through. He was beginning to slide down into a corridor. Alan put his legs through and lowered himself down. Holding onto the table with one hand and cradling William with the other, Alan tried to swing his son's head round as he caught sight of an arm lying in the corridor. There was no one attached to it. Then the windows exploded, filthy, muddy, freezing cold water crashed in and the lights went out. Although dark, there was just enough light to see. A nearby woman had her head split open.

Dazed and shocked, Alan carried a crying William back to his mother, fighting his way through the chaos. Sue passed their daughter Emma to Alan so she could focus on baby Adie. His buggy had rolled and come to rest at the leg of the table. Sue watched in horror as a man fell downwards and grabbed the buggy handles to save himself. This flipped the buggy up in front of her and she somehow managed to cling to it, Adie still strapped in. She took him out and held him up above the water.

Holding onto his twins, Alan grabbed his wife's collar as the water was now up to her neck. Holding all three children above their heads between them, with freezing water up to their necks, they were finding it difficult to breathe. After a while, Sue feared their baby Adie had died. He had gone so quiet and still. 'Keep hold of him', Alan told his wife, 'At least we'll all die together.'

Eventually the family found a ledge and handed the children along a line of people where they could be safe. About forty people were trapped with them. The eerie scene was illuminated by the occasional flashing lights of circling helicopters. Not being able to see each other, people were shouting. Sometimes there was a splash in the darkness as someone lost their grip and fell.

Lorry driver Alan Hawkes (54) of Peterlee, County Durham, was on board with his stepson Stephen Scott (15). Alan knew that the ferry was tipping over and wedged himself up against a fixed chair and table in the TV lounge. 'It seemed as if the ferry suddenly went hellishly fast and made a sharp right-hand bend. I was in the video room and everything started coming towards us. Children, objects, people. People were flying past me like bullets,' he said, 'they were shooting through glass windows and getting ripped to pieces.' When the water came in he was swept away but managed to grab a ledge.

Somebody yelled that their baby was in the water. Hearing a cry, Alan reached into the water and grabbed an anorak with a baby girl inside. After passing the baby to a woman on the ledge above, he heard a man shout that he could not hold onto a girl he had saved because he was losing too much blood. 'He dropped her into the water and I nearly lost her but I was able to grab on to her before she was swept away.' Alan then picked up another little girl. 'Amidst all this panic and chaos she just sat on my knee smiling. She was amazing and I will never forget her for as long as I live.'

Baby Michael Drury, in the TV lounge with his parents and two sisters, was thrown to the other end of the room in the capsize. Julie Drury's big toe was severed by a sheet of glass but was caught in the stockings she was wearing. Despite the fall, Michael was uninjured and later reunited with his family.

Also in the TV lounge were army Private Chris Fowler (20) and his wife, Irene. Chris recalled, 'At first everyone thought it was a great laugh and they were all cheering as the glasses slipped all over the place. Then when it didn't stop and kept going people started shouting and screaming. They were hanging onto anything to stop themselves falling down.'

Aft of the TV lounge was the B-deck lounge. Miles Southgate, his girlfriend Cath and their friend Stuart Orpwood had been relaxing in the almost empty lounge waiting for their friend Martin Spooner to join them for a few drinks and a game of cards. The ferry suddenly took on an ominous list and objects began to fall off tables. Miles caught sight of a man smiling at him through the railings of the iron room divider. 'You're not much of a seafarer,' the man must have thought at the look on Miles' face.

Suddenly everything shifted to port, and everyone found themselves thrown from their seats. A fire shutter came crashing down and Cath screamed. She was sliding down the deck to port and Miles knew he needed to keep her in sight and stay with her. A 'heavy' man on the starboard side of the railings lost his grip and crashed into the bars. Miles said to himself, 'Can't worry about him – sorry!' as the group of friends found themselves struggling for survival. Miles noticed that the dark night outside the windows had been replaced with sea water and suddenly realised that the ferry had listed so badly the windows were now under water.

The windows caved in and a wall of water thundered through, submerging the whole area in freezing seawater within seconds. Cath was hanging on to the belt of Miles' trousers trying to pull herself up but he felt himself being pulled down. Miles tried to throw his haversack and coat above him in a vain attempt to save his belongings, but the strap broke and they fell into the water. 'You're gonna die anyway,' he thought, 'so I wouldn't worry about it too much.' He took a deep breath and said to himself, 'I just hope it doesn't hurt too much.'

Miles was now thigh deep in water which was 'so bloody cold'. He and Cath managed to stand on fixed seating and tables. The water, he realised, had stopped rising, and he thought they were in an air pocket, not knowing that the ferry had stopped sinking. They were temporarily safe and it was giving him valuable 'thinking time'.

Passing through the B-deck lounge at the time was army Captain Brian Bunker, who was looking for the Salad Bowl cafeteria. He had left his wife Diane and Nadine, 9 months old, in a corner of the C-deck lounge below while he fetched some drinks and snacks. He had just arrived on B-deck when he felt a 'violent shake' and was thrown downwards, sliding into the area of the lounge opposite the TV room. Brian found himself in sea water which was steadily rising. He didn't panic or struggle. His army survival training kicked in and he rode the water as the level rose. After the water level stopped rising, and in total blackness, Brian was shouting, attempting to calm people down in the water around him. He was desperate to be with his family but he realised that the stairway from which he had come was now deep under water. He needed to get out and find them.

In the petty officers' mess, Steward Mick Stickler had just ordered a meal. He assumed the roll of the ferry was a violent turn to avoid something. Being naturally nosey, Mick went over to the door to see what was happening. This saved his life. As he got to the door, he could see into the galley. People were falling down and plates and kitchen utensils were crashing down around them. Suddenly, behind him the seawater burst through the windows of the petty mess. Mick found himself in the alleyway, which was now directed upwards. There were no handholds to climb up. Then the main lights went out. Somehow, he managed to go forward through the officers' mess and reached an alleyway running behind the ship's bridge. The last thing he saw before the emergency lights went out was water pouring in and up through the ship's office and up a stairway. He was on his own in the dark and the ferry moved a little more. Mick thought this was it, they were going right over. And he could hear screams – from where, he didn't know.

Using a row of doorways leading to toilets as a ladder, Mick climbed up the alleyway, all the time being followed by rising water. Reaching the door at the top, he had already given up hope and was doubting why he was carrying on, believing there was no way he could get out. Through the doorway was an alleyway running forward and aft. He knew there was a foyer lobby on the starboard side that led to the open deck. His escape route was blocked by a fire door which had shut automatically. He couldn't open it so moved along the corridor, feeling his way across a row of showers. A chair fell through a cabin door above, hitting him on the head.

From the galley and the cafeteria, he could hear shouts and screams. Suddenly, he also heard the voices of fellow crew members. Totally lost in the darkness, he called out, 'Where am I?' He realised he was by the lift. He tried to find the door which he knew was nearby, but it was now above him. From behind the door there was a faint glimmer of light. The water was still rising and was now up to his legs. 'It's OK, we can ride the water up to the door', someone said.

There were at least ten people in the crew's mess. Seaman 1A Mark Squire was just about to tuck into chicken tandoori when the ferry began to turn over. There was swearing from the galley next door as pots and pans clattered to the floor. The ship stopped for a few seconds at an angle of 40 or 45°. Everyone thought it would come back but it then carried on rolling. The main lights went out. Storekeeper Max Potterton cried out, 'She ain't coming back! Let's get the hell out of here!'

Across the room, Deckhand Leigh Cornelius fell on top of Seaman 1A Brian Kendal. Assistant Steward Nick Delo (35) was also in the crew's mess:

Plates and cups started sliding off the tables and within seconds we were vertical and clinging onto anything we could get hold of. People were being thrown up against the walls and then all the lights went out. Then, the water started coming in. That was the most terrifying bit because we couldn't see anything. We could just hear the water gushing in.

Steward Clive Bush (50) was pinned against the port bulkhead under a pile of fallen chairs:

The water rushed over my head and whipped my glasses off. I said to myself: 'This is it. I hope it's going to be quick.' Somebody else was hanging onto my belt. I didn't know who it was. When I first came out of the water I remember complaining about losing my glasses and not being able to see, to which Max said, 'You silly sod! None of us can. It's pitch black.

Leigh Cornelius and Brian Kendal managed to get to the door by side-stepping along the edge of the table. The door, now 6ft above them in the ceiling, was opened by Cornelius, who helped Kendal out. Kendal held the door open for Phil Naisbitt. Just outside the door there had been a row of lockers, which now formed part of the floor. Cornelius stood on them, and Kendal stood on Cornelius's shoulders. Mark Squire climbed up their backs and grabbed at a lip jutting out like a bulkhead near the lift shaft. Realising that it would be easier if there were two of them up there, Kendal held onto Squire's ankles and hauled himself up. After going through another door, Squire ran to fetch a bridge hose, tied it to a rail and threw it down into the crew's mess, where more of their colleagues were trapped. Senior Stewardess Moyna Thompson was lifted out, followed by Max Potterton, Nick Delo, Billy Walker, Clive Bush, Danny Morgan-John and Steve Greenaway.

Steward Graham Merricks and a woman were being swept up the alleyway. Mick Stickler and Able Seaman Billy Walker (22) grabbed the woman and held her head above water while Billy gave her the kiss of life, eventually reviving her. He then tried for fifteen minutes to resuscitate a girl aged about 10, without success.

Danny Wyman, 17, of Dover, was one of only two crew members to get out of the *Herald*'s galley alive. The other, Chief Cook Paul White had been elsewhere placing an order with Assistant Purser Stephen Homewood. Seven colleagues perished in the ship's kitchens.

Wyman told of his escape, 'I was swimming in 20ft of water when it suddenly pushed me through a serving hatch [into the crew's mess]. I knew then I would be saved.'

Mechanic Kevin MacLean (33) of Southampton had been on the open deck of the *Herald* as it capsized. After the ferry settled onto a sandbank, Kevin found himself standing on what had once been a wall. He didn't even get wet.

Gillian Baddeley, who had left her family to also go up on deck, was leaning over the rail when the capsize began. 'I felt I must be imagining it'. She was knocked unconscious as she was thrown against an outside wall and after she struggled to her feet was knocked down again, again knocked out. When she came round, she found herself in pitch blackness:

> There was a terrible creaking and groaning of metal, and people screaming in the darkness in sheer terror, shouting for help. Everything was the wrong way round. I was lying across some chairs fixed to the deck. I didn't realise at first that the ship was on its side and the chairs were vertical, almost like a ladder. Above me I could see doors leading back inside and wanted to go and find my family, but I couldn't get over the chairs.

Anthony Ray (20) of Wembley, had watched his sister Karen and future brother-in-law Alan walk off hand in hand to the cafeteria. 'I wanted to walk on deck,' he said, 'all of a sudden the boat started to roll. At first I thought it was waves. People were cheering. They thought it was funny. Then, as the ferry started to capsize, people started screaming and smashing windows.'

John Mancini (47) of Faversham, Kent, was on board with friend Harry after a day trip to Belgium. John said, 'People who couldn't hold on to something dropped vertically. One young lad fell on a table so hard, he smashed it. Then he fell through a window into the gangway.'

George Lamy was looking after his grandson's pram while the rest of his family were queuing for food and drink. When the ferry began to roll over, he let go of the pushchair and grabbed hold of the table in front of him. Using the edge of the table as a ledge, he climbed up to the windows and kicked one of them through, ignoring calls from other passengers not to break the windows as he may get into trouble.

Civil servant Noel Arnold (23) from London said, 'The water was rising but you couldn't get through the glass with your bare fists. I punched and punched but couldn't make a hole to get out. I saw one woman go flying right through one of these glass sheets and disappear into the water. She's most probably dead.'

Social worker Richard Smith (28) spoke of the panic after the capsize, 'People went flying past me hitting the walls as they went. They just couldn't stop themselves. One survivor had been in the freezing water so long he just couldn't put his arms back down.'

In the C-deck lounge, security guard Peter Martin (53) of Lancing, West Sussex, cried out to his wife, 'Oh Kay, what is happening?' as the ship went over. Kay, also 53, last saw her husband 'falling straight into the sea'.

The Zutic family became separated in the chaos of the disaster. Julie was trapped against a metal grille. 'I felt Carly fall away from my arms,' Julie recalled, 'but just managed to catch her. It was terrifying, complete mayhem, with people flying past us into glass partitions and everyone screaming and crying. Water was rushing up towards us and we all felt we were going to die.' Handing Carly to husband Petar, she felt the baby would stand a better chance of survival with her father. 'I held on to Carly and managed to pass her to Petar before I was carried away. As we became separated ... I didn't know what had happened to Petar or my baby. I hated to do it but I thought Carly's best chance was to stay with him.'

Third Engineer Keith Brown (23) of Ramsgate, was praised by many survivors for his efforts in the moments leading up to the rescue:

> I had just come out of the engine room and was halfway through my meal when, without warning, she went straight over. I was chest high in water and I suppose I must have been in there for about half an hour. But there were a lot of people who needed help and I just pushed and shoved them as quick as I could out to where the boats were.

Patricia Fox (26) of Forest Hill, south London, described how some passengers scrambled over her to escape. 'It was like a human pyramid with me at the bottom.'

A Hungarian lorry driver known as 'Charlie' was driving for haulage company Caspar Hangartner. He was on his way home to Scotland when he found himself on board the *Herald*. During the capsize, Charlie had been in a lounge. He wedged himself against a table and managed to kick out one of the windows. Once outside he helped haul out passengers who were still trapped.

Soldier Peter Williamson (26) of Portsmouth, was plunged into the freezing sea water pouring in through the smashed windows. His friend was struggling for life in the water but there was little Peter could do to save him. 'He was so cold he couldn't stay afloat; he weighed too much. I held onto him for as long as I could, then I had to let him go. My hands were freezing. It was terrible but there was nothing I could do.' After a while, Peter managed to grasp onto a chair fixed to the floor [now the wall] and grabbed at others still in the water with his free hand. A young girl who was screaming with fear was pulled to safety, as was a woman, who was dragged to safety when Peter grabbed her coat.

Steward Martin Barnes (18) had been looking after lorry drivers on H-deck before making his way upstairs. He told of how an old lady fell across his legs. 'I was underwater for some seconds and then managed to struggle clear, climbing up from table to table. I held on for about one and a half hours.'

Andrew and Eleanor Parker were on a family outing with their daughter and two family friends. Eleanor recalled the moment of disaster:

> We heard a crashing of cutlery and suddenly everything went black. My daughter was underneath and we were all lying together in a heap, with my husband telling everyone to keep calm. We were quite calm because we were all together ... then we could hear the water rushing in and could feel the ship sinking. Even then I don't think we felt scared. We just thought everything would turn out all right.

It was only when their 12-year-old daughter Janice saw that their way to safety was blocked by a gaping chasm that she began to get hysterical, convinced she was going to die. The chasm was a cross-corridor, running from one side of the ferry to the other and was rapidly filling with water.

Clearly, passengers and crew who had survived the initial capsize of the *Herald of Free Enterprise* were still in serious danger of dying of injuries. Many of them were slowly drowning, some were suffering from the first effects of hypothermia. They needed to get out – and quickly.

3

RESCUE

Trapped

Rescuers were on the scene within minutes of the *Herald*'s capsize. The crew of the dredger *Sanderus* had witnessed the ferry in trouble as she passed through the Outer Mole, and watched in horror as, moments later, she heeled over to port for the final time, with half of her superstructure plunging into the waves and settling in about 10m of water. Immediately, the captain of the *Sanderus* radioed Zeebrugge harbour authorities, who put into action a well-rehearsed disaster plan.

About 12 miles away, at the mouth of the River Scheldt, the naval hardware of four countries were participating in a NATO minesweeping exercise in the English Channel. Two Royal Navy Sea Kings, carrying four Royal Navy divers were on their way from RAF Culdrose in Cornwall, and the destroyer *Glasgow* and frigate *Diamede* were also called to the area.

Bosun Terry Ayling was shouting at stewardess, Gail Cook, 'Come on, you've got to get up!' They had been chatting with Ship's Carpenter Mick Tracy in Ayling's cabin when the ferry capsized. Gail had fallen heavily and was obviously injured. Finding a piece of glass in her shoe, she refused to go anywhere without putting her shoe back on. The three crew members made their way along the now upturned corridor to a set of pneumatic doors, the two men pulling the injured Gail along, now in near darkness. They squeezed through a 3ft wide gap next to the stairs that had been a passageway, and crawled along until they came to the door that led to the outside.

Outside, 'everything was quiet and absolutely still. It was dusk, so there was still enough light to see what we were doing', Ayling said. They went over to the bridge, where they saw Able Seaman Tony Down and Quartermaster Tom Wilson, who had managed to escape from the bridge, get a rope out of one of the lifeboats and lead it down into the doorway. Tony Down had actually been outside when the ferry capsized. Had Leigh Cornelius not gone to get a glass of milk in the crew's mess, Down would have been on his way there in the lift.

Captain Lewry said, 'The bosun and quartermaster threw a line down but I was too cold to tie a bow so they had to pull the rope back up and tie it for me. They hauled me up and I blacked out again.' Once Lewry was out of the water, Wilson said, 'The captain was badly injured but at least he was alive, so I left him there.'

Brian Kendal and Nick Delo had escaped from the crew's mess along with nine others, all of whom were now on the upturned hull. At this time, Chief Officer Leslie Sabel and Second Officer Paul Morter were pulled out, with Lewry next. There was no sign of Quartermaster John Hobbs, who had vanished below the water.

They learned that no 'Mayday' had been sent before the capsize. Unsure if any help was on its way, Kendal retrieved a flare from No. 3 lifeboat. 'In the midst of all this tragedy,' Ayling said, 'the farcical bits still stand out. I thought Brian had blown his head off. It just disappeared into a cloud of orange smoke.' It worked – Kendal said, 'I remember seeing a ship just off the starboard side and he blasted his horn back to let us know he'd seen us.'

Ayling said, 'What I will never forget is having to walk on the windows. It was like a scene out of a horror film, set in an asylum. We were walking on people's faces and fists hammering at the windows.'

Grabbing hammers, axes and ropes from the upturned, and now useless, lifeboats still fixed in their davits, they began to smash their way into the *Herald* in an effort to free those who were trapped inside. Shouting and signalling with their hands, they motioned for the stricken to move aside to dodge falling glass. Windows began to cave in and ropes were quickly secured and dropped down.

Fireman's son, Alan Firbank (21) of Doncaster, South Yorkshire, was amongst the first of the dead victims recovered from the wreck. His body was pulled out at 1945hrs. When his body was examined later, it appeared that there had been attempted signs of CPR (cardiopulmonary resuscitation).

At about the same time, tugs were arriving and pulling up alongside the ferry. One of them bumped the side of the ferry between A and B decks. Kendal was thrown a fireman's axe which he used on the middle panel of one of the lounge windows. He hit it twice, 'The first time it blew sparks everywhere; the second time the glass cracked and broke. Soon people were climbing out. I rounded up some of the people who had been rescued plus some of the Belgian tug crew to help pull others out.'

Bosun Terry Ayling said, 'Passengers were scrambling over each other to get out. One stewardess was knocked off a rope by a male passenger. There was considerable confusion, but we shouted not to panic and "She's settled – she's not going any further down". Many more passengers started to assist.'

Captain David Lewry was in a very bad way – Assistant Steward Nick Delo said he had no idea where the captain came from 'but he literally fell into my arms. He was obviously very badly injured and we decided we should get him off as soon as possible.' However, he kept pulling away from Delo, saying 'Let me stay with my ship. I must help the people'.

Lewry later testified, 'There was a tug coming alongside the ship. The next thing I knew I was on the tug and then I was in hospital in Bruges. I had no idea what happened.'

Gillian Baddeley (16) had been outside on deck at the very aft end of C-deck. The outdoor seating area was half enclosed, that is, it was sheltered above by the B-deck outside seating area which was completely exposed. Clinging to seats, the water rose up to her waist. Scared, her hands numb with cold and feeling sick and confused from briefly being knocked out, Gillian had crazy thoughts that she could swim to the shore, so she leapt into the waves. She struggled back to the surface and realised the waves were much bigger and the current stronger than she expected. She realised her only chance of survival was to stay with the ship. 'I swam back to where the decks had formed an alley full of water. I saw a terrified woman holding a girl of about two. I hitched my skirt to a hook to stop me going under then held my arms up to help keep the girl out of the water.' The woman told Gillian that the child wasn't her daughter; she'd grabbed the child as she escaped. For the next half hour Gillian and the woman held the girl between them while they bobbed in the water.

When they heard a helicopter above, Gillian knew that they couldn't be seen because they were in the sheltered area of the open deck. As she let go to swim out into the open sea again, the woman shouted, 'Gillian, please don't leave us, help us!' but she knew it was their only chance of being seen. Suddenly she heard a shout and Gillian knew that she would survive. A boat came alongside and she was pulled on board. She told her rescuers 'There's a woman and a child in there, please save them!' but she doesn't know if they were rescued. It still haunts her.

Unbeknown to Gillian, the woman and child did survive, although the following account suggests the child was a boy, rather than a girl. The child was probably dressed in winter clothing and it was very dark, but the two were undoubtedly the same people in Gillian's account. Able Seaman Brian Kendal and Steward Ken Hollingsbee went together to the same area of the C-deck open area. Kendal said:

> There was a woman and child holding onto the chairs. I ended up hanging from the rail trying to prise the child away from the woman. She wouldn't let him go at first, even though, as I found out later, it wasn't her child. Luckily, the child was thin enough to squeeze between the two rails and I passed him up to Ken.

Next, they pulled the woman up, part way by a fire hose around her body and partly on her own, using the seating to climb up. They had difficulty in getting her over the railing. 'We were both dangling in the air like monkeys.' Kendal grabbed the belt loops in her jeans, got hold of her and pulled her stomach onto the railing and Hollingsbee pulled her over the rest of the way.

Kendal and Hollingsbee then heard shouting from a doorway on E-deck, just aft of the winches. Kendal looked inside and saw a man hanging onto a sprinkler unit 20ft below, with a lifejacket slung around his neck, in the water. Kendal saw that he was losing his grip so he shouted to the man to tie his lifejacket to the sprinkler in case he let go. He told the man the divers would come and get him out. Kendal saw the man the next day in Zeebrugge, with a broken arm. He had survived.

Kendal then went to an entrance on C-deck, where a ladder and a rope had been lowered down through a window into one of the lounges. Seeing that Tom Wilson was extremely tired, he told him to take a breather. Kendal climbed down the ladder and started pulling people out. He was joined by Ayling, and then Wilson came back to help. Kendal worked the bottom half of the ladder and Wilson the top half. Sometimes people who were almost at the top slipped out of the rope and fell on top of Kendal, 'I was hanging there at times supporting people on my back. There was no way I was going to let them go.'

Lorry driver John Ward had been in the cafeteria with his friend, Tony. He watched as a man suddenly appeared from nowhere, gripped a table and began to climb the wall that had been the floor. The man fell back into the water but climbed back up as if nothing had happened. When the man was alongside John, he smashed a window and they all climbed out. John was one of the first survivors who made it on to the side of the ferry. The man who had climbed up the inside of the ferry, smashed their way out with seemingly no effort and then vanished into the night. John remained on the ferry long enough to help a couple and their baby by smashing a window and getting them out.

One by one they came. Few were able to climb ropes of their own accord – climbing ropes is difficult enough for those not used to it at the best of times. The circumstances they found themselves in were incredible, to say the least. Instead, those that could be saved were hoisted up from where they were clinging, both in and above the water. Where able, the ropes were fastened around the waists or arms of those waiting in the freezing dark below. Their fingers numb with cold and most did not have the strength to lift themselves.

Salvage expert David Beerman spoke at the time of the rescue:

Lamps, ladders, safety harnesses and all kinds of safety equipment have been brought into the vessel. The rescue operation is proceeding with all force possible. There are clear signs of people inside. Rescuers have to go in through doors and windows of the starboard side, and the people inside have to climb up vertically to reach the doors and windows.

Emmi Smith was trapped on a stairway after being pushed there by a man who drowned saving her. She had last seen her husband and four-year-old son as they were leaving the vehicle deck. 'The window [above] chipped over me. A ladder was pushed through. Two hands pulled me up. I was taken on a fishing boat. There I cried. Where were my child and my husband?'

Ambulances lined up waiting to receive casualties from the capsized ferry.

The injured are rushed to a waiting Belgian Red Cross ambulance.

A survivor, with fluorescent lifejacket, is winched to safety by a helicopter as rescuers, including some survivors, prepare to pull more people out of the wreck. (Courtesy of Fred Vandenbussche)

Shortly after the *Herald* capsizes, rescue workers are on the scene: a race against time to save as many people as possible before they succumb to the cold of the North Sea. (Courtesy of Fred Vandenbussche)

Rosina Summerfield and Julie Clark were trapped in a stairwell between the car deck and the lounge where they had last seen Rosina's son, Ryan (4), and her boyfriend Kevin Batten. They had listened helplessly to the cries of their fellow passengers in one of the ferry's busy lounges on the other side of the wall. They guessed they had been there for about an hour:

We saw flashes of light above us, which had to be helicopters. There was a commotion above us and we screamed and screamed to get someone's attention. The glass was broken on top of us and a rush of cold air came in. A little wooden ladder was lowered to a ledge above us and we had to climb to the next level. I seemed to vault up leaving poor Julie behind. She was quite small and couldn't reach. All I wanted to do was get out, under any circumstances. She was calling me and I hesitated to turn round and help her. It's something that I have never forgiven myself for. She would have been fine but at this stage I didn't know that.

A helicopter shone its searchlights on the boat and we could see the water rushing towards us. We could hear people screaming. It was horrible. We shouted for help and banged on the stairs. Someone threw a rope to us but we couldn't reach it. Then they dropped a ladder and we climbed onto the deck.

The two women found themselves outside on the ferry's side:

The lights from the helicopters and boats were so bright, like a film set. I always remember a big stack of lifejackets on the side of the ship, then along came a helicopter and blew them all into the sea. I ran along the ship looking into every porthole and window, screaming for Kevin and Ryan. I was terrified that they had drowned. Running towards me was a total stranger carrying two very young children, one of which was my four-year-old. I stopped him and he told me to get into a fishing trawler. The air was bitter and Ryan was hysterically screaming. I got into the trawler and went downstairs with so many other people. The captain gave me his coat and I wrapped it around Ryan as he was soaking wet and half-dressed. I didn't know what was wrong with him and he just wouldn't be consoled. It turned out that his father had fallen the full width of the ship with him and would not let his hand go. This saved his life but also dislocated his arm. Sitting in the trawler with a child that I couldn't help was probably one of the worst moments.

Maria Hasler (19) and Sharon Stanton (20), of Waltham Abbey, had been trapped in the ladies' for twenty minutes, hammering on the windows above their heads, until they were rescued. Maria was the mother of a 2-year-old daughter, but found herself caring for others that night, 'We were freezing and injured but our first thought was to help everyone else. When I got two babies out I just cuddled them.'

Miles Southgate and his girlfriend, Cath, were holding onto each other in thigh deep water in the B-deck lounge. It wasn't until rescue workers were on the upturned hull shining torches through the windows above that Miles could begin to think about their next move. Illuminated by the torchlight was their friend Stuart Orpwood, who was clinging to iron railings that had once been used as a room divider. He was trying to keep buoyant in the freezing water. Miles began to climb upwards, helping Cath towards the windows above, which seemed to be their only means of escape. He called down to his friend, 'You'll have to look after yourself, Stuart', as his hands were full with looking after Cath. He knew that their other friend on board, Martin Spooner, would manage to get himself out because he was used to swimming in cold water.

Army captain, Brian Bunker had been walking through the same lounge on his way to get drinks for his wife and daughter one deck below. After being thrown into the rising water, he had helped calm panicking survivors in the darkness around him. All the time, he had been extremely worried about his family, having no idea what had happened to them. Brian managed to climb onto a TV stand that was protruding from what had been the ceiling and was now the wall. He reached down and pulled others up, helping them to climb out of the water and towards the windows above. He was now just below a toughened glass window, when someone on the outside smashed it through. Miles and Cath also found themselves below the same window. Shards of glass showered down on them. Brian was cut by the glass. Miles was pulled out first so that he would be in a better position to help his girlfriend. Cath was then pulled out next, on a rope. It was a bit of a struggle as she was a 'big girl'. Both were out within twenty minutes of the capsize. 'I'll send the rope back down after Cath', he called to Stuart, who was still inside the flooded ferry.

Miles and Cath were not injured but they were freezing cold after being submerged in the water inside the B-deck lounge. They were no use to anyone in this state so they were given blankets and ended up in a tug moored next to the hull of the *Herald*. Whilst in a cabin trying to get warm, he thought he saw their friend, Stuart Orpwood, being ushered past the doorway. During the course of the evening they lost track of him and intended to look for him.

Once Brian Bunker had climbed through the smashed window onto the upturned hull, he helped pull more people out. There was total chaos. He could see that the side of the ship where he had left his wife and baby daughter was now lying under water. He took a few steps to the windows of C-deck and, although unsure if it was the exact spot where his family would be, he began to shout for them through another smashed window. With the help of another man, who Brian believed may have been a crew member, they located a rope ladder and let it down through the window. They also threw some ropes down and encouraged the people still trapped below to tie it around themselves so they could be pulled up.

After about half an hour, the Bennetts, who were standing in water chest high in the cafeteria, became aware that there were footsteps above them on the side of the ferry. There was some knocking and vague shouting. They realised that rescue was near. Suddenly windows were smashed above and torches were shone down onto those still trapped below. Michael Bennett noted that some passengers were injured by the falling glass but reasoned that this seemed minor when life was at stake. 'Ropes were let down and when I managed to grab the first one I tied it round my wife, the next one around the nurse who was still beside us and finally I had myself hoisted up.'

Once outside the ferry, crew members of the tug *Burgemeester Vandamme* guided them to their boat. After the tug had taken on as many survivors as they could find, they were taken back to shore where they were transferred immediately to St Jan's Hospital.

Among the rescuers were Bosun Terry Ayling and Quartermaster Tom Wilson. Wilson had already helped rescue three men on the bridge and had now turned his attention to the trapped passengers inside the ship, below where he now stood. Their priority was to free those trapped as fast as they could before hypothermia could claim any more victims. Ayling spoke of their rescue efforts, 'There was no question of getting women and children off first and keeping the men to the end. We had to get people out as they appeared'.

Wilson, working in a makeshift rescue team alongside him, said:

I shouted to everybody to be quiet because all the shouting was causing panic. One girl would just not stop shouting and was getting people more upset, so I got her out first. It was very, very cold. Some of them were so paralysed by the cold that they slipped through the ropes and slid back into the water.

Wilson recalled one young survivor, 'I took a baby to the tug. He was in a little blue romper suit and was soaking wet. He never cried. He just wanted to pull my hair.'

Working alongside them was senior barman John Hudson (32), he said, 'Passengers were trapped in water up to their necks. As soon as we got out we started handing down ropes and ladders and dragging them out. Once they were out on the side of the ship they started to calm down.'

Second Engineer Nicholas Ray illuminated an escape route using the headlights of cars on the vehicle deck.

Andrew Simons, a 30-year-old self-employed motor mechanic and his friend, Clifford Byrne, of Tooting Bec, south London, had become trapped in a corridor and were convinced they were not going to make it. Andrew recalled that moment, 'Before we saw the helicopter lights we looked at each other and thought we were going to die. We said to each other, "live together, die together".'

Caroline Harley was beginning to feel the effects of hypothermia before she was rescued, 'I couldn't feel my legs or my feet. We were in the water for about twenty-five minutes.'

Philip Wilson and his young family managed to escape from the ship, but became separated in the confusion, '… we got out. We passed Sabrina to the rescuers outside. Afterwards she just disappeared.'

Jenny Pierce had managed to hold onto her daughter, Emily, after watching her boyfriend and his 7-year-old son drown in front of her. When rescue arrived, a ladder was lowered through a broken window. Just as they were about to be lifted to safety, Jenny said, 'I lost my grip and fell into the water'. Emily started screaming. Mother and daughter became separated and eventually Jenny was hauled to safety and taken to a tug. 'A man came up to me and said "your daughter has ginger hair, hasn't she?" I said yes, and he replied "We've got her out, she's in another boat."' Tragically, Emily Pierce, 4 years old, was certified dead as the rescue boat reached shore. After sustaining a severe head injury, Emily had developed a blood clot and choked on her own vomit as rescue workers fought in vain to save her young life.

Assistant Purser Stephen Homewood (34) and another man began lifting people upwards and they, in turn, helped him to safety:

> There were people without lifejackets. Some were holding on to the end of a ladder. There was an accumulation of dead bodies at the base of the ladder and I am sure some people were floating on top of them. I told them to tie ropes underneath their arms so that the crew and passengers above could pull them out. We should have in our lifeboats a harness which is used by the helicopter services, like a baby's cradle with straps that pass underneath the arms and between the legs. Undoubtedly, if we had used this method, we could have saved more lives.

Crewman Glen Butler was in the water when Homewood spotted him and talked to him, 'He said he was all right, but when the diver reached him he was dead.'

Homewood, having climbed out onto the hull of the ship, was amazed and alarmed to see 2-year-old Matthew Conway wandering around, apparently alone. Pretty soon, however, Matthew's dad appeared to claim his son; he had already rescued Matthew from inside the ship and, making sure he was out, had gone back to save his heavily pregnant wife Debbie.

Homewood went over to 29-year-old Assistant Bosun Mark Stanley to help with the rescue efforts. Stanley, in an obvious state of shock and distress, kept saying over and over, 'It's my fault, it's my fault. I didn't lock them properly.' Homewood knew it was Stanley's job to make sure the bow doors were closed. He realised with horror why the ship had capsized.

Homewood told the court he had recently read a book about the sinking of the *Lusitania*, 'I might have been more prepared than most for the aftermath.'

George Lamy didn't know where his family was. Four of them were missing. He just knew he had to get out and try to find them. With the help of another man,

George smashed a window with part of a table and climbed onto the upturned hull. 'I thought that perhaps we shouldn't do it because the boat might right itself and we were causing damage. It was a stupid thing to think. I prayed. I don't know who to …' Then he went along the upturned superstructure, below his feet, smashing windows as he went, hoping that among those emerging from below would be his family. His daughter Tracy later said, 'He always said he wasn't thinking, "I am saving all these people", he just wanted to clear the way hoping that the next person would be family. He pulled so many people out, but in his eyes he let the family down and he never did enough.'

Lorry driver John Wickham (46) of Guildford, Surrey, found himself in the water with Sheila Perkins and her 18-year-old son Simon; both were clinging to him for life. 'I tried to pull a life jacket over the boy but he was too tired and cold to help me. I couldn't save them both – it was one or the other. Without a word, he slipped beneath the water while his mum looked on, crying quietly.'

Bank worker Andrew Parker (33) of Herne Hill, south London, was trying to save his family from the freezing cold water. Their way to a ledge above the water was blocked by a cross-corridor, leading from one side of the ship to the other. It had now become a vertical shaft, a sheer drop into an abyss that had partially filled with water. It was too wide to jump. The 6ft 4in tall Parker spreadeagled himself across the chasm with his feet and hands across two metal bars for support. Daughter Janice (12) was the first across, followed by wife Eleanor:

Andrew has a very large frame and he started shouting at me to step on his back and jump to the other side. But the rails were wobbly and I was worried that we would go down together and both die. He wouldn't let me say no. I felt as though I had to do it because there were so many people waiting. If it failed the rest would be left behind for good.

Andrew maintained the human bridge, which he himself later described as more like a 'stepping stone', for half an hour. More than twenty people crossed to safety this way, including family friend Oriana Gomez and her 12-year-old son Jonathan. The order that the group were pulled out of the ferry meant that the family became separated for almost twenty-four hours, Mr and Mrs Parker each thinking that the other was dead. Andrew said:

There was a lot of screaming in the ship. But luckily we were all together and because of that we were quite calm. What surprised me was that so many of the men were just thinking about themselves. They were not thinking of those who were injured, or young. Several young men who had been drinking were particularly selfish, and two tried to climb the rope together but they fell into the water.

After Andrew eventually got out of the ferry, he was given an injured baby to hold that had been found on the floor. 'The baby wasn't crying and we were told later that she had a fractured skull.'

Jan Willis had become separated from her friends in the cafeteria. She had been trying to calm 12-year-old Wayne Pinnells, whose family were missing:

> The lights had gone out and sometime later, time had no meaning, there was smashing glass from above. Someone threw a rope down and by this time I was very weak. I put the rope loop around me and I was told to jump. I did and they didn't pull me up. I recall falling into the cold water and lots of things floating about. I like to think that they were life jackets but for years I thought they were people. They then pulled me up and I hit my head on a metal bar but was pulled to safety.

Suddenly Jan found herself in the night air:

> The sight that met me was like something out of a Bruce Willis movie. I have rarely thought of it and I can picture it in my mind as I write this. There I was sitting on the side of a massive ship. The wind was freezing and helicopters with massive lights were flying around. Up until this time I had been calm. Strangely they gave me a woman with a dislocated arm to look after as we sat there. I grabbed her by the dislocated arm – what was I thinking? At that point I started to shiver and lose it. Someone said this one's got to go. A rope had been put down the side of the ship, now I guess the floor, and I managed to climb down onto a tug ship. Sometime later we were transferred to shore.

Paul Fisher's wife, Barbara, had been clinging to his legs as he was clinging to the counter in the duty-free shop when she had lost her grip and fell into the water. He was convinced that she was gone forever. Paul continued to hold onto the counter 'for what seemed like an eternity' when he heard footsteps above him, outside on the ferry's side. Suddenly the sealed windows caved in as they were smashed by the rescue workers and Paul was pulled to safety. His wife was missing. So was his four-year-old daughter and the two family friends who had been looking after her.

Soldier Terry Smith (23) had been returning to his young wife Sharon, and 6-month-old son Robert in Southampton, from his base in Germany. He had been in the duty-free shop when it literally fell in on him and the people around him. 'Twelve of us were trapped in one little place. The water started rising, then stopped. I thought we were going to drown. People were clinging to anything – clinging on to life. It was unreal. People were panicking. There were no announcements. People knew nothing. No one had a clue what to expect.' Terry had almost reached safety when he slipped and fell 30ft back into the freezing water. He had to save himself twice, barely making it back up again for the second time. 'Eventually rescuers got to us, smashed the windows and got us out, thank God.'

Julie Zutic was holding her two-month-old daughter, Carly. 'I held onto Carly and managed to pass her to Petar before I was carried away. As we became separated, I was up to my knees in water before help arrived. Somehow I got out with the help of rescuers.' Petar made his way across upturned tables handing Carly to strangers, who in turn handed the baby to others who were above them in the abyss. 'It was a struggle to move forward but the others made a wonderful effort to keep Carly safe. In the end a diver appeared and took her, strapped in a baby nest, away from me'. It was to be another ten hours before the parents were reunited with their baby daughter.

Soldier Nick Moore (20) had the opportunity to climb to safety just moments after the capsize, but instead stayed behind to help those floundering in the icy water. Nick was based in Germany as a Transport Corps driver and was on his way to visit family in Caerphilly. He had already reached a window after climbing up tables and seats and had smashed it. Smashing the window, he looked back down at those still struggling to survive and helped pull them to safety.

Struggling in the freezing cold darkness, it wasn't until the arrival of the helicopters and their searchlights that Sonia Saunders saw a man standing on a small ledge above her. 'Can you get me out?' she called. By this time she was so cold that her body had gone numb in the water. She pulled herself up and nearly slipped back in but the man shouted at her to grab his pullover. Sonia made it to the ledge where she found herself standing face to face with the man, both of them illuminated in the lights of the helicopter:

> The man said he could see another ledge, much bigger and I let go of him as he jumped over to this other ledge. He called me over but I fell into the water once more. He got me out again, this time I was freezing cold. He took off his lumber jacket and put it around me. I told him I had pains in my chest and he replied 'you're only imaging it – think of something nice, just talk about anything that comes into your mind.' As they took me out on the helicopter rope, I saw my husband in the water with lots of other bodies.

All she knew of her rescuer was that he was a lorry driver.

Brian Bunker and a crewman had been on the upturned hull for 'quite a while' and had formed a small group, pulling as many survivors as they could see from inside the ferry. An official rescue team arrived on a helicopter and they told Brian and the others that they would have to leave as they were evacuating everybody. 'Fuck off!', Brian shouted, as he continued to pull terrified people out, 'Take the women and the children but we need the men to stay and help.' Brian was hoping that the next people that would appear at the windows were his wife and daughter, but he knew that it was like looking for a needle in a haystack.

Four-month-old Kerry Mason, by this time, was white with cold, so her dad Stan kept moving her arms and legs and rubbing her body to keep her blood circulating.

Stan, and the others on the ledge took it in turns to try and keep Kerry warm. For forty-five minutes, the group of freezing cold survivors huddled together for warmth and waited for someone to get to them.

Suddenly a helicopter overhead shone its powerful searchlights down through the windows, high above them. The huddled survivors heard a rescue worker's boots scraping against the windows, his torch criss-crossing the darkness. It suddenly caught Kerry's yellow romper suit, held for a second, and then carried on. Seconds later, hammers began to beat into the windows above them, sending shattered glass showering onto them. A thin rope was dropped down. Someone above shouted down to them, 'Tie it round the baby!' A man next to Stan couldn't tie a knot as his hands were so cold. Still holding Kerry, Stan eventually managed to tie the rope around his daughter and she was winched to safety, swinging around in mid-air.

After everyone else on the ledge had been lifted to safety, Stan was the last to be rescued. He was suffering severe pain in his back, not knowing then that he had badly injured his spine. All the time, he was hoping that his wife, Cath, who he had last seen during the capsize, would be outside, safe and waiting for them.

Stan had last seen his wife when they had all been thrown downwards during the capsize of the ferry. He knew his daughter was safe; he had carried her to safety in his teeth only to watch her being winched away from him by rescuers. 'I wanted to find Kerry and Cath. There was no sign of them.' He first went to one tug, looking for them and then heard that another tug was about to leave. He went to that one and at first could not see them. 'Then suddenly I saw a little flash of yellow and a tiny hand sticking out from under a blanket. I pulled back the blanket and it was Kerry.'

Dave Hawken was rescued from the ruins of the duty-free shop, where he had been clinging onto shelving for about twenty minutes. Only seven people were pulled from the shop alive – Hawken, David Matthews from the bureau de change, one of Hawken's colleagues from duty-free and four passengers, including Paul Fisher. Once Hawken was out, he walked along the hull to the *Sea Horse* tug and was taken to a private clinic in Knokke for treatment for his broken shoulder, deep lacerations to his head and body, and severe bruising.

As they clung to a rope 30ft above the water inside the ferry, Andrew Golding (23) of Dartford decided to propose to his girlfriend Sarah Breare (19). 'Things were looking very grim and I thought I had better ask Sarah to marry me before we died.' Seconds later, Andrew lost his grip and fell back into the water. But, determined to fulfil his promise to Sarah, he bobbed back up to the surface and clambered back up the rope. Once he knew Sarah was in safe hands, Andrew decided to stay and help others still trapped, guiding them to rescue teams.

Susan Hames, separated from her boyfriend, was looking after two young children, 9-year-old Claire and her 11-month-old brother Christopher, on a ledge in a water-filled corridor. The children's parents, John and his wife, were nearby. Rescue workers eventually located them and smashed windows above their heads:

The broken glass was falling on some people. I was all right. I was trying to shelter the children. John's wife, still holding the baby, was opposite me. I was able to reach across and take the baby from her. The mother was pulled to safety. A man appeared from somewhere and he and I were able to get the baby and Claire onto a ledge above our head. I shouted 'Are there any more children?' Someone said yes and we were able to get them up onto a ledge. A canvas bag was lowered on a rope. We put the children in the canvas bag and they were pulled up one by one. Rescuers threw down a rope ladder and I persuaded John to climb up. I climbed up last but two.

Brian Gibbons lifted two injured lorry drivers from the corridor below into his own cabin on H-deck. He, Jock Calderwood and Roger Broomfield contemplated their fate as sea water continued to pour into the ferry below them. Jock told them that he had seen the ferry leave port with the bow doors open. There was no confusion in their minds as to what had happened. A fourth lorry driver had decided to try and get out himself in the pitch darkness and, before they could stop him, the unfortunate man had plunged into a cross-corridor, which had become a well full of water. They could only listen in horror to his shouts that he couldn't get out. The corridor walls had become a shaft with nothing to hold onto and the man quickly drowned.

The row of drivers' cabins that Brian had settled down in had ironically been below the water line when the ferry had been upright. Now these cabins were above water. The three lorry drivers did not know that the ferry had settled and was no longer sinking. Convinced that the sea water was still rising, they discussed amongst themselves how far the water had risen. Jock handed Brian a book, and he dropped it through the open cabin door to listen to the splash. The water surface was a lot closer to them than it had been before they had climbed into the cabin from the corridor.

Ship's Carpenter Mick Tracy and Assistant Bosun Mark Stanley spent two hours smashing windows and helping pull people out of the ferry. Justice Sheen later told Tracy at the inquiry, 'Many people are much indebted to you and we owe our gratitude for all your work.'

Rescue

On the night of Friday 6 March 1987, the Dutch-built 4,970 tonne dredger, *Sanderus*, was at the entrance to Zeebrugge harbour, dredging inwards between the New and Old Mole on the western side of the channel. The tide was ebbing when the *Herald* passed them at 8 knots, heading for the open sea. The crew of the *Sanderus* could see that the bow doors of the *Herald* were clearly open. At 1928hrs, when the ferry was about 3,000 yards away, Chief Mate Elias Van Maren saw the *Herald* sheering to starboard and heeling to port. Thirty seconds later, the brightly lit ferry was plunged into darkness as the *Herald* capsized.

Robert Heinemann, acting master of the *Sanderus*, also saw the lights of the *Herald* tilt and go out. He immediately gave the alarm with a VHF radio call to Zeebrugge pilotage control, who in turn informed the Coastguard:

> I was about a mile away watching the ferry. I had seen nothing wrong. But suddenly when next I looked, it was aslant in the water. It was obviously in very, very serious trouble. I sent out a 'Mayday' and told control help must come very soon.

Then the *Sanderus* raced towards the ferry and pulled up alongside, the first rescue vessel on the scene, with the aim of rescuing any survivors.

Three minutes later, at 1931hrs, the first rescue boat left Zeebrugge harbour. These first rescue boats were joined very quickly by the tugboat URS *Fighter* Vlissingen, the rescue boat *Javazee*, and two tugboats, the *Sea Lion* and the *Letzer.*

Robert Compernolle, captain of the dredger *Vlaanderen XXI*, had finished for the day, but immediately restarted the engines on the salvage tug, *Zeebrugge 1*. He called his divers, Dirk Van Mullem and Piet Lagast, both of the Norma Ltd salvage company, and recalled Chief Master Marcel Rutjens, also of Norma, who had just arrived home.

At 1935hrs local time, the coastguard radioed Search and Rescue (SAR) at Koksijde, which alarmed all ships at sea. SAR Koksijde despatched three Sea King helicopters, carrying eighteen naval personnel and several divers. Ten minutes later, the coastguard alerted CRC 100 (Call and Rescue Centre – 999 in the UK) and gave the message 'pre-alarm – ferry out of control in front of Zeebrugge'. At around the same time, the first survivors were being taken aboard the tugboat *Burgemeester Vandamme*, which had pulled up alongside the *Herald*. It would be an hour before this first group of survivors was to reach land.

The Zeebrugge Port Control informed the 538-tonne British cargo vessel *River Tamar*, which was due to leave Zeebrugge at 1930hrs, about the emergency. British skipper Billy Budd (32) and his five-man crew were unloading in Zeebrugge harbour when the *Herald* capsized. The boat first searched down tide for fifteen minutes before pulling up alongside the *Herald*. They transported eighteen people to ambulances waiting at the quayside, some of whom they had pulled from the water. Among those they rescued was a 4-month-old baby.

At Zeebrugge's naval base, one rating and one lieutenant were on duty in the first floor duty room. Next door, overseeing 'paper problems', were a large number of naval officers, as part of a NATO exercise codenamed WINTEX. Upon receiving the *Sanderus*' 'Mayday' call, the duty lieutenant contacted the Belgian air force base at Lesseweg, 25 miles inland. A helicopter was immediately scrambled and was hovering over the capsized *Herald* just fifteen minutes later. The pilot of that helicopter then sent a report back to the duty lieutenant, who ran into the WINTEX control room. Operation WINTEX was immediately cancelled and all its on-site personnel were ordered into the duty room. Operation 'Harbour Rescue' was now in full swing.

At that moment, the phone rang at the home of West Flanders Provincial Governor Oliver Vanneste. Just two words from port control – 'Zeebrugge Alarm'. Leaving his dinner, Vanneste ran to his car. 'We had practised this many times. I knew where to go – the crisis centre. But I didn't at that time know why.' Vanneste arrived at Van Hamm House, the preordained crisis centre. The city's fire chief was already there. It was only then that he learned that a ferry had capsized. 'That is the way our contingency plan is made. No one is permitted to ask questions about where or what has happened. That wastes time, and whether it is a sea disaster, a major fire, a rail crash or a nuclear accident, lives will be wasted.'

Zeebrugge's crisis plan – an immediate meeting of eight leaders is called, controlling the police force and gendarmerie, fire brigade, all hospitals, ambulance service, army medical corps, Red Cross and volunteer civil defence force. Telephone calls are cascaded down in a pyramid system – each man, on receiving his call, alerts those on his designated list, saying just the two words, 'Zeebrugge Alarm' and then leaves for his post.

'It is a good simple plan, which we have practised again and again so we know that it works.' It was reformulated in 1985, after the Heysel Stadium disaster in Brussels. 'But of course we could only wonder if on the day it would work.'

Thirty-five ambulances were already lined up on the Mole within fifteen minutes of the distress call. Red Cross workers, most of them teenagers in their grey uniforms were waiting nearby for the survivors to come ashore. As soon as the first of the survivors reached the Mole, they had blankets thrown around them at either of the two reception quays. The injured and the severely shocked were put into ambulances and driven off immediately. The others were bussed away from the scene. Vanneste said:

It was our decision, on medical advice, that in such temperatures, no one must be on the quay for more than sixty seconds. We had thirty-five ambulances and two mobile medical units. But what of those unhurt? There were such numbers, more than in our plan. I sent the police to the railway station to turn the passengers off the city buses and sent them [the buses] to the dock. It was drastic but I don't think the people of Zeebrugge will complain.

Relaxing at his seafront home in Blankenberge was the 52-year-old head of Belgium's pilotage and sea rescue service, Captain Marc Claus. His peace was shattered with the phone call that brought news that a ferry had capsized off Zeebrugge just minutes before. Claus drove straight to his office and began to co-ordinate the rescue. His staff had already summoned help from every available craft in the area, and soon tug boats were racing to the scene from Zeebrugge, Flushing and Derneuzen, as well as ships from the NATO exercise in the River Scheldt. 'This is my job', said Claus, who had previously witnessed burning oil tankers and other accidents at sea. This was by far the most serious incident of his career, in terms of loss of life. 'I am glad we were able to do our bit,' he added.

Navy Lieutenant Guido 'Gie' Couwenbergh was the duty officer at Zeebrugge Naval Station. The chief petty officer had taken a call informing them of the disaster, saying that helicopters were on the way and that an appeal had gone out for divers. Gie immediately retrieved his diving gear from his car, which he had used the day before when a French ship had had an accident with a propeller shaft. He shouted to his colleague to get the helicopters to pick him and two others up to take them to the *Herald*.

At 6.37 p.m. local time in the UK (1937hrs in Belgium), just nine minutes after the *Herald of Free Enterprise* capsized, the Dover Maritime Rescue Co-ordination Centre received a 'Mayday' signal from Ostend Radio. Twenty minutes later, the regional controller and district staff officer of the Dover coastguard had arrived at the centre, followed by a liaison officer from Kent Police. The centre's automatic telex network relayed information from Belgium to emergency services contacts.

As well as helicopters and Hercules aircraft out of RAF Manston, Kent, a Hoverspeed hovercraft was put on standby, along with RNLI lifeboats at Margate and Dover. HMS *Glasgow* and HMS *Diomede* were despatched to Zeebrugge to await instructions.

At RAF Brawdy, Dyfed, and RAF Coltishall, Norfolk, Sea King helicopters were scrambled, just seconds after the alert. They were joined by two more from Royal Navy Air Station Culdrose, in Cornwall, and two from RAF Bulmer in Northumberland. Each helicopter carried diving teams and equipment. RAF Manston, in south-east Kent, was chosen as the nearest UK base to the disaster scene and the helicopters were ordered to land there. An RAF Nimrod was put on standby at RAF Kinloss, Tayside, to act as an airborne communications centre but was not required in the end for that purpose. It was, however, used to transport a specialist team with cutting equipment from Hull to Zeebrugge.

At 1945hrs, having overheard the 'Mayday' communications, two Zeebrugge tugs, the *Burgemeester Vandamme* and the *Sea Horse* sailed to the *Herald* and stopped just aft of the ferry's funnels. At the same time, the No. 1 lifeboat was launched from Zeebrugge, and a control centre was established at the pilot station. Various small boats and fishing vessels had now joined the search for survivors. The 7,635 tonne RORO ferry *Gabriele Wehr* and the Townsend Thoresen ferry, *European Trader*, were sent from Zeebrugge. The *Gabriele Wehr* anchored about a third of a mile west of the *Herald*, whilst the crew prepared the ferry's helipad on the upper deck. The stern ramp was lowered and was made ready to receive survivors.

At 1955hrs, the first 'Mayday' relay to Ostend Radio alerted Dover Maritime Rescue Co-ordination Centre. One minute later, the Townsend Thoresen ferry, *Nordic Ferry*, left Zeebrugge harbour to assist the rescue efforts, supplying harnesses, Aldis (signal) lamps and other gear.

Fifteen minutes later, in Plymouth, Squadron Leader Ian Challas logged the disaster call, 'Dover coastguards have informed us that a vessel, the *Herald of Free Enterprise*, is believed to have capsized off Zeebrugge … it was obviously a terrible catastrophe and we immediately alerted helicopters and divers.' Royal Navy Clearance Diving teams were despatched to the scene.

In September 1986, armed forces chiefs had ordered air/sea search and rescue contingency plans to be drawn up. The Plymouth centre commander, Squadron Leader Mike Norris said, 'The air/sea search and rescue co-ordination have been concerned about an incident involving a ferry for some time. Our two senior commanding officers have both voiced their concern and decided we must develop a plan.' The plans were co-ordinated in a bombproof underground bunker in Plymouth. A skeleton plan, covering 50,000 miles of sea around southern Britain was ready.

At 2000hrs, the salvage tug *Zeebrugge 1* arrived on the scene. Divers Dirk Van Mullem and Piet Lagast set out in a rubber dinghy to search the sea for survivors. 'We made everything ready on the *Zeebrugge 1* so that we would be able to haul up as many people as possible from the water. Yet practically nobody fell overboard. As soon as we realised there was nobody to be rescued from the water we returned [to their boat] in our dinghy'. The *Zeebrugge 1* then manoeuvred near to the upper body of the ferry and served as a pontoon over which dozens of survivors would be able to walk to safety.

Telephones at crisis centres were inundated with calls from people offering clothing. Hotels in the area offered free beds, and even sent their own cars to pick up their new guests. A number of survivors were not reported for some time because the sailors of fishing boats and private launches who picked up survivors from the scene had taken them home for hot drinks and fresh clothes.

The *Sanderus* had rescued the first forty survivors. Acting master Robert Heinemann had manoeuvred the dredger as close as possible to the *Herald* and then launched a dinghy.

Marcel Rutjens of the Norma Salvage Company had been recalled to work just after arriving home for the day. 'I raced as fast as I could from my home back to the office. When I arrived there every place was full with the injured, which the *Burgemeester Vandamme* had brought ashore. This portion of the harbour is best suited to quick unloading of small craft. It was a scene out of hell!'

An urgent call was put out for naval divers, with two being flown directly to the *Herald*. Others from an Ostend-based crack diving team were flown in as soon as they reported for duty.

At 2025hrs, Gie Couwenbergh, a navy lieutenant and experienced diver, and his two colleagues, sports divers but not fully qualified, were airlifted to the *Herald*. They became the first Belgian diving team searching for survivors in the wreck. Gie could see 'flickering things' in the darkness below and a white shirt moving around. Someone was obviously alive down there. Gie Couwenbergh was lowered into the cafeteria of the ferry though a broken window on the end of a 10m long ladder. The ladder was too short for Gie to be lowered into the water and he had to drop the rest of the way. Gie quickly saw that the flickering came from the reflectors of lifejackets bobbing on the water. Unfortunately no one was in them.

The first person that Gie saw in the water was a young woman with blonde hair and blue eyes. She had bruises on her head. 'She looked straight into my eyes and didn't say anything.' There was only room for Gie to manoeuvre amongst the life-jackets and bodies in the water, so his two colleagues stayed on the hull. Gie shouted for a rope to be lowered down and he tied it lasso-style. He slipped the loop around the arms and shoulders of the woman and she was the first to be lifted out.

Another man had managed to get a lifejacket on but the straps had wrapped around the neck of another passenger, almost strangling him. Suddenly there were many people around him who needed his immediate help and he was the only one there to help him. He was overwhelmed.

It was a race against time to get the survivors out of the water. At first, the survivors were very vocal and animated but as the minutes went by, they grew quieter and still. Most of them were suffering hypothermia and were slowly succumbing to injuries, shock and exposure. To save time he would always take the person next to him. One woman was shouting 'Help me! Help me! Get me out!' but Gie figured that if she could make that much noise, she would be OK for a few more minutes. He gave the signal for one man to be lifted, but halfway up the man slipped out of the lasso and fell right back down onto Gie, pushing him underwater. When they surfaced, Gie asked the man if he was all right and the man simply replied, 'Where are my glasses?'

Suddenly a diver carrying a sling came down a wire and asked if Gie needed any help. There was only room for one rope and the diver's wire was still attached to a helicopter. There was also only one window to pull survivors up through so the diver got one man into the sling and took him back up, telling Gie that because of the danger involved with being linked directly to the helicopter, he wouldn't be back.

Half an hour later, a lifeboat was launched from the RORO ferry *Duke of Anglia* after receiving the 'Mayday' relay requesting that all vessels render assistance. The *Duke of Anglia* had been approaching the Schleur Zand buoy on the journey from Chatham to Zeebrugge. The ferry's lifeboat was commanded by the chief officer with the second engineer, three seamen and the cook. The chief officer saw lights in the *Herald*'s upper car deck so the lifeboat was manoeuvred into the stern area as the lights were hope of signs of life. However, the lights turned out to be those of an overturned lorry. The lifeboat was unable to go into the ferry any further because overturned cars were blocking the entrance.

Berthed at nearby Ostend was the British minesweeper *Hurworth*, of the NATO Standing Force Channel. At 2100hrs, the captain of the *Hurworth* ordered Able Seaman Eamon 'Ginge' Fullen to collect together all the diving equipment aboard. Two other divers, Lieutenant Simon Bound and Sub Lieutenant John Cox, had been ashore, but were contacted by the *Hurworth*, and all three divers made their way to Zeebrugge sep-arately by road. At 2120hrs, the Belgian Navy's *Ekster* left Zeebrugge with more divers.

St Jan's Hospital, near Bruges.

The A&E entrance at St Jan's Hospital.

Six hospital staff on duty or called in on the night of the disaster at Blankenberge Hospital. *L–R*: Chris Mahieu, Pier Levecke, Ria Proot, Linda Bill, Freddy Doom, Gisele de Bruyner.

The temporary mortuary at St Jan's to care for the bodies after the *Herald* was raised.

Zeebrugge marine base, where survivors and victims arrived on the night of the disaster. Bodies were also taken here after being found on the raised ferry.

The sports hall in Zeebrugge, scene of the first temporary mortuary the day after the disaster.

The *Herald of Free Enterprise*, in the process of being raised by *Smit Tak*. (Courtesy of Fred Vandenbussche)

Volkmar Asboe, a 26-year-old German Navy diver based with a NATO squadron in Ostend, arrived at the scene two hours after the capsize:

> It was a horrible vision, very dark, and you could see bodies of women and children floating past in the middle of the … bottles and cigarettes from the duty-free shop. I think it happened too fast for anyone to do anything. I hope I never see anything like this again. I saw the cars in the holds, piled up like children's toys. There was a lot of fuel about so we did not go in there because it was too dangerous.

A Hercules transport plane which had landed by chance on its way to RAF Lyneham, Wiltshire, was commandeered to fly to Zeebrugge with underwater lighting equipment, divers, diving equipment and a team from the Kent Fire Brigade, along with their breathing apparatus and cutting gear. Accompanying the fire service personnel was junior BBC reporter Triona Holden, along with a cameraman and soundman. Triona had been on duty at the BBC Television Centre in Wood Lane, London, when news of the disaster broke. The newsroom had erupted, with everyone 'jumping around like lunatics'. Her colleagues, chief reporters Kate Adie and Martin Bell were already on their way to Zeebrugge. Triona was sent to RAF Manston on a 'no hope' trip – a long shot. Whilst there, she had become friendly with the RAF commanding officer and had charmed and nagged her way aboard the Hercules.

Channel 4 News editor, Stewart Purvis, had been on duty in the newsroom when news of the disaster filtered through. Reporters, producers, camera crews and satellite dishes were immediately despatched to Belgium to be ready for the next day's programmes, whilst telephone interviews were arranged and graphics put in place to broadcast the first reports. Normally Channel 4 News, produced by ITN, only broadcast the news headlines on weekends but Stewart persuaded his bosses to prepare for a special thirty-minute programme for the next day.

Later that night the rescue centre in Edinburgh co-ordinated the plan to move helicopters within Britain to make sure there was adequate cover for air/sea rescue operations to fill gaps left by those helicopters sent to Zeebrugge and Manston.

Able Seaman Ginge Fullen arrived in Zeebrugge at 2200hrs, an hour after being sent from his ship, HMS *Hurworth*. He and his colleague, Lieutenant Bound, were immediately flown to the *Herald* by helicopter and they were the first divers who went into the most accessible lounge on the ferry. Finding only bodies, he reported it clear of any survivors. Fullen and Bound then swam along a rope into the next lounge where they found only more bodies.

Salvage divers, Dirk Van Mullem and Piet Lagast had already donned their diving suits and were navigating their dinghy towards the vehicle deck entrance. Armed with anything they could break windows with, they knew there were people still inside. 'We heard the screams of those who were still trapped in mortal agony.' On board the ferry, they came across an open wooden door and they could see people below.

Casting down ropes, they saw that the people down there did not have the strength to grab them. They found a ladder and lowered it through the doorway. 'That one ladder saved dozens of lives.' Piet remembers a boy of about 16 or 17 holding a baby. Too petrified to move, the boy had to be practically carried up the ladder. Then Piet again went down the ladder and pulled up another seven people.

A 14-year-old girl had spent two and a half hours in the icy water next to the body of her mother. Piet and Gie Couwenbergh had tied a rope around her, as she was unconscious and close to death. 'Three times I lifted Nicola Simpson out', Piet said, 'and twice she slipped from me at the last moment. The third time I had to push her, step by step, up the ladder before me to make sure that she wouldn't fall back in the water again.' She was then evacuated by helicopter to St Jan's Hospital, receiving external cardiac massage on the way. At this point, she was clinically dead.

The Dutch minesweeper HNLMS *Middelburg* arrived on the scene at 2220hrs with a diving team to offer help. Twenty minutes later, the tug *Burgemeester Vandamme* made its second trip back to Zeebrugge with another group of survivors. At 2253hrs a British helicopter with twenty divers arrived. They were joined a short time later by underwater search teams from the Belgian ships *Bellis* and *Jenie* and the Dutch ship *Bittelberg*. The German ship FGS *Goettingen* and the British Royal Navy's HMS *Hurworth* had been berthed at Ostend but, after the *Hurworth* had sent three divers by road to Zeebrugge, the ships had sailed for the scene. The Belgian Navy's auxiliary ships, *Spa* and *Crocus*, were on standby next to the *Herald*, taking survivors and bodies from the sea. Divers were also supplied by the Belgian ships *Krexel*, *Valcke*, *Zeemeeuw* and *Bij*.

The tug *Holland*, skippered by Mark De Riddier, arrived at the scene of the disaster at 2300hrs from its base at Terneuzen, on the western Scheldt. They found two victims and recovered them with a boat hook, unable to pull them from the water as they were too heavy. They held them there – a girl of 14 or 15, and a woman aged about 35 – until a lifeboat came to pick them up. The *Holland*'s sister tug, the *Zeeland*, commanded by De Riddier's engineer Peter Steel, picked up another two bodies. The *Sea Horse* took another 150 people to shore, dead and alive.

Captain Andre Pape told of how his tug, the *Sea Horse*, and his crew took part in the rescue of the *Herald* survivors. 'What I remember most vividly is the horror of seeing so big a ship on her side. It was just not possible. We see these ferries every day in our harbour. How could this have happened?' Captain Pape and his crew could see people's faces behind the glass in the windows of the upturned ferry, illuminated from the glow of cigarette lighters and from torches above. 'We took hammers and smashed the glass and started pulling the people out on to our decks. Some of these people were wonderful, never thinking of their own cold or fear. They immediately turned to help us in our work.' Passengers constantly asked Captain Pape to take them ashore and away from the disaster scene. 'No', I said. 'We must wait. We must take as many people as we can on board. The tide was running in our favour but would turn. Not to wait would have meant certain death for those we left behind.'

Captain Pape and the *Sea Horse*'s crew, along with the Breckens vessel *Javazee* are credited with rescuing 140 survivors from the *Herald of Free Enterprise*.

At this time there was much confusion at the wreck site because of the lack of lighting, the sheer number of rescuers and the noise of helicopters overhead. Verbal communication at the scene was almost impossible. From around 2300hrs that night, for the next forty minutes, more survivors were taken to shore by the tugs *Burgemeester Vandamme* and *Fighter*. Helicopters were taking the most seriously injured by air, direct to hospital.

Reporters had found their way on board the two tugs, asking to view and photograph the bodies of the deceased that had been brought to shore. They were immediately ordered off.

By 2341hrs, helicopters from the United Kingdom arrived at Zeebrugge – a Sea King from RAF Coltishall, with further helicopters from Bulmer, Tyneside, Brawdy and Culdrose.

When the helicopters arrived at Zeebrugge, forty-six service divers were already within the hull of the *Herald*, engaged in rescue and recovery. Five warships had launched smaller boats to conduct search patterns in the surrounding waters. 'Some chaos,' ensued on the side of the ferry about this time, according to on-board Dutch divers.

Lieutenant Steve Wild, leader of the Royal Navy divers involved in the rescue, refuted claims that co-ordination by the Belgians had been 'chaotic':

> If the Belgian people had not used their initiative and reacted spontaneously and enthusiastically, the number of survivors would have been reduced dramatically. There were a lot of people pulling survivors off the wreck so it was obviously a little disorganised, but the priority was speed. As soon as the accident happened there was an appeal for help on the radio and the rescue services, merchant seamen, people with boats and members of the public rushed to the ship to get people off.

At 2350hrs, Lieutenant Gie Couwenbergh was hauled up on a rope through the window of the cafeteria where he had spent three hours rescuing people in the freezing cold water. He couldn't feel his hands on the rope ladder as he'd had to remove his gloves to help the survivors. His diving suit had also cut into his wrists and had partially cut the blood supply off to his hands. He had tied a rope around fifty people in total and they had been lifted out to waiting rescue workers on the ferry's side. Thirty were OK, ten were unconscious but he knew that the last ten people he sent up were dead because they had been floating on the water. By the time Gie was pulled out, the tide had started to rise and the ferry was filling with more water. When he got back outside, the blonde girl he had first rescued was still there. 'She was dead. That I won't forget.'

At that point, Lieutenant Couwenbergh had been co-ordinating the rescue effort on board the *Herald*. Gie was exhausted. The role of on-scene commander was given to Chief Officer Malcolm Shakesby of the *Duke of Anglia*, with the ship nominated as the co-ordinating vessel. At this time, Shakesby was unaware of any shore centre and he was in VHF communication with his own ship. It appeared that this actually worked well, as language difficulties were eliminated.

At the same time, the *European Clearway* anchored near the wreck, offering assistance. Shakesby appealed for people with knowledge of the *Herald*, and crew members of the *European Clearway, European Trader* and *Free Enterprise VI*, which had arrived from Dover and was conducting a search of the sea, came forward. Shakesby now had overall control of the situation and continued to make requests for lights, ladders, stretchers and plans of the *Herald*. All the requests were met, although the amount of lighting proved to be inadequate. The *Arco Avon* had supplied hand lamps but these did not arrive until later.

Brian Bunker spent up to four hours on the upturned hull, pulling one survivor out after another, together with a team of survivors that had formed on a rope gang. After a while the only people that remained in that area were dead bodies. Exhausted, soaking wet, freezing cold and having been injured by glass, Brian had to concede defeat. He had helped save the lives of dozens of people, but had not seen his wife and baby daughter since before the capsize. He was led to the tug, *Burgemeester Vandamme*, alongside the *Herald*.

Some crew members who had been rescued from the *Herald* had insisted on staying aboard the wreck to assist in the rescue efforts. They were persuaded to go aboard the tug *Burgemeester Vandamme* for food and drink. Suffering from cold and shock, it was thought advisable for them to be taken to shore.

After more than five hours of pulling people to safety, Bosun Terry Ayling and Quartermaster Tom Wilson could do no more. 'By the finish we were so tired that even seven of us could not pull one person up between us', Wilson said, 'Our heads wanted to but our bodies would just not react.'

By half past midnight in the early hours of Saturday morning, it became clear that most of the survivors above water level had been rescued. Divers were then organised to begin recovering bodies while still looking for the living.

At 0035hrs, the tug *Fighter* and the *River Tamar* were back alongside the *Herald*. Reporters had jumped aboard the *River Tamar* in Zeebrugge and had refused the master's request for them to get off his ship. Shortly after the *River Tamar* arrived, the reporters climbed aboard the *Herald* and got in everyone's way. Still refusing to leave, they finally left after Shakesby threatened to physically throw them off. Meanwhile, the *Fighter* was preparing to take more bodies on her foredeck as there was no space left on the side of the *Herald*.

By 0050hrs, the hand lamps were failing. A request was sent out for more. Most of the bodies that could be seen were recovered, and most of the divers had withdrawn from the darker areas of the wreck. At 0130hrs, an inflatable raft carrying divers was sent to hammer on the bottom of the wreck as there was no obvious access to the engine room. There might be crew members still alive in the hull. Officers and crew members from other Townsend Thoresen ferries were arriving. Many of them were familiar with the layout of the *Herald*. As more hand lamps became available, further searches were carried out.

On H-deck, deep inside the *Herald*, three lorry drivers – Brian Gibbons, Jock Calderwood and Roger Broomfield – had been trapped for hours. Their shouts for help had gone unanswered, and they realised that unless anyone knew they were there they would be overlooked and would probably die. They decided that Brian Gibbons, being the only one of the three that was uninjured, would try to get to safety and let rescuers know where the others were.

So, wearing just the underpants that he had gone to bed in, Brian lowered himself onto the floor below the cabin, which had been the corridor wall before the capsize. Inching his way along the corridor in darkness, using pipes to hold onto, he came across a heavy metal door above. Cracking it open and letting fresh air flood in, they knew that they were not in an air pocket after all and that somewhere in the darkness of the ferry above there might be rescue.

Still shouting for help and with their calls going unanswered, Brian suddenly caught sight of the wrist watch he was wearing. He thought he might use the watch to tap on the pipes he was holding onto and give some kind of signal to people further down the ferry that they were trapped and needed help. They had listened in horror to the sound of people deeper inside the ferry that were screaming for help. They had also heard some of those same people dying unseen around them. They had heard the noise of rescue helicopters above but had been unable to make themselves heard. Now the noise of rescuers had died away, Brian knew this was their chance to be heard. He began tapping away on the pipes, no particular signal but just a noise to let people know that they were still alive in the ferry.

As he tapped away, bits of his watch began to break off and thinking he could save the bits for later if he needed to use them to carry on, Brian began to store them in his underpants. It just seemed the right thing to do. 'I just started tapping away, but I couldn't tell you how long I was down there for.' As he tapped he wondered if he would ever see his family again. He wondered if he would ever see his next birthday. 'At the end of the day it was just mind over matter. You tell yourself that if you're still breathing then you've got a chance of surviving.'

Jock suddenly called out, 'Did you hear that?' Brian became aware that there was another tapping, louder and heavier and not his own. Somebody had heard them! Somebody was answering them! All three drivers shouted and screamed in newly found strength. There was a shout from above. It was the young navy diver Ginge Fullen. Brian shouted back that there were three of them down there. He said he was going to go back to get the others but he was told to stay where he was. A rope was thrown down and he was winched to safety above. Once out of the ferry Brian had a blanket put around him. He waited there until his two companions, Roger and Jock, were brought up from the hull below.

Able Seaman (AB) 'Ginge' Fullen and other divers had found only bodies in one of the ferry's lounges. They then arrived in a flooded corridor on H-deck where they rescued the three trapped lorry drivers. It was 0215hrs on Saturday morning. Almost seven hours after the ferry had capsized, Brian Gibbons, Jock Calderwood and Roger Broomfield were the last three survivors found on the ferry.

Fullen and Bound were replaced by Sub Lieutenant Cox after five hours of 'extremely dangerous' conditions. Cox then oversaw rescue operations aboard the ferry for the following six hours. He organised a search of the *Herald* after plans of the ferry arrived. British and Belgian clearance diving teams took part. At 0245hrs, diving was suspended until more lights were available. They arrived at 0315hrs, and the search continued as helicopter movements were halted to aid communications and to listen for signs of life inside the ferry.

Belgian rescue diver George Decock (43) was on scene shortly after the last of the survivors had been rescued in the early hours of Saturday morning. He said:

There were bodies everywhere, I counted at least seven. There must be dozens down there … there was blood all over the cabin walls. The people inside had fallen on top of each other and were crushed as their bodies were pressed against the sides of the cabins. You couldn't see more than an inch in front of your face. We had to use torches and felt our way round. We had been tapping on the bulkhead to listen for any response but there has been none so far … all the bodies I saw were of young people in their twenties. One of them had obviously tried to swim as the water level rose but he had nothing to grab hold of on the wall to support himself. Exhausted, he just slipped under the water and drowned.

By 0300hrs on Saturday morning, with rescue operations being wound down, the Belgian naval crisis controller was able to turn down offers of help from diving teams from France and Finland. Lieutenant Commander Wilfried Van Kersohaever, said later:

Those who were saved were lucky to choose the day of Operation WINTEX. We were able to begin within fifteen minutes. Otherwise it would have taken thirty minutes, and fifteen minutes in those conditions in that cold sea is maybe the difference between 400 saved and 200.

The rapidly rising tide led to the suspension of diving aboard the *Herald* until the first daylight and a fall in the water level. At 0415hrs, the *Duke of Anglia* handed over rescue operations to the HNLMS *Middelburg*. After a final search, which included the *Herald*'s engine control room, the operation was completed. All of the rescue teams left the *Herald* at 0425hrs.

Divers Piet Lagast and Dirk Van Mullem were among the last rescuers to leave. 'The last hours were murderous, almost nobody was left alive and corpses were floating about. We pulled back eyelids and felt jugular veins. Whoever we thought had any chance we tried to bring out.'

Interviewed for the *Independent* newspaper on the twenty-fifth anniversary of the disaster, Peter Still, a former Royal Navy diver who had received the Queen's Commendation for Brave Conduct, said:

> It was around five in the morning. We were taking out people who had died and there were very, very small children, two or three years old. And I came across the bodies of a couple of old ladies who had ruined their fingers and fingernails trying to get out of the windows. Things like that stick in your mind. The hardest thing to take is the fact that it needn't have happened – the waste of life because of stupidity.

The armed forces minister, Mr Stanley praised the joint forces response, 'They responded marvellously and the whole operation was superbly well run throughout.'

NATO exercises, where the navies of various nations had regularly worked together, also benefitted the rescue operation. 'Our training is very, very similar and we all intermingle with very little difficulty. Speed was absolutely vital, because the water was so cold and people could not have survived more than half an hour in it.'

On the morning of Saturday 7 March, another Hercules brought the firemen of the Kent Fire Brigade, along with BBC junior reporter Triona Holden. Squadron Leader Norris said of the plan, 'The plan worked well and the decision to concentrate assets close to the accident, so that we could respond to requests quickly, proved to be very fruitful once the operation got into full swing.'

The naval governor of West Flanders, co-ordinator of the rescue efforts, Jacques Thuis, said he hoped that the achievements of the men under his command would help to reverse the memory of the Heysel Stadium disaster two years before, when the Belgian authorities were blamed for reacting too slowly. At that time, the Belgian Parliament had been one of the biggest critics.

In 1993, V.G. Vandermoere, summed up the rescue efforts in a presentation as part of an evaluation of the overall disaster:

> At sea, the early stages of the operation's manpower would involve tugboat crews, divers from the heli' air force, the navy, fishermen and physicians from the armed forces. Later, NATO divers and divers from the Engineering Corps would assist. Blankets, ropes, lights and ladders would be needed to locate survivors within the wreck and to extract them from the interior of the ferry. The rescue workers and the survivors would need to be transported between the disaster scene and safety on shore by utilising helicopters, tugboats, fishing boats, minesweepers and civilian boats.
>
> Once these helicopters and boats had transported their human cargo to the port, the Britannia dock, they would be looked after by the physicians, the Red

Cross and the Flemish Cross, the police and gendarmerie, the fire brigade and the medical services. Due to the conditions that the survivors had been subjected to, i.e. freezing cold water, blankets were on hand for everyone in the very first instance. Survivors were then to be taken to hospitals and reception centres via a fleet of clinic-mobiles, ambulances and commandeered city buses.

In the Hinterland zone, five hospitals were put on standby, along with three reception centres (social and tourism centres, including the De Haan holiday camp). An information centre and co-ordination centre were both established and the navy base was set aside to receive the bodies of the deceased. Personnel (physicians, nurses and the Red Cross) were to be mobilised in the hospitals, as well as personnel and physicians in the reception centres.

The Britannia dock was established as the sole meeting point, as a hinge between land and sea. All aid services on land, and boats at sea were ordered to go to this point. The local police and the gendarmerie were to keep the roads free of heavy traffic, particularly between the Britannia dock, the hospitals and reception centres, in order not to impede rescue workers and those injured being transported to hospitals. Despite the large number of onlookers, *ramptoerists* (disaster tourists), all of the crossroads were immediately under control and the road was cleared for ambulances and clini-mobiles.

By 0345hrs, the 'Mayday' distress signal was downgraded to the lower key 'Pan-Pan' signal. Just before 0500hrs, the search for survivors was called off until first light. By 1034hrs, the seventh and penultimate situation report was circulated.

Rescue workers continued to search for survivors in the wreck of the *Herald* all through the night. At any one time, there were up to forty divers – British, Belgian and Dutch – working in the hull. The British diving team consisted of twenty-nine men from two of Britain's elite clearance diving units, based at Plymouth and Portsmouth, a handful of clearance divers from the minesweeper HMS *Hurworth* and six search and rescue divers from the naval air stations in Lee-on-Solent and Plymouth.

Commander Jack Birkett, superintendent of diving with the Fleet Diving Group at HMS *Nelson* in Portsmouth spoke of the conditions that the divers had to face:

There was a hell of a lot of oil and diesel pollution from the cars and the ship. There was floating debris, no lighting, and there were rows and rows of dead bodies. The men are used to dealing with dead bodies but not in these sort of numbers. When you actually do meet a dead person – young children as well – in the dark, it's very unpleasant. I would have thought that all those who were involved will remember it for the rest of their lives. It will certainly scar them, even though they were trained to do it. I think they did bloody well.

Chief Petty Officer Eddie Kerr spoke of having to walk along the tops of overturned lorries on the vehicle deck. Only seeing dead bodies, he had to turn away and concentrate on finding the living.

A Belgian diver who was on the scene less than one hour after the capsize, related his experience. 'I could not describe it. It was hell, chaos. People were doing their best to save lives, as many as they could.'

Belgian Navy Commander Willy Herteleer (46) masterminded the rescue operation. It is largely down to his planning that lives were saved, but he gave the credit to his rescue team, 'The heroes are the divers who made the decision to jump into the water when they could not see anything and it was full of debris. The heroes are the passengers who risked their lives to save others.'

Two divers from Sealift marine contractors had flown into Belgium aboard an RAF Hercules on Saturday, with diving equipment and cutting gear in the hope of finding survivors. John Webb and Eric Styles were soon confronted with the realisation that there were no living people to be found. 'Our lights picked out bodies submerged in corridors which drifted away from us and we were unable to reach them. There were old people and babies. For the sake of the families I wish we could have recovered more bodies.' They eventually managed to recover seventeen bodies. 'Having dived on the ship and seen the devastation, it was a miracle that they got so many people out as they did.'

At the same time as Buckland Hospital was preparing to take the repatriated bodies, more than one hundred relatives of the *Herald*'s passengers and crew travelled to Belgium, many of them still not aware whether their loved ones had died or survived. All day on Saturday, frogmen aboard the *Herald* were tying bodies to railings and ledges for retrieval later, all the time hoping that they would find survivors in air pockets.

Later, in the afternoon, an RAF Sea King helicopter, using an infrared thermal imager, detected moving hotspots in the hull of the *Herald*. Hopes of finding anyone else alive were soon dashed, however, as it became increasingly apparent that only a miracle would save any of the missing in the freezing water and cold temperatures. On high tide, the *Herald* lay two thirds submerged.

Later on Saturday night, the search for survivors was reluctantly called off due to bad weather. Choppy seas caused by high winds were preventing the divers from continuing their search safely.

During the day, the Dutch salvage firm Smit Tak positioned a floating pontoon with an enormous crane alongside the wreck of the *Herald*. Negotiations between Townsend Thoresen and Smit Tak had begun late on the evening of the disaster. Now they were in position to begin salvage operations, as soon as rescue workers gave the go-ahead. But first the weather would need to improve.

4

AFTERMATH

Ashore

Emergency doctor Karel Vandevelde had left St Jan's Hospital for the day at 1600hrs. By 1930hrs he had returned. He was despatched to the Zeebrugge seafront where he assumed the role of triage doctor, Triage 1.

At 1952hrs, CRC 100 (999 in the UK) despatched the first medical rescue team from Bruges (known as MRT 1 Bruges) to Zeebrugge. MRT 1 Bruges consisted of one doctor and two nurses, and was joined upon arrival in Zeebrugge by a similar rescue team and five ambulances from Blankenberge. As far as they were aware, they were there to help with 'a few victims'.

At 2000hrs, Senior Nurse Rene Tytgart of St Jan's Hospital, Bruges, began a series of phone calls to members of his staff, both on duty at the hospital and those who had already gone home for the weekend. One of the first people he contacted was his boss, Nadine de Gendt, nursing director of the hospital, who was at home, relaxing with her family.

Twenty-four-year-old Koen De Meester was in the gym working out when he got a phone call from his mother. She was passing on a message to him from his boss at the volunteer Flemish Cross, which had existed in Bruges since 1934. He immediately left the gym and made for the organisation's ambulance station just four minutes from his home by bicycle.

With driver Maurits Stalpert at the wheel, the Flemish Cross ambulance arrived at a chaotic Zeebrugge harbour at 2000hrs. They headed for the Britannia dock to await the arrival of the first survivors from the *Herald*. Ten or fifteen ambulances were already there, eagerly awaiting their charges. On their way to Zeebrugge were Koen's brother and sister-in-law, also driving one of the organisation's ambulances.

Around thirteen minutes after the first MRTs had been sent by Bruges CRC, they, along with the ambulances, were in the harbour of Zeebrugge, awaiting the arrival of the first casualties. A reception centre was established on the pontoon of the Britannia dock after consultation between medical teams, the coastguard and the fire department. By 2010hrs, Triage Point 1 had been established. A minute later, CRC 100 formally announced the incident as a ship disaster with in excess of 400 victims. This launched the disaster plan known as 'Harbour Zeebrugge'. At exactly the same time, St Jan's Hospital activated its disaster plan, Phase B, with thirty anticipated casualties. Four minutes later, at 2015hrs, the second medical rescue team from Bruges (MRT 2 Bruges) was despatched to Zeebrugge, with two doctors and two nurses.

News of the disaster had just begun to be broadcast by the international media, but Belgian television seemed very slow to broadcast any news. Most of the Belgian people got the first news of the disaster from television stations based in France and the Netherlands. The rescuers in the harbour did not hear or see them, and still did not realise that the ferry had capsized; as far as they knew they were dealing with the victims of a ferry that had run into trouble.

The news broadcasts prompted offers of help from towns all over Belgium. At 2020hrs, MRT Jan Palfijn Hospital in Antwerp offered its assistance to St Jan's. Five minutes later, St Jan's was radioed to advise exactly what they were dealing with. Suddenly the extent of the disaster had become clear. The offer of help from Antwerp was accepted.

In Zeebrugge, the Disaster Co-Ordination Centre was set up in the harbour's office near the Vandammelock, under the command of the province's governor, Oliver Vanneste. The time was now 2025hrs, almost an hour since the *Herald* had capsized. Public transport buses were commandeered and blankets supplied by the army in order to warm the survivors upon arrival and transport them to makeshift rescue centres as necessary. Meanwhile, back at the wreck site, divers who had been taking part in NATO exercises a little way up the coast were busy saving lives within the *Herald*.

Linda Bill, a nurse at Knokke, had arrived as normal for the late shift at 2030hrs. She didn't believe the stories that she'd been hearing of a boat sinking off the coast, and carried on with her duties.

At 2030hrs, the Britannia dock was full of hundreds of rescue workers and at least fifty ambulances. The Command Post Operations (CPOPs) was activated to make some sort of order for when the first victims of the disaster were brought ashore. Disaster plans had been implemented by this time in all hospitals in Bruges, Ostend, Blankenberge, Knokke and Sijsele. The Red Cross Association was also informed by the CRC 100 to be ready to look after the survivors. At 2040hrs, the CRC 100 summoned the help of MRT Torhout.

Five minutes later, at 2045hrs, the first tugboat, *Burgemeester Vandamme*, arrived with fifty survivors at the pontoon of the Britannia dock. The survivors were reported to be in 'rather good condition', with a few injuries, shock and exposure. Triage 1, set up thirty five minutes before, assessed the level of treatment that they needed.

The *Vandamme* had brought the most mobile survivors with lesser injuries, who were able to leave the *Herald* of their own accord, or with little assistance. Many of the more able-bodied survivors chose to remain at the scene helping with the rescue efforts.

The first group of survivors had escaped the *Herald* by using the salvage ship, *Zeebrugge I*, as a 'stepping stone' to the three tugboats, two fishing boats and two rescue boats. By 2045hrs, the boats, carrying numerous survivors were ready to return to Triage 1. Three survivors were placed into the back of the two-bed Flemish Cross ambulance. Following the directive issued by the Disaster Plan, the ambulance headed straight for St Jozef's Hospital in Bruges. Koen De Meester recalled that those first three survivors were apparently uninjured, but suffering from shock and exposure.

MRT 1 Blankenberge boarded the *Vandamme* on its return to the wreck at 2050hrs, after it had offloaded its human cargo, at the same time as MRT Antwerp, 100km away, departed with one ambulance and one helicopter. Offers of assistance from Centre Hospitalier Regional Universitaire (CHU) Lille, 60km away across the French border, were also accepted. At 2100hrs, University Hospital Brussels sent a group of ambulances and one MRT. The whole of Belgium, and beyond, was responding magnificently to the disaster.

In Zeebrugge, at 2110hrs, MRT Torhout boarded a tugboat bound for the wreck, to assist MRT 1 Blankenberge with the treatment of injured casualties on board the upturned hull of the *Herald*. CPOPS called MRT 3 Bruges to the harbour office to give assistance to a group of victims, but the eleven survivors were uninjured. Feeling their expertise was needed elsewhere, they returned to Triage 1, arriving at 2150hrs, and moved on to Triage 2 ten minutes later.

After dropping off three survivors at St Jozef's Hospital in Bruges, the Flemish Cross ambulance crewed by Koen De Meester and Maurits Stalpert attempted to make the return journey to Zeebrugge, working hard not to crash into ambulances screaming past in the opposite direction. These ambulances had been forced to drive down the wrong carriageway due to the huge jams piling up with '*ramptoerists*' – disaster tourists.

Arriving back in Zeebrugge, the two men stood on the sea wall, awaiting the next boat load of survivors. Eventually they came to shore, and another three patients were placed in their ambulance, one with a clearly broken leg. They were immediately despatched to the military hospital in Ostend at around 2130hrs. Upon arrival at the hospital there, Koen observed that one doctor had literally just arrived after being called in; rushing across a hospital corridor in just his underpants on his way to get changed.

Dr Luc Huyghe had also been at home when he heard the news. Not believing it at first, he listened to radio reports that confirmed that a ferry had sunk off Zeebrugge, and that many casualties were feared. When he arrived at the accident and emergency department of Knokke Hospital, all of the twenty-eight patients that Knokke would receive that day had already arrived, at around 2130hrs. Radiologists, surgeons and orthopaedic surgeons were all called together to treat the survivors. Most appeared to be uninjured but were suffering from various stages of hypothermia and exposure. Some were still soaking wet from their immersion in seawater. Some had broken arms and legs. All were extremely quiet, and shivering from the bitter cold.

The smell of oil and diesel was very much present on the survivors' clothes, which Dr Huyghe described as a 'very stinky business'. It was quickly recognised that the immediate priority for the vast majority of the apparently uninjured survivors at Knokke was to re-establish warmth. Nurse Linda Bill recalled that blankets were briefly warmed in ovens and then placed around the still shivering patients. Wet and fuel-soaked clothes were stripped off and fresh, clean clothes were distributed. In fact, Piet Denorme remembers how he and his wife went through their own wardrobes at home and brought clothes to the hospital. He later saw a little girl on television, a survivor, wearing the clothes that had once belonged to his own daughter. Townspeople and shops in Knokke also donated clothes, and anything they could think of to help those who had lost everything but their lives.

One survivor was taken to intensive care suffering from a pneumothorax after an injury which caused one of his lungs to collapse. This would be the most seriously injured survivor to be treated at Knokke. The majority of the remaining twenty-seven survivors were made as comfortable as possible in a first-floor room at the hospital (the cafeteria). The hospital managers had reckoned it would probably be beneficial to keep them all together, where they could comfort one another. Television screens were set up, and the kitchens were opened.

At 2130hrs, MRT Roeselare was called in by CRC 100 and at 2145hrs, MRT Blankenberge was called to Zeebrugge Naval Base where three search and rescue helicopters had just landed on the base's runway. With thirty seriously injured victims who required immediate medical attention, the navy established the naval base as Triage Point 2. There had been no time to warn the civil authorities. Ambulance 100 Blankenberge quickly assessed the situation and called for immediate assistance from MRTs and ambulances. Upon hearing the radio call for assistance, St Jan's asked at Triage 1 (Britannia dock) to send reinforcements to Triage 2 (navy base). St Jan's also immediately despatched MRT 4 Bruges (comprising three doctors and two nurses) to Triage 2. Upon arrival at 2215hrs, the seriously wounded were treated and four victims had to be resuscitated, including 14-year-old Nicola Simpson.

At the various triage centres, people with no injuries were guided to warm buses, and many were taken to the Novotel and Europa hotels in Bruges, where they were offered rooms free of charge. Others were accommodated in the newly commandeered Duinse Polders holiday centre. Jim Garvey and his girlfriend Manuela Meltschack were allocated a small room at the Novotel, sharing with a woman who had apparently lost members of her family. All they wanted to do was to rest and change out of the orange overalls they had borrowed after their clothes had been discarded inside the *Herald*. The couple felt guilty that they had survived intact and uninjured while the woman was weeping uncontrollably for lost loved ones. They tried their best to comfort her, and in the end an official came to look after the woman.

Injured victims received first aid in ambulances, and were transported to hospitals if necessary. The idea of transporting patients to several hospitals on a rotation basis was to prevent any one hospital from becoming overwhelmed, when several could share the workload and therefore give patients the dedicated care they needed. Unfortunately, not all of the ambulances followed this directive and as a result of this, the A&E department of one hospital became overcrowded.

Many nursing staff had already left for the night when the *Herald* went over. Johan Bruneel, a radiologist at Knokke-Heist Hospital, was at home next to the hospital with his wife, painting a door, when he received a phone call from Dr Goeminne at around 2200hrs. The phone call was the first time that Bruneel learned of the disaster. Quickly washing his hands, he arrived at the hospital just five minutes later. Bruneel was joined by the head of nursing at the hospital, Eric Dobbelaere, who had also been at home. Dobbelaere was anxious to get to the hospital to test that the new ventilation machine in the six-bed intensive care department was working before any patients arrived.

The number of rescued victims was rising rapidly, and more MRT reinforcements and ambulances were requested by CRC 100. At 2200hrs, University Hospital, Ghent, despatched one MRT and one ambulance to the scene, while MRT Roeselare boarded a tugboat at Triage 1 at 2215hrs to render emergency medical assistance at the wreck site. At the same time, a helicopter from MRT Antwerp had arrived with one doctor and one nurse, and five minutes later, MRT Jan Palfijn, comprising two doctors and two nurses, arrived at St Jan's, to pick up a guide to direct them to Triage 2.

At 2230hrs, two medical teams were transported to the wreck via a search and rescue helicopter. They found that the exposed starboard side of the *Herald* was slanting at such an angle, along with the slippery and freezing conditions, that it was impossible to medically treat any of the casualties in situ. The best chance that they would have to save anyone was a quick evacuation by helicopter to Triage 2, where the medical teams were in a better position to do their work.

At 2240hrs, MRT Jan Palfijn Antwerp arrived from St Jan's at Triage 2. At 2245hrs, the low tide forced the closure of Triage 1 at Britannia dock, which meant that no more rescue boats could tie up alongside the pontoon there. At the same time, MRT Torhout, which had departed for the wreck site an hour and a half earlier, returned to the harbour aboard a tugboat. Unable to land at Triage 1 because of the low tide, they made their way to the small lifeboat station, where Triage 3 was established. MRT 1 and 2 Bruges then departed on the tugboat for the return journey to the wreck site. Meanwhile, over at Triage 2, a rescue helicopter (Helicopter Samu Lille) had arrived.

Marcel Vanparys, the hospital's administrator, had been attending a show organised by a youth group, of which his two children were members. He and the other parents had been invited to be part of the show and, after it ended, they were enjoying drinks in the bar. Hearing news of the breaking disaster on the radio in the bar, Vanparys immediately left for the hospital. He arrived at about 2300hrs, still wearing the make-up that he had worn for the show.

Piet Denorme had been dining in a restaurant when he became aware of the disaster. He left for Knokke Hospital immediately, arriving at about the same time as his colleague, Vanparys. Freddy Doom was also called in to stand by and prepare for arriving casualties.

By 2300hrs that night, MRT Ghent, who had been despatched an hour earlier, arrived at Triage 2. MRT 5 Bruges, comprising two doctors and four nurses, was sent to Zeebrugge's ferry terminal after CRC 100 relayed a message that a 'RORO ferry will arrive with victims on board.' The message proved to be a misunderstanding. Ten minutes later, medical teams and ambulances arrived from Brussels and were sent immediately to Triage 4. At 2315hrs, there was a call for help at the North Sea Ferries terminal. MRT Brussels tried in vain to resuscitate a victim. This victim was taken to the sports hall at Zeebrugge, which was being used as a temporary mortuary.

MRT 3 was put on standby on a rescue vessel near the wreck site, whilst MRT 4 found themselves on the minesweeper *Crocus*, which had been searching for victims in the sea. At about the same time, an ambulance arrived from Lille but was stood down, as it was no longer needed. The Flemish Cross ambulance which had taken three patients to Ostend arrived back in Zeebrugge after calling into the military base in Ostend for critically needed fuel supplies. After waiting around for an hour to take more survivors, the ambulance was finally stood down around midnight.

Between 0100hrs and 0300hrs on the morning of Saturday 7 March, almost all of the medical teams and ambulances that had been despatched from Blankenberge, Lille, Bruges, Brussels, Antwerp, Ghent, Torhout and Roeselare had returned to their respective hospitals. There was nothing more that could be done. Everyone who could be found was either in hospital, or being looked after in hotels and makeshift rescue centres. The last three survivors were the lorry drivers who were rescued after a British diver heard their knocking from the driver's cabin section. Before the helicopters had left, they had not been able to get themselves heard. They were taken to hospital with minor injuries and low body temperatures. Finally, at 0415hrs that morning, MRT 4 and 5 Bruges arrived back at St Jan's.

At St Jan's, the biggest hospital in the area, Nadine de Gendt and her team kept a meticulous record of the arrivals and discharges of every patient admitted and of every phone call she received concerning the people in her care. Nadine noted that three victims had died after CPR administered at the scene in Zeebrugge, and that two people had died at St Jan's. At least one of the victims had sustained such devastating chest injuries that CPR had been extremely difficult. In total, 164 survivors had been admitted to St Jan's and ultimately discharged – nine through Triage 1; 117 via Triage 2 and thirty-six through Triage 3. Of these 164 patients, fifty-one had been hospitalised (nine from Triage 1, thirty-one from Triage 2 and eleven through Triage 3). A total of 166 people had been hospitalised – sixty-eight at Kliniek Fabiola Blankenberge; fifty-one at St Jan's Bruges; twenty-eight at Kliniek Onze-Lieve-Vrouw Ter Linden Knokke; eleven at AZ St Lucas, Bruges; six at Kliniek St Jozef, Bruges; one at Kliniek Elisabeth Sijsele and one at Kliniek AZ St Jozef ,Ostend.

The medical rescue teams' roll call consisted of twenty-six doctors and forty-six nurses, of which St Jan's and Bruges provided eight doctors and thirteen nurses.

Injured passengers and crew were taken for treatment at several local hospitals. Dr Luc Huyghe, looking after survivors at Knokke Hospital, described their pitiful state. 'They are very, very shocked with severe hypothermia. They have taken in a lot of sea water.'

Distraught survivors found themselves wandering through hotel and hospital corridors desperately looking for their missing loved ones.

Two young children were taken to hospital separately, and without their families. Little Martin Hartley was taken to hospital with leg injuries and suffering from shock. He had not seen his parents, grandparents and family friend known as 'auntie' since the *Herald* went over. Likewise, 5-year-old Kerry Smith arrived back on shore, telling nurses, 'My name is Kerry Louise Smith. We were on a big boat … and then there was a lot of water. My dad said he would buy me some sweets if I was good on the boat. But he's not here now.' A rescue worker misheard the little girl and recorded her name as Terry instead of Kerry. Fortunately, Kerry's aunt, Dolores Hinsley, saw Kerry on television back in their home town of Manchester. She made immediate plans to travel to Zeebrugge to comfort her niece.

The Drury family were missing their 4-year-old daughter, Emma. They had seen her being lifted to safety onto a tug, but from there they didn't know where she'd been taken.

Fifteen-year-old Wayne McKenny and his half-sister, Lynette Carvley, were missing their mother, Sheila McKenny. The last time Lynette saw her mother, Sheila had been trying to stop a woman rolling away in her wheelchair. Lynette told reporters, 'I am still waiting for my mum. I don't know where she is.' Wayne was equally distraught, 'I've lost my mum; I don't know what's happened to her.'

George Lamy had become separated from his wife, mother, daughter and grandson even before the *Herald* had capsized. Now he was searching for them in all the hospitals in the area and constantly consulting lists of survivors, but his hope was fading fast. 'The lists of survivors are very inadequate. They don't even have *me* on them.' he said.

After spending four hours saving lives on the upturned hull of the *Herald*, Brian Bunker was taken to a hostel at Zeebrugge Naval Base. He wasn't there for long before he 'scrounged' a car and drove around the local hospitals with a Belgian Navy diver, looking for his missing wife, Diane, and baby daughter Nadine. He had last seen them in the C-deck lounge, where he had left them to get some drinks. His frantic search in the early hours of Saturday morning proved to be futile.

He eventually located a telephone and called his parents to break the news. Then he reported in to his army unit in Germany. The army flew in his father and Diane's brother, Keith, later the same day. A British Army padre, Father Crosby, arrived in Zeebrugge to support Brian and the family.

Piet Denorme was approached by Philip Wilson, who was looking for his 18-month-old daughter, Angelina. He knew that she had survived – he had carried her in his teeth – but Angelina had become separated from the rest of her family when the boat that had rescued them arrived at one of the landing stages. Angelina had been wearing a Mickey Mouse T-shirt. The call went out for a girl wearing such a T-shirt but none was found. With rising concern and desperation, Philip was driven by Erik Dobbelaere and Piet Denorme to survivor reception centres in the area, driving from one to the other in a search for the missing child. Eventually Angelina was recognised by her father in another hospital, with her wet Mickey Mouse T-shirt replaced by warm and dry clothing. The family were reunited once again.

At Knokke Hospital, as the effects of the cold and shock began to wear off, the survivors realised that they may have been injured after all. People began to limp, and cuts and grazes were noticed. Medical staff began to treat the apparently uninjured survivors for knee and ankle trauma, and cuts, most likely to have been caused by broken glass from when the rescuers smashed windows. Radiologist Johan Bruneel X-rayed several patients and discovered fractures and broken bones, of which the survivors had not shown any earlier signs.

By the early hours of Saturday morning, several hours after the disaster, all twenty-eight patients being treated at Knokke had been put in contact with their missing family and friends. It was extremely fortunate that that they had all been reunited. The success rate of reunited people at Knokke would prove to be unique that night.

Many of those who were caring for the Knokke survivors did not leave until 0300hrs or 0400hrs in the morning. With their patients in the safe hands of the night shift, and with no more survivors expected, the late shift staff finally began to go home. Many of them were exhausted, after what had effectively been a double shift.

The youngest survivor treated at Knokke had been 6-month-old Sabrina Wilson, who returned to Cumbria with her recently reunited family. The patient with the pneumothorax (collapsed lung) remained in hospital for several days. He had wanted to go home as soon as possible but wasn't discharged until his condition had been stabilised. When he returned to the UK, he unfortunately had to travel by sea as a journey by air could have caused further health problems.

Nurse Ria Proot, had helped look after the survivors at Knokke and, as a Red Cross volunteer, had also helped organise the collection and distribution of clothes and blankets. Ria's Red Cross role also took her to the sports hall at Zeebrugge, which had been converted to a temporary mortuary holding the remains of the fifty-eight victims who had been recovered in the first hours of the disaster. 'I will never forget it,' Ria said, shaking her head, 'Nothing could prepare you for what we saw.' She spoke of faces of the dead contorted in terror, the last seconds of the *Herald*'s victims frozen in time. She imagined what they had gone through before they died – and that's when the nightmares began. Ria now works at Blankenberge Hospital (which has since merged with Knokke).

Piet Debuyser was working in the emergency room, whilst Pier Levecke, upon hearing of the disaster, was despatched along with a doctor and nurse to Zeebrugge. They treated survivors who were taken to the triage centre at the naval base.

Chris Mahieu, working in intensive care at Blankenberge, did not know how many patients he was supposed to prepare for, and so began to call other hospitals as a back-up. He wanted to borrow ventilators for his intensive care department. As Blankenberge was closer to the site of the disaster than any other hospital, Chris reckoned that the majority of the injured would be brought to Blankenberge. Nothing could have prepared him for the influx of survivors. Describing the scene as total chaos, he would open the back door of an arriving ambulance to find five or six patients crammed into the back. There were several arrivals like this. Naval base buses were also used as ambulances, and it quickly became apparent that the numbers and condition of people arriving at Blankenberge suggested that people were being shipped off to hospitals whether they were injured or not. The confusion in the immediate aftermath of the disaster was now leading to a chaotic situation. Too many ambulances were being summoned for the number of casualties needing them.

Pier Levecke remained at the Zeebrugge naval base until the early hours of Saturday morning, performing four or five reanimations (resuscitations). After checking over the last three survivors (the lorry drivers) pulled from the wreck, he finally made his way back to the hospital.

Blankenberge hospital administrator, Gisele de Bruyner, faced a tough task in dealing with the communications side of the disaster's aftermath. The press had already interfered with the efficient running of the hospital through their overbearing presence and non-stop phone calls. She remembered how the press tried to invade the hospital to interview and take photographs of the survivors, and it became a priority to establish order within the hospital. From then on, news of the hospital's new and unexpected admissions was channelled through Gisele, seemingly placating the newsmen 'lying across the hospital entrance'.

Chris Mahieu confirmed that one victim, a young black girl, had died very soon after arriving at Blankenberge in the back of a VW Transporter belonging to the Belgian Navy.

Three patients were admitted to intensive care, all with lung problems consistent with swallowing sea water.

The last patient at Blankenberge, believed to be a crew member, was released after ten days.

In all, at least sixty-eight patients, and maybe as many as seventy-five, were treated at Blankenberge. The hospital, like the others, had responded to and coped with the aftermath of the tragedy magnificently. Several people have since said that if the disaster had to happen, it happened at the right place at the right time and involved the expertise and compassion and professionalism of the right people.

It soon became apparent to the rescuers involved in the disaster that no one actually knew how many people they were looking for. There was no passenger list available, despite Townsend Thoresen's insistence that they knew exactly how many were aboard. The numbers simply did not tally. A claim was made that there was no record of 147 foot passengers on board, or even the names of any car passengers. It seemed only drivers' names and vehicle registration numbers were recorded.

Early reports suggested that passengers not only came from Britain but also Belgium, Holland, Germany, Italy, Denmark, Austria, Sweden, Norway, Poland, Hungary, Romania and Turkey. But who were they, and how many?

All through the evening, survivors were comforted by their rescuers and carers. Not one person had a bad word to say about the way the Belgian population cared for the people of the *Herald*. The speed and efficiency with which the Belgians put together the rescue and care operation was nothing short of extraordinary.

As the last minutes of 6 March 1987 passed, the governor of West Flanders confirmed that twenty-six people had died on the *Herald*, and that another 240 people were missing. By the time the search was called off in the early hours until first light, the toll had risen to fifty-one. The incident was declared 'a 'national disaster'.

Waiting for News

Chef Steven Helkvist (24) of Llanrumney, Cardiff, had left home at the age of 18 to attend naval college, and had settled in Dover with his partner, Pauline. He had been transferred to the *Herald* after his normal ship, on the Dover–Calais run, had been taken out of service for a refit. His mother, Maureen, had watched the newsflash on TV, unaware that her son was on board, as the *Herald* was on the Zeebrugge run. She waited for five minutes before phoning his flat. Steven's partner, Pauline, answered and confirmed Maureen's worst fears.

Worried relatives crowded into the arrivals lobby at Dover harbour. Amongst them was Victor Stanley, looking for information on his son Mark (29) assistant bosun on the *Herald*, 'I simply can't find out anything. Obviously I am terrified that he might have been killed.'

'My father-in-law has worked on the ships for five years,' said supermarket storeman Richard (20), in Dover, trying to find out about Barry Allen (48), a cook on the *Herald*, 'so I am praying that he has used his knowledge of the vessel to escape.'

Becky Ede (16) was at friend Katie Hosking's house when they saw a newsflash on television. Her parents, and seven of their friends from a village social club were aboard, returning from a day out. 'I broke down, but, with my friend I travelled to Dover. I spent £16 ringing hospitals in Zeebrugge, before I found out that my mother had head injuries but was alive. I had to go through three more hospitals before I learned my father had also survived.'

Crewman Dave Hawken's girlfriend, Sue Gurr, heard about the disaster from a friend who had seen it on television. 'I had no idea what to do, and phoned Townsend Thoresen but they could not help.' Sue then phoned every hospital and clinic in and around Zeebrugge until she found him.

On hearing news of the disaster, Jenny Pierce's father, Vic, rushed to Belgium to find his daughter and her new family. He broke the news to his wife that, although Jenny was safe, their granddaughter Emily had died and that Jenny's partner, John Bray, and one of his sons were missing. By the end of that night, it was confirmed that Jenny Pierce (24) and Mark Bray (12) were the only survivors from the family.

Rosina Summerfield was desperate to let her mother know that she and her 4-year-old son were safe. After ensuring her son was being treated for his dislocated shoulder at St Jan's, where they'd been taken, she tried to find a phone:

I was really concerned about her not knowing if I was alive or dead so I asked the nurse where I could make a phone call. Of course, I had no money or documents as I had lost them all. The nurse told me to go to the telephone exchange in the building. I found the room and there was a very upset receptionist trying to manage the phones when so many people were ringing in for information. She said that there were no lines available because of all our [British] press had blocked the lines ringing in. She said 'please, can you talk to them'. So I answered one call that happened to be from the BBC. I begged the man to ring my mother and tell her we were OK and explained that it was urgent as she had recently had a stroke. He took the number and said he would, but only if I told him what had happened.

She did not realise that her telephone conversation would be broadcast to the world on the late night television news as an 'exclusive interview'. 'So *after* the shock of hearing me on the news, my mother got a phone call!'

Jan Willis had hit her head on a metal bar as she was being rescued from the *Herald*:

I had been injured on the head. I had blood on me and my clothes were ruined. Because I guess my injuries were not severe or even noticed I just cleaned myself up and that was that. The Red Cross gave me some clothes and months afterwards I would wear these clothes at home. They were tired and old fashioned. It was a sad day when the jeans I wore that day were too indecent to be seen in.

Jan realised years later, from her psychology studies, these were called transitional objects. Jan continued, 'From the boat we went to a school. Here I took control of the telephone phoning England, to notify everyone's family. I only broke down in tears when I spoke to my own. I also made friends with a German lorry driver. We shared a radiator and spoke only through sign language.' The survivors at the school were then transferred to the Novotel:

> I shared a room with a young girl who I had never met. She had been travelling with her friend's parents on a day trip as well. The father sat crying and rocking in the chair all the next day. His wife and daughter were missing. I do remember on that first night that life seemed so insignificant. I recall telling the girl that her friend was probably dead and it just seemed so normal. We believed at that time we were the only few survivors.

The girl who Jan was sharing with was 14-year-old Cheryl Taylor, whose school friend Nicola Simpson was missing. Nicola's father, Tony (41), was grieving for his lost daughter. Unbeknown to them all, Nicola had been rescued, on the point of death, and was receiving lifesaving treatment at nearby St Jan's Hospital.

Stan Mason was taken to St Jan's Hospital. His daughter Kerry was safe, but his wife, Cath, was missing. As he lay in a hospital bed racked with pain, he wondered when someone would tell him what had happened to Cath. 'I just felt so hopeless lying there. There were different stories coming through all the time. I kept thinking I'd lost her, but then you don't give up. You keep hoping that someone is going to walk into the room and say everything is OK.'

Meanwhile, back in Wigan, Stan's sister, Jean, and Cath's aunt, Rita Williams, had seen newsflashes of the disaster on television. They called Townsend Thoresen in Dover, but they could tell them very little. Preparing for the long drive, the family received a phone call from Stan at midnight, 'I'm OK, Kerry's here. They can't find Cath.'

'Hang on in there, lad, we're on our way', they told him, and then immediately started out for Zeebrugge.

Stan was initially stopped from going to the mortuary at Zeebrugge's sports hall in an effort to find Cath. Some bodies had already been identified, and the lids of their coffins had been screwed down. Stan began looking at those coffins that were still open, hoping that if Cath was dead, she would be here and not floating around in the wreck of the ferry. Cath was not among those bodies recovered on the night of the disaster. His sister, Jean, had arrived from the UK to search for Cath but had not found her. Shortly afterwards, Stan was transferred to a military hospital in Germany because of his spinal injuries.

The last time Susan Hames had seen her boyfriend, Robert Heard, was in the Blue Riband restaurant when he had shouted her name. Now she was waiting to hear if he was safe. 'My father's coming to meet me and I just want to look over the bodies to find out whether he's died. It's looking desperate but it's the not knowing that hurts so much.'

Miles Southgate and girlfriend, Cath, were taken to a reception centre where they thought their friends, Stuart Orpwood and Martin Spooner, would be taken as well, but they never appeared. The couple were then taken to the Novotel, outside the centre of Bruges, and given a change of clothes. Their shoes had also been ruined and so they were given a choice of shoes which had been donated by local people. Miles was pictured in several national newspapers trying on a pair of shoes to see if they fitted. 'The Belgian people were absolutely fantastic', said Miles, after they supplied hot drinks and cigarettes to the beleaguered survivors.

Stuart and Martin were still missing. After finding the name 'Steward Orderwood' on a list of survivors, and convinced they had seen him go past their cabin door on the tug that had brought them to shore, their friends Miles Southgate and his girl-friend Cath called Stuart's parents and told them, 'We think he's all right.' Martin's parents were at a dinner party and had had no idea that their son had been caught up in a disaster.

It wasn't until the Sunday morning that journalists took Miles and Cath to Stuart. Stuart had been hospitalised after being cut by falling glass. When they found him at the Novotel, Miles described Stuart as having 'quite an easy-going attitude.'

At the Novotel, two telephones were placed at the disposal of the survivors. However, British reporters were using the lines to transmit their stories. They were physically thrown out of the hotel by the enraged relatives.

Lynnette Carvley had seen her mother Sheila McKenny killed as she tried to stop a woman rolling away in a wheelchair. Shocked and traumatised, Lynnette and her daughter Rebecca were taken to shore by a tug. 'I don't remember an awful lot about how we were treated, only being given some black coffee. As soon as I drank the coffee I was physically sick.' They were then taken to the Novotel where they were reunited with Lynnette's half-brother, Wayne, and her stepfather, Richard.

As soon as Maureen Bennett arrived at St Jan's Hospital, she made enquiries about her missing daughter, Theresa, and her boyfriend Mark Webb. The hospital staff searched in vain for Theresa Bennett on the patient lists but they should have been looking for Theresa Gander. She was eventually found after being brought to another hospital by helicopter. Theresa had enquired after her mother and stepfather and, after they had been traced to another part of the hospital, an American priest went to the Bennetts' room at around 0200hrs whilst they were being interviewed by a tele-vision news crew. The priest leaned over and quietly spoke to Maureen. She shielded her eyes from the glare of the TV cameras and listened intently to the stranger. She suddenly burst into tears and shouted to her husband in the next hospital bed, 'She's alive! Theresa's alive!' About three hours later Theresa's boyfriend, Mark Webb, was found at the Novotel. He was unhurt.

The family of 24-year-old crew member Ian Lawson received the news that he was safe and being treated in hospital for injuries but otherwise '100 per cent alive and kicking'. His brother, David, had persuaded his bosses at the Dover import/

export firm where he worked to telex Townsend Thoresen in Zeebrugge to make inquiries about his brother on the ferry. 'Ian Lawson in hospital. He is alive', came back the reply. Another telex came later advising that Ian was alive as of 0030hrs on Saturday. However, despite constant telephone calls to the hospitals in the Zeebrugge area, they could find no evidence that he was at any of them.

Ian's brother, David, was engaged to the sister of another crew member, 17-year-old Danny Wyman. When Danny arrived at 1100hrs on Saturday to an emotional reunion with his parents and sister, they expected Ian to walk in with him. Soon afterwards the Lawson family were told that Ian was officially listed as missing. Ian's name was still appearing on updated lists of survivors and the injured in hospital.

Ian's wife, Sally (23), was too upset to be alone or to meet the incoming ferries carrying survivors, and was staying at her mother's home, waiting for news. Sally's mother, Pat Henworth, said, 'It is absolutely awful, like being on a seesaw that you can't get off.'

The world's press were swarming all over the Novotel lobby in Bruges. They were accused by some survivors of trying to trick their way into the hotel to get to the survivors. However, Lynnette Carvley said:

> The newspaper men were very helpful and kind as I remember. There was one in particular I will never forget. He bought a brandy for someone in shock, as we could not have free spirits and no one had any money on them to buy their own.
>
> Rebecca and myself did a few interviews for the local TVS [Television South. Their interviews were shown on network television first on Saturday morning]. After the inquest I was interviewed by 'News at Ten' and also did an interview on TVAM with Anne Diamond. It was very therapeutic.

Emmi Smith had been rescued from a stairway near the vehicle deck, and taken to the Novotel since she was uninjured. A Red Cross helper told her later that her missing husband was alive, and was being treated at St Jan's hospital. It was there, fifteen hours after the disaster, that Emmi learned the fate of her son. The waves had torn the boy from the arms of his dad – 4-year-old Mike had drowned.

Graham Lennox's mother, Gwen, had received a call from her son two days before the disaster, full of excitement about his forthcoming trip with his girlfriend, Pat Dockrill, his son Mark (13), and Pat's two children Emma (18) and Andrew (8). 'Mum, I'm going to bring you back some Belgian chocolates – the biggest box you've ever seen,' he'd told her. 'But that's Graham for you. He's one of the most generous people you'd ever meet.' Gwen went to the Townsend Thoresen headquarters at Dover to await news, with four other family members, including her common law husband, Bob Townsend, and Graham's younger sister, Dawn. They had gone to Dover in three cars from Basildon, Essex. 'They enjoyed their lives and they had everything to live for. I just hope that wherever they are, they are still all together, because I'm sure that way they have a better chance of survival.'

Twenty-year-old Jane Hind had been unable to go to the Netherlands with her mother and uncle because she was working and had to earn commission. Instead, Margaret Pelling (58) had asked her other daughter, Shirley Lopez (38), to go in her place. Margaret's brother, Terence Maloney (56), needed some help packing up a house he was selling in Eindhoven. Instead, Jane had arranged to go for a drink after work in London on Friday evening. Upon arriving at the family home in Beckenham, Kent, later that evening, she was met by her stepfather and brother-in-law, Shirley's husband:

> My stepfather didn't even give me a chance to sit down, and started saying there's been an accident with a ferry and we think your mum, sister and uncle are on it. I couldn't understand what was going on. I said that I wanted to call my brother and sister but they wouldn't let me. They said they didn't want to worry anyone else until they knew for sure. All I wanted was to have someone I loved around me so I just locked myself in the bathroom with my black Crombie coat on (funny the things you remember), and just sat there crying and praying that they were safe.

By the next morning, there was no news of Jane's mother, sister and uncle, and then they knew for sure that they were aboard the *Herald*. They had not been due to take that particular ferry, as they had planned to sail from another port, but they had apparently been running early.

Tracy Edwards was at home ironing and watching over her 5-month-old daughter, Sarah, while her husband, a London tube driver, was on late shift. At 7.15 p.m. she suddenly began to shiver. 'A horrible feeling fell upon me, which to this day is hard to describe.' Twenty minutes later, there was a newsflash on television that a ferry had been in an accident. She realised at that moment that it was her family, and that they were hurt. She knew her mum, dad, nan, sister and baby nephew were on that ferry. Tracy called her auntie Pat, her dad's sister. She had seen the newsflash too. The television news was scant, and she waited for the next bulletin.

She knew then that their lives were about to change forever. 'I was overcome by a feeling of sadness and sorrow.' Then she suddenly pulled herself together, an attitude of 'right, let's find out and do something'. She drove to her sister, Christine, who didn't have a phone. They then drove to their maternal grandmother, Nanny Lily's home and left Christine's dog there. Next they went to their parents' flat in Bow, east London, to collect their mother's dog. 'The flat seemed so empty, and the plates from dad's birthday meal the night before were still there.' They returned to Tracy's home to wait to pick up her husband at the end of his shift. All the time they were waiting, they had been calling the emergency telephone number shown on the television for news, without getting through. But their auntie Pat had, although as there was no passenger list, they couldn't give her any information.

Tracy Edwards and her family, the Lamys, had been to Townsend Thoresen offices many times, as they were regular passengers to France and Belgium. Now they were there for completely different reasons. It felt uncomfortable. Upon arrival in reception at about 2 a.m. on the Saturday morning, the first question they were asked was 'Are you a relative?'

'Yes', Tracy replied.

'Are you next of kin?'

The only reason to ask such a question was because they were dead. 'It was at this point that my husband's post-traumatic stress or mental illness started. My sister wasn't far behind. I found a hidden strength. My husband calls it nurse mode, where my nursing training kicks in and I become a fully functioning professional with no emotion or release.'

Tracy was told that she was next of kin to her mum, dad, sister and nephew and her aunt was her grandmother's next of kin. Tracy's sister, Christine, was put on a boat within hours, with her sister Kim's partner. Tracy, her husband and their baby daughter, Sarah, and Tracy's mother's dog, were left in a waiting room, along with other worried relatives, to wait for news of their loved ones. The family worked out a system between them. Those waiting at Dover would collate information to Nanny Lily. Their aunt Pat would call Dover for news, knowing that all the family would contact their Nanny Lily, as she was the one they always called. They were allowed access to a telephone and called back home about every hour. Christine was halfway to Zeebrugge when Tracy received the news she had been dreading. Tracy had called their Nanny Lily and the conversation still haunts her.

'Is there any news?' Tracy asked.

'Yes', replied Nanny Lily.

'Dad?'

'He called.'

'Who have we lost – mum?'

'Yes.'

'Nan?'

'Yes.'

'Kim?'

'Don't know.'

'Stevie?'

'Yes.'

She told her husband. The next three hours of memory and life were blanked out.

After spending that Saturday night at a bed and breakfast organised by Townsend Thoresen, they drove back to the waiting area of Townsend Thoresen House. 'I always felt they wanted us just to go home, disappear maybe.' The press were everywhere, and even followed Tracy into the toilets. Firing questions at her through the cubicle door. 'They even put a microphone boom, which looked like a foot long grey fluffy brush, under the door. So I pulled it and shoved it down the loo.' Tracy stormed back to reception and demanded they were let back into the waiting area. They looked at her, and she remembers saying, 'Unless you would rather me talk to the press?' They were back in the waiting area immediately. They were looked after by the Salvation Army and Red Cross volunteers. Nappies and special soya milk for the baby were provided, as her daughter was on a special diet. They even obtained fresh chicken and cut it into small pieces for the dog, as she wasn't eating.

Their Nanny Lily was still the co-ordinator of events, and had told them she was getting more information from the television than she had from officials. She had even seen Tracy and the family on the news. Tracy and the other relatives asked for a television. Townsend Thoresen provided a television set and some videos. They couldn't have vetted them very thoroughly – one of the videos was *The Poseidon Adventure*. 'I remember relatives fighting over who was going to jump on it and destroy it ...'

Despite everyone's best efforts, some reporters managed to gain entry into the waiting area, posing as volunteers and counsellors. They were immediately thrown out.

Meanwhile, in Zeebrugge, George Lamy spoke to waiting reporters about his family, 'I cannot believe that Kim, my darling daughter, is dead. Everything tells me she is. But I have to believe somewhere there is a miracle.' He then talked about Frances Lamy, 'This wonderful woman, my wife, was the best a man could ever have. She looked after me, she babied me ... yes she did.'

On Sunday 8 March, George Lamy returned to Dover with his daughter, Christine, and Kim's boyfriend. George was effectively being deported, as he did not want to leave without the bodies of his wife, mother and baby grandson. His 20-year-old daughter Kim was still missing. Tracy and her family met them at the ferry terminal. 'My dad looked so weak, grey and had aged so rapidly. He was only 54 and one day old, yet he looked at least 70. He was smoking a cigarette and lighting one at the same time. He hadn't smoked for over seven years.'

The AA (Automobile Association) towed the car home with the family. They were not up to driving themselves. 'The conversation in the lorry was so strange. Dad was allocating cars and possessions and deciding things that seemed to be so important to him. It was as if he was verbally making a wish list or will.'

They arrived at the family flat in Bow to the empty kitchen and the dirty plates they had left behind on Thursday night, when they had been happily celebrating George's birthday for the next day. Nanny Lily and Grandad Matt arrived, and the surviving members of the family had a meal of Chinese takeaway. 'The rice first seemed to stick in our throats, we were all so shocked.' Tracy, her husband and daughter went home the next day.

Soon afterwards, they had a phone call from Belgium. Her dad, George, had managed to get back to Belgium. He wasn't there long before he was deported again. This happened again and again, until a few days had passed. The British Army were called in to look after him and the other relatives who were determined to stay in Zeebrugge. George's family went to Zeebrugge to meet up with him, and they were asked if they could control him. The whole family was under virtual house arrest at the hotel, as the soldiers had orders to detain them for their own safety. This tense situation was making George increasingly angry and frustrated.

George had vowed to stay in Zeebrugge until the body of his daughter Kim was found. Bodies were still being recovered and he wanted to check every one that was brought back to see if it was Kim. Interviewed on television, he explained that by being in Belgium he felt closer to her. After that, the family was flown back to the UK from Belgium. Christine began to make funeral arrangements for Victoria, Frances and Stevie Lamy. Arrangements for Kim were put on hold as they still did not know what had happened to her.

The six children of Billy Schmidt and Brenda Lamb were convinced that their parents were coming back home to Reynes Park, south London. Both were on the missing list. The children's aunt, Pamela Williams, blames herself for their fate. She had talked the couple into taking a romantic break. 'How I wished I hadn't suggested it. I feel so guilty.'

Alison Gaillard's mother was in Australia, and her father had left to join his wife there at about the same time as the *Herald* capsized. Alison's younger brother and sister were at the family home in London. As the news of the disaster broke, the 20-year-old sister travelled to Dover to try to find out the whereabouts of Alison, and Alison's husband, Francis. After hours of making enquiries to authorities, she had no option but to return to London alone, exhausted and distressed. Maurice and Margaret de Rohan, upon learning of the disaster, and finding that their daughter and son-in-law were not on the list of survivors, immediately set out for London to be with their younger children.

Failing to get any definitive news of his sister and brother-in-law, Alison's younger brother decided to go to Zeebrugge but was told categorically by Kent police that under no circumstances were any relatives allowed to go there as there was 'total chaos'. By 11 p.m. on Sunday, 8 March, relatives in Britain were being told that all bodies that had been recovered and taken to the morgue had been identified. As Alison's parents arrived at Heathrow on the Monday morning, the information being given by Kent Police was that thirty-four of the bodies had been positively identified, but a further eighteen had not.

The family decided the only way to find out for sure was to ignore Kent Police and go to Zeebrugge. With the help of the Australian Consulate in London, the de Rohans arrived in Bruges on the morning of the following Wednesday. Contrary to everything they had been told by the police in England, they found that the Belgian authorities had actually been waiting for relatives from England to arrive to claim the bodies of their loved ones. Shortly after arriving at St Jan's Hospital, the de Rohans found the body of their daughter. Apparently she had been rescued alive from the ferry, but had died from the ordeal. Furthermore, her parents discovered that she was wearing a watch that bore her full maiden name. They were understandably angry that despite the family's repeated contact with the police in Britain, the police had failed to identify Alison.

Care

Madame Nadine de Gendt, Nursing Director of St Jan's Hospital, spoke of the city's 100 page '*Rampplan*', literally translated as 'disaster plan':

> It was vital for us all to keep our nerve and remember our training. Some of the unfortunates who arrived here were close to death, either from hypothermia or from their injuries. Some were quite badly hurt, others in deep shock. All of them had had their emotions shattered.

Among the patients treated at St Jan's was fourteen-year-old Nicola Simpson, who was unconscious when she arrived, with a heartbeat that was barely detectable. Her body temperature had plunged to 23°C, as the schoolgirl struggled to survive in the freezing water. By all the laws of medicine she should have died, but the surgeons at St Jan's were determined to save her life. She was airlifted to St Jan's Hospital. They cut into her chest and massaged Nicola's heart with their fingers. The ECG (electrocardiograph) showed ventricular fibrillation. Attempts to defibrillate were unsuccessful and extracorporeal circulation was used to perfuse, oxygenate and rewarm Nicola's body. At 30°C the heart could be defibrillated. There was also massive pulmonary oedema, and it took another three hours before the extracorporeal circulation could be stopped. The following morning, at 0900hrs, Nicola was conscious and was able to write her own name. She finally left the hospital on 31 March, the last survivor to be discharged from hospital in Belgium.

In the operating theatre next door, a 4-month-old baby girl was having a blood clot removed from her brain after suffering a fractured skull. Her parents were still missing.

After being rescued and reunited with her 4-year-old son, Rosina Summerfield and her friend, Julie Clark, were glad to be on land:

> We arrived at the dock and I was carrying Ryan down the stairs. An ambulance man ran up to me with a blanket and said, 'give me the child'. I handed Ryan to him and he ran off through the crowd so Julie and I followed. The press were there in force getting in the way of all the people that were trying to help us. The photo on front of every newspaper in Britain was of Ryan being held by the ambulance man.

Rosina and Ryan were taken to St Jan's. Ryan had suffered a dislocated arm as his father had tried to hold onto him during the capsize. Rosina's boyfriend, Kevin Batten, was still missing:

> By this time I was hysterical because I thought Kevin had drowned. They sedated Ryan, took him to X-ray and set his arm there so as not to upset me further. Eventually we were taken to the ward as Ryan was in danger because they couldn't get a drip into his tiny arm because of the hypothermia but he was sedated and quiet.

Rosina thought the staff at St Jan's were 'fantastic'. 'Nearly all of the staff had some English and they could not have helped us more.' She knew she had to contact her mother at home as soon as possible.

Nadine de Gendt was asked by reporters if the local community had come forward with flowers or gifts for the children. With inner calm, she replied, 'They came in to give their blood, they came in with warm clothes, they came in with blankets. But flowers, no, they did not bring.'

In Kent, eight hospitals prepared to receive the bodies of the victims.

Lorry driver Joseph Kay was being treated for injuries to his hands and feet after smashing through the windscreen of his cab to escape from the *Herald*'s car deck. After receiving stitches, he told reporters, 'I am not a religious man but I thanked God for saving me. I prayed my thanks to the nurses. They were angels.'

When Shirley Laverick was safe on land, the army nurse, heading to Newcastle, spoke to her boyfriend on the telephone for fifteen minutes, '… but he wasn't able to speak. He broke down and cried'. Shirley befriended Sue Hames, whose boyfriend Robert Heard was still missing. 'I don't know how Sue is coping. It is such a terrible time.'

Corporal Conrad Wilson (24) survived, with his family. It was his son's sixth birthday. 'We were planning a real celebration before all this. The whole point of us travelling home was to attend my parents' silver wedding party. We have nothing to celebrate now – except being alive.' Conrad added, 'I believe an investigation will show most of the deaths were in the cafeteria and duty-free areas.'

On Saturday, dozens of people thought to have perished in the disaster turned up alive and well after spending Friday night in the homes of townspeople in Zeebrugge and surrounding areas. They had arrived at the quayside shocked and dazed, and were driven away by concerned locals who just wanted to help. A heavily pregnant woman, her husband and son – most probably the Conway family – spent the night at the home of a doctor in Knokke, who examined her and found she was fine.

From Moerkerke, 50 miles from Bruges, came a family of five who simply wanted to visit those who had no one to visit them. Robert Kerport, his wife Daniela, and their three children had seen reports on television and read in the newspapers of children who had been orphaned in the disaster. They arrived at St Jan's hoping to offer some comfort.

The following story was related by Lady Marie-Louise de Zulueta, writing to *The Times* on 20 April:

A young couple who had survived the disaster were lying in hospital beds when they were approached by a couple. After chatting for a while, they were asked if they had lost anything in the disaster. The young man admitted he had lost his watch and his young wife her ring. They quietly went away and returned later with a magnificent watch for the husband and a ring for his wife and refused to give their names. A touching story.

The aunt of 5-year-old Kerry Smith, whose parents and baby brother were missing, flew from Manchester to Belgium when she heard news of the disaster. As Dolores Hinsley spoke to reporters at the hospital where her niece had been taken, another orphan, 12-year-old Mark Bray came in and held her hand. Dolores then went to Kerry's room where her rescuer, lorry driver Roger Broomfield, was at her bedside, 'He refused to leave her side. He was combing her hair and chatting to her.'

Twenty-year-old conscript Philippe Barremaecker had gone home for the weekend from his desk job in the ship's supply service at Zeebrugge's naval station. As the disaster unfolded, he and his parents had been aware of the sirens of ambulances from the nearby fire department. On Saturday morning, Philippe received a phone call ordering him back to the base to relieve colleagues who had been working all through the first night of the disaster. They received just half a day's basic training. Not quite knowing what was ahead of them, he knew 'we are going to be part of something big.' When he and his colleagues arrived, they became very quiet when their job became apparent. 'This is all about humans, defeated and powerless.'

On 9 March, Michael and Maureen Bennett, of Crawley, were discharged from St Jan's Hospital. Before they left, Maureen told reporters, 'I would have liked to have seen the captain for just a moment, but it's not possible. I just want to tell him not to blame himself for what happened.'

Before Captain David Lewry's wife, Patricia, arrived at his bedside at St Jan's, Lewry had received limited visits from Margaret Thatcher, Belgian Prime Minister Wilfried Martens, the Civil Police, the Harbour Police and Arthur Dhoest, the local Judge of Investigations. Lewry was put on an intravenous drip in intensive care, suffering from broken ribs and a punctured lung.

On Saturday afternoon, 7 March, the Duke and Duchess of York, Prince Andrew and his wife, Sarah, and Prime Minister Margaret Thatcher were among the official visitors to Queen Fabiola Hospital in Bruges. The Fisher family of Northamptonshire spoke to the royal couple of their experiences during the disaster and rescue. Prince Andrew was pictured holding 4-year-old Lisa Fisher, who survived with her parents.

Amongst those visited at the hospital was 8-year-old Martin Hartley, who had lost his parents, grandparents and an aunt. When the Duchess of York asked if there was anything she could do for him, Martin replied that he wanted a Rolling Thunder toy truck. His mother had planned to buy it for him. Sarah promised to bring one to him. 'She spent a long time with me,' Martin said. 'She was very nice.'

After they had visited Blankenberge, Prince Andrew told reporters, 'Complete shock is the only way to describe our first impression. I am amazed that so many people got out. One extends sympathy, but there is not much you can do for them.'

Prime Minister Margaret Thatcher said, 'I think an accident like this at sea has something in common with a mining tragedy. Everyone involved in that kind of work goes immediately to the scene. The feeling was, "This might have been us so we must do everything to help the victims"'.

At Queen Fabiola Hospital, Martin Hartley's nurse, Doreen Brouse, said, 'He seems to understand what has happened but the hardest part is when he still says he wants his mother.' Barbara Fisher, who survived with her husband and daughter, was often looking in on Martin. 'Martin's a lovely little kid. He gets a bit tearful now and then but he's incredibly brave.'

Martin's bed was next to a man who had lost two daughters. The man spoke fondly of Martin, 'Every time I was upset and started to cry he would come across and give me a drink of pop and tell me not to show my hairy chest to the nurses. People have been very kind.'

A few days after Martin arrived back home in Derbyshire, the toy truck that the Duchess of York had promised him in Zeebrugge was delivered. With the toy truck was a note – 'Here is your roller truck. I hope you have fun with it. Do let me know how you get on in the future. Love, Sarah.'

In Zeebrugge, a memorial service was held at St Donaas on 11 March, for those who had died aboard the *Herald*. A coach arrived with a number of survivors, bereaved families and friends, and those who had not yet been able to identify their loved ones. In Flemish and English, the Bishop of Bruges, Roger van Gheluwe, and the Right Reverend Richard Third, Anglican Bishop of Dover, conducted the ceremony together:

> In the midst of tragedy, how our little dreams crumble and seem no longer of any importance and we begin to grieve for other people's joys. Yet may we derive some comfort from knowing that at the worst moment of the disaster, men and women were giving each other great comfort and support. Our thanks go out, too, to the people of Belgium for their infinite love and kindness.

The *Herald*'s mourners were joined by Prince Phillipe, heir to the Belgian throne; Mr Peter Petrie, British ambassador in Belgium; General Sir Martin Farndale, commander in chief, British Army of the Rhine; Air Marshal Sir David Perry-Evans, RAF commander in Germany; and Townsend Thoresen executives, including Sir Jeffery Sterling, chairman of P&O, recently arrived from New Zealand.

In early April, a Belgian police spokesman gave this advice for relatives thinking of going to Zeebrugge to see the bodies of their loved ones, 'It is only natural that after reading about others who have made that terrible journey they will feel that they must come too. All we can say to them is that they would be causing themselves unnecessary distress. They should feel no shame about waiting in Dover.' Despite the police's gentle but firm advice, about twenty-five relatives and survivors arrived in the town.

On 9 April, Nadine de Gendt of St Jan's said:

Once we knew there were at least twenty-five had come here rather than wait in Dover for identification procedures there, the hospital called in the same medical staff and nurses that were on duty in the hospital on the night of the disaster and stayed with the same patients and their families until they were able to return to Britain. Some of my nurses have gladly cancelled leave to come back to be part of the special roster so that they can be reunited with those patients and families who are arriving here, many of them survivors themselves, asking 'why did we survive and others didn't?'

The bodies were being cared for in the mortuary at St Jan's Hospital. After witnessing the ordeal of several relatives who had insisted on seeing their loved ones, nursing co-ordinator Mr Maurice Bauta said, 'They wanted to go ahead even though we told them what five weeks in the sea would mean. They were clearly desperately shaken.'

Nadine de Gendt confirmed that the plan to have nurses and medical staff available as 'familiar faces' to the bereaved was working well. Speaking of the bereaved, Madame de Gendt said they had been dignified and serene 'but obviously they were not in a very good state'.

Victim Lita Harris's brother, Alan (31), from Dartford, said no one would have stopped him from seeing his sister. He spoke of the 'nightmare' ordeal of being in the mortuary but would not have given up those few seconds with her. 'I just stood there, seeing her in that mortuary and I was that close to the little girl I grew up with. I had to be there because of my mother … all that time I could think of nothing but Lita in that dark ship. I had to come back here as soon as they got the ship up.'

Nadine spoke of the after-effects of the disaster:

There are two periods of difficulty in a disaster of this scale. There is the first acute moment of that Friday and Saturday morning when the ship went down, and now there is the very difficult second period where psychological help is badly needed. On the first period, we are just professionals doing a job without time to think. In the second, we get closer to the survivors and their families and this is when it begins to hit us.

Oh yes, I cried all night. Sometimes I cried in front of them when we had to tell them, as was the case all too often that children, wives and whole families had been wiped out. This is what is now uniting us. These moments that brought us so close together and made us realise that the patients are the ones who have suffered. We are the professionals here to help them.

At this moment, everyone is very calm, but the emotion comes when the relatives see for the first time a piece of jewellery or a watch, that tells them the worst. It is a very cruel moment – as cruel as the sea. It is the worst moment also for the nurses.

Over the course of the disaster, 151 bodies were taken to the mortuary at St Jan's Hospital, Bruges. One person died there, after being rescued from the ferry, from 'catastrophic chest injuries' shortly after being admitted. Meticulous records collated by Nadine de Gendt show that, the day after the ferry was righted on 7 April, ten bodies were recovered and taken to the mortuary, another twenty bodies arrived there the next day and the body count rose to more than sixty a day later. On 11 April, four days after the *Herald* was raised, the total number of bodies in the mortuary rose sharply to more than 100.

Principal psychologist Peter Hodgkinson, of Bexley Hospital in London, said:

Maritime disaster is the worst. After any natural or manmade disaster, the levels of psychological problems among the bereaved and survivors are around 30–40 per cent at the end of the first year. There are only a few studies of maritime disaster and some show levels of up to 70 per cent. So we know we're working with absolutely the worst situation.

In August 1987, six months after the disaster, Michael and Maureen Bennett travelled from their home in Crawley, West Sussex, to Bruges, to personally thank their rescuers and the people that cared for them. They offered a commemorative plaque to the matron, Nadine de Gendt at St Jan's Hospital, before going into the Maraboe Hotel to meet up with the people who had helped save their lives – Henri Vermeesch, and four crew members from the Zeebrugge tugboat, *Burgemeester Vandamme* (Alfons Compernolle, Bruno Van Massenhove, Daniel Degraeve and Theophile Pape). They were welcomed by Charles Claeys of Townsend Thoresen, Zeebrugge, and Paul Goris and Christian de Block, of the Tug and Rescue Services Union.

On Christmas Eve 1987, a large bunch of tulips, carnations and freesias was delivered to Nadine de Gendt from a family in England. 'I felt I shared my Christmas with all these people', she said, talking of all the people that had contacted her and the hospital since the night of the disaster.

Reaction

On the day after the disaster, once it was established that there was no evidence of a mechanical or structural failure, Townsend Thoresen's deputy chief public relations officer, Paul Ovington, said:

> We don't know the cause of the accident. We are holding our own investigation, but it will be for the official Department of Transport inquiry to establish the reason. Water did ingress into the main vehicle deck and it does not appear that the ship was holed. … There is no Department of Transport requirement for them to be shut in calm and stable waters before a ship leaves the harbour entrance.

This was immediately disputed by maritime experts in Dover. One expert claimed, 'Regulations of this sort are not vague, they are quite specific that when a ship puts to sea its structure must be intact – in other words the wood must be put in the hole.'

Ovington went on to say that sometimes doors were left open after a ferry left the harbour to clear exhaust fumes from the vehicle deck. It was at the master's discretion whether or not vehicles were chained down, depending on weather reports. 'On Friday evening [the night of the disaster], there was no reason to secure the decks.'

The Zeebrugge Harbour Authority had witnessed previous incidents when ferries had left the Belgian port with their vehicle deck doors open. An official said it was 'not uncommon. Many rules are considered too strict by seamen and tend to be often overlooked.' The official added that sometimes vehicles were not tethered, meaning that if a ferry rolled in heavy seas, vehicles could move around on the car deck.

Barry Gilmour, former European Ferries deputy chief marine superintendent until 1979, was part of the Townsend Thoresen team that was responsible for bringing the *Herald of Free Enterprise* and her sisters into service. Gilmour said there was nothing wrong with the doors. 'One can only draw the conclusion that if the doors were shut when that ship left her berth and are subsequently open, then there is one great mystery to open. But if they were not shut, I think that it is relatively conclusive that the open doors were as a result of operator error – and a significant factor in the loss of the ship.'

Former Townsend Thoresen captain Oliver Elson (63), who had been master of the *Spirit of Free Enterprise* for six years, said that he would never have sailed with the doors open. '… and I don't think Captain Lewry would either. He is not that sort of character. I am sorry for Lewry, he is a grand chap.'

The Queen sent a message to the transport secretary, John Moore, 'I have been deeply shocked and saddened by the news about the terrible disaster at Zeebrugge. I send my deepest sympathy to the families of all those who have lost their lives so suddenly and tragically.'

Margaret Thatcher praised the rescue efforts as 'the greatest international help I think I have ever known'.

P&O chairman, Sir Jeffery Sterling, was on a promotion visit to New Zealand and Australia when he heard the news of the disaster. He immediately cancelled the trip and flew straight back to the UK, and on to Zeebrugge.

Archbishop Robert Runcie in Canterbury thanked those involved in the rescue efforts:

We owe a special debt to our friends in Belgium. The total commitment and excellence of their rescue and hospital services figure in every account I have heard or read. As so often in the past, tragedy at sea has displayed the human qualities of courage and generosity in all their splendour.

The Lord Mayor of Birmingham said, 'We owe Belgium a great debt. Many people of Birmingham were on that ferry and they would be dead today had it not been for the splendid rescue your people organised.'

Prime Minister Margaret Thatcher also praised the people who cared for the survivors:

I want to thank the president of the hospital, all the doctors, nurses and staff for the tremendous care which they have given. The quality of the treatment they are receiving is second to none. Some of the doctors have been up overnight and are still working. I think it was a high degree of organisation which enabled the best of treatment to get to the cases which most needed it, immediately.

In the publication *Loss Prevention Bulletin*, it was concluded that 'the Zeebrugge ferry disaster will be remembered for many dramatic reasons but also it will be seen as a superb demonstration of emergency preplanning, of international co-operation and the thoroughness of one nation's emergency response to a critical situation.'

Cardinal Basil Hulme heard the news of the disaster on German radio whilst at a meeting of European bishops in Frankfurt. 'Everybody at the meeting of the European bishop conference was deeply saddened. Special prayers were offered during our service at Mainz Cathedral.' He added that he would go to Belgium 'like a shot' if he thought it might help. Hulme presided at a requiem Mass for the victims at Westminster Cathedral on Wednesday 18 March.

The finals of the 'Miss Kent' contest were due to take place on Saturday evening, 7 March. The fifteen finalists boarded the *Pride of Free Enterprise*, the sister ship of the *Herald*, and helped raise more than £1,000 for the Channel Disaster Fund by passing round buckets and boxes amongst the passengers on the journey from Dover to Calais. 'Everyone wanted to give something', said Louise Hodges (19), from Medway. 'Twenty pound notes were dropping into my bucket. There was a lot of foreign currency too. Senior Purser Ian Brading thanked everyone on the ship's tannoy.

At midday on Sunday 8 March, the *Spirit of Free Enterprise* made its return journey from Calais to Dover. Among the passengers were many people who had first learned of the disaster to the *Spirit's* sister-ship, the *Herald*, by reading the Sunday newspapers on board. For one reason or another, they had not been aware of the capsize on Saturday, probably already travelling across Europe towards home. Those that knew of the disaster were understandably worried and nervous. 'I'll be happy when we get to the other end', said one. Another added 'If we worried about it, we would never go outside and do anything. The chances of two accidents on identical ferries is impossible, isn't it?'

A Townsend Thoresen company spokesman said, 'we are quite satisfied there is nothing wrong with the design of the three ships in the *Herald* [*sic* – *Spirit*] series. We have no plans to modify the other two ships or make alterations to two very much larger ones currently being built for us in West Germany.'

Later that day, several long-distance lorry drivers arriving on board a Townsend Thoresen ferry at Portsmouth Continental Ferry Terminal from Le Havre, blocked the off-ramp, preventing other vehicles leaving for about an hour. Several drivers had friends aboard the *Herald*. They were protesting at another safety aspect, that their cabins were below the waterline and, in the event of an accident, they were vulnerable. A Townsend Thoresen spokesman said their cabins were as safe as other passenger's cabins on higher decks. 'We feel they are safe wherever they are and the ferries are as safe as they ever were.'

The next morning (9 March 1987) in the *Sydney Morning Herald*, the assistant secretary of the Victoria branch of the Seaman's Union, Mr Michael Doleman, said, 'There is no way in the world an Australian ship would leave their stern doors open. The regulations in this country are the highest in the world, as a result of the *Straitsman* Inquiry.' This was referring to Australia's only vehicle ferry disaster, in 1974, when the 100-ton *Straitsman* capsized and sank in the Yarra River, Melbourne, just as it was about to berth. Two seaman were killed. An inquiry found that the ship's rear door had been opened before it reached dock.

During a debate in Parliament on 9 March, at 3.31 p.m., John Moore, the Secretary of State for Transport, said the following:

… immediately the tragedy occurred, the Belgian authorities took charge of the search and rescue arrangements, with assistance from Her Majesty's Coastguard and the Ministry of Defence rescue co-ordination centre at Plymouth … I wish to pay tribute to all those involved in the rescue arrangements, especially to the Belgian authorities and the Belgian people, without whose speedy response the casualties would have been much greater. I should also like to pay tribute to the police, hospitals and fire services on both sides of the Channel, the staff of Townsend Thoresen and the British ambassador and his staff in Belgium, for their assistance to the injured and bereaved.

He went on to reveal that the admiralty judge, the Honourable Mr Justice Sheen, would oversee a full formal investigation into the disaster:

> It will be for the formal investigation to investigate the causes of the disaster and to make recommendations to ensure that all possible lessons are learned. But the preliminary reports which I have received suggest that the cause of the capsize to the vessel was an inrush of water through the bow loading doors. I have no evidence to suggest that this was due to any fundamental design of the ship.

The Department of Transport was instructed to immediately introduce safety checks on all RORO ferries leaving ports in the United Kingdom. These checks included ensuring that all loading door mechanisms were in full working order, that all officers and crew were aware of the operating procedures, and that all openings in the hull and superstructure must be closed before ships reached the open sea. Moore also advised ferry owners to fit warning lights on the bridge to show whether the loading doors were properly closed.

He told the House that he was considering this as a statutory requirement. He next addressed the question of financial support for the injured and bereaved in the immediate aftermath of the disaster and for the long term:

> As regards immediate needs in Zeebrugge, the British consul and his staff are offering all possible consular assistance. In this country, the Department of Health and Social Security is providing emergency arrangements so that people arriving at Gatwick and Dover can be given immediate help. As regards to concerns about long term financial entitlements, a team from the DHSS is going out to Zeebrugge today to give advice on the spot.

Moore added that £250,000 had been made available by P&O to meet the immediate personal needs of those immediately affected by the disaster. The fund was handled by Townsend Thoresen in Dover. He explained that the company would be advertising in the national press the next day with details of the central point for claims.

The Channel Ferry Disaster Fund was set up on the initiative of Dover District Council. Designed not to affect compensation claims, the fund aimed to assist the victims and relatives.

The government also announced a contribution of £1 million to the fund from a contingency fund. 'Every year some 26 million passengers are safely carried on United Kingdom ferries and it is tragic that our fine record of safety has been marred by the disaster. I share the grief and anguish of those who are bereaved, and those who are still uncertain of the fate of their friends and relatives … '

Mr Robert Hughes, MP for Aberdeen north, said, 'I also pay tribute to individual passengers and crew members. Reports are coming in of individual acts of heroism and it is clear that passengers and crew alike put their lives at risk and may, indeed, have lost their lives trying to save other people.' Addressing the issue of ferry safety, he asked the secretary of state, 'Will he not hesitate to use section 21 of the Merchant Shipping Act of 1979 to insist that this is done?'

He went on to further enquire about a Europe-wide directive on the same revised safety procedures proposed by Moore, along with the possibility of securing vehicles on the car deck to aid the stability of ferries, and that the safety lessons from interim reports be put into effect without delay. 'Whatever lessons come out of this, under no circumstances can commercial pressures be allowed to mitigate against the safety of our people and our passengers'.

Moore, in reply, said:

... The honourable gentleman was right to pay tribute to the passengers and crew. It is difficult at this stage to be precise but in my conversations at Zeebrugge and again this morning with Jeffery Sterling, it is clear to me that there are many, as yet untold, heroic actions by both members of the crew and passengers. I am sure that the former would have done their duty in the standards and traditions of the British Merchant Navy.

Mr Peter Rees (Dover), asked, 'Will my right honourable friend accept that many people in east Kent will wish to be associated with the tributes he has paid to the rescue services, and with the expression of gratitude that he made to our neighbours in Belgium, for their prompt and sympathetic response.' Rees also addressed the lack of news and misinformation that followed the immediate aftermath:

... The methods of contacting and informing the families of those directly involved could be sharpened up. I know that my honourable and learned friend, the member for Folkestone and Hythe, and I came across one or two distressing cases over the weekend, of families who were left in considerable uncertainty for a long time. One appreciates that, when an incident has occurred in foreign waters, and the primary responsibilities for the rescue lie with foreign authorities, that the difficulties may be considerable ...

Mr Terence Higgins (Worthing) said, 'While joining in the expressions of sympathy to the bereaved, may I ask whether my right honourable friend is satisfied that steps to recover and identify the remaining bodies in the wreck are being taken without delay?' In response, Mr Moore replied:

I have spoken to Jeffery Sterling and to the people involved and there is no question but that the only criterion that concerns them is the raising of the vessel in such a way to obtain the bodies of those currently entombed in the ship. That is the first, last and only important criterion that they are addressing and that must be right. It is a very difficult operation, as those that have been involved know. Therefore, I am afraid that it will take time, but we wish them speedy success.

MEP Christopher Jackson said:

I speak today as the representative of east Kent, and in particular of Dover, the home port of the *Herald of Free Enterprise*, of Folkestone, and the other towns and villages where bereaved families grieve for those who will never return, where yet others come to terms with injuries. I express deep gratitude and admiration to the Belgian authorities who were superb and to the ships, helicopters, divers and rescue teams from Belgium, Britain, Holland and NATO. Without their heroic and speedy efforts the terrible death toll would have been vastly greater. To the people of Zeebrugge especially, I say your work and your care which made so much difference will long be remembered on our side of the channel.

On 9 March 1987, the chairman of Cavewood Transport, of High Wycombe, sent a letter to the Belgian Ambassador in London, Jean-Paul Van Bellinghen, expressing his thanks to the Belgians. He wrote:

Sadly our company had two trucks on the *Herald of Free Enterprise* which sank off Zeebrugge on Friday night. To date, the drivers are still missing. On Saturday morning, I travelled to Belgium with our traffic director and representatives of the families and I am writing to formally thank you on behalf of everyone involved for the help and co-operation we received from the Belgian authorities. I would ask you to convey our thanks to the immigration staff who arranged immediate entry at Brussels Airport for the three relatives who were travelling without passports and above all to the numerous workers of the Belgian Red Cross who worked so hard to ease the situation for the relatives. As a token of our appreciation, we will be making a donation to the Belgian Red Cross and the Belgian Hospital in London.

By Tuesday 10 March, Townsend Thoresen chairman, Peter Ford, urged distressed relatives to return home. Between sixty and seventy relatives remained in the town waiting for news of their loved ones. Ford said:

It's better to remember them as they were when they were alive. We have spoken to the families about this. They seemed to accept it. Doctors and psychologists have advised us that, in many cases, it would be strongly inadvisable to see the bodies. Relatives could even be forbidden, perhaps by the introduction of a local bylaw, for reasons of compassion. We consider now that the welfare of the relatives coming to visit is our number one priority. It is obviously extremely difficult for them.

We have a situation in which fifty-three bodies have been recovered, but there are eighty-one still trapped in the hull of the ship. We have opened a hotline at Dover now because many people coming here will not find the persons they are looking for. In many cases it is probably best to go back home. Obviously we will give people every possible help and assistance to go back.

On 13 March, the National Union of Seamen General Secretary, Sam McCluskie, also wrote to the Belgian Ambassador:

The loss of so many passengers and crew on board the *Herald of Free Enterprise*, has filled our two nations with great grief and sense of loss. However, much relief and comfort has been given by the care, comfort and sympathy with which the Belgian people responded to the catastrophe. This was matched by the calm efficiency with which rescue activity was undertaken and the many acts of individual bravery and sacrifice. We know this not from press reports, but from the first-hand experience of our two representatives who went to Zeebrugge on the night of March 6. They have nothing but praise and admiration for the manner in which so many people from so many different parts of the Belgian community joined together in a common endeavour to save life and to relieve suffering and pain. I would be extremely grateful therefore, if you would convey in appropriate fashion, our appreciation and gratitude to the Belgian Government, to the local authorities and to the many organisations and individuals who gave so unstintingly of their time and energy in helping our people at such a critical time.

London resident John Morgan, also wrote to the Belgian Ambassador, expressing the feeling of many:

I write with heartfelt thanks for all the tremendous, absolutely extraordinary support that the government gave in only fifteen minutes. I cannot believe it, how quickly your superb government moved to help the UK. It would give me extreme pleasure if as an ordinary citizen old enough to have lost in Belgium two uncles in the First War, this warm love of Belgium is passed to the King.

The *Sun* newspaper, on whose tokens many of the *Herald* passengers had travelled, organised the recording of the Beatles hit 'Let it Be' – a charity single performed by a combination of 1980s music industry artists, over three days between 14 and 17 March, a mere eight days after the disaster. Produced by Stock, Aitken and Waterman, the ensemble were known as 'Ferry Aid', and included Paul McCartney, Boy George, Kate Bush, Edwin Starr, Kim Wilde, Mel and Kim, Bananarama and Frankie Goes To Hollywood. The record was released on 23 March and went to number one in the British charts.

On Monday 23 March, the EC (European Community) Commissioner for Transport, Stanley Clinton Davis, in Brussels for two days of routine EEC (European Economic Community) talks, spoke of a review of the international maritime laws currently limiting the compensation levels which could be claimed by next of kin to passengers killed at sea. The Athens Convention, to which Britain belongs, limits compensation to approximately £38,000 for death or personal injury. These limits can only be exceeded if the ship's owner is proved reckless. The limits for deaths in train accidents is £57,000, and aircraft deaths £82,000. Commissioner Davis said, 'It is never too soon to turn our attention to the wholly inadequate insurance limits imposed internationally.' An interim report on the ferry disaster was being prepared for a meeting of the IMO (International Maritime Organisation) on 27 April.

Norman Fowler wrote the following letter to Mr Heer Van Oyen at St Jan's Hospital on 27 March:

> I would like to express my very sincere thanks, and those of my ministerial and National Health Service colleagues for the prompt and professional manner in which you provided for those who had been injured and had undergone such terrifying experiences.
>
> We in the United Kingdom were appalled and saddened by the extent of the disaster but it is of considerable comfort to hear of the kind and effective help you were able to offer at such short notice. I am sure that there are many survivors who will remember with gratitude and admiration the assistance they received from you when they most needed it.

At Bremerhaven in Germany, Townsend Thoresen's latest addition to the fleet, the *Pride of Calais*, had launched in a ceremony tinged with sadness. Originally commissioned to work alongside the *Herald*, the new ferry inadvertently became the *Herald*'s replacement.

On 10 November 1987, Lord Brabazon of Tara, the aviation and shipping minister, said in the House of Lords, 'I shall not stand up here and say ... whether or not RORO ferries are safe. They are not intrinsically unsafe.'

In contrast, Commodore Gordon Greenfield on 17 February 1988, wrote:

> The Nautical Institute would be failing in its duty if it did not bring to your attention the inherent vulnerability of the RORO ferry whose uninterrupted car deck is so close to the waterline that it may be assumed it will capsize and sink almost immediately, in the event of a collision.

Greenfield's comments were echoed when, on 21 March 1988, the Royal Institute of Naval Architects, in a considered statement, said that the existing RORO ferries are 'unacceptably vulnerable'.

In February 1988, a delegation from the *Herald* Families Association (HFA) met with Paul Channon, the Secretary of State for Transport, after writing to him a number of times on the issue of ferry safety and vulnerability.

Another meeting, on 12 May 1988, was held with Lord Brabazon. After these two meetings, and in numerous written communications with the government, the HFA released a statement which criticised the government, and expressing the HFA's dismay at their response. The immediate cause of the disaster, the HFA said, was common knowledge – that the *Herald of Free Enterprise* went to sea with the bow doors open, and water entered the vehicle deck. But the HFA believed that the reason why so many died, that the ferry capsized and sank in just ninety seconds, was not being given adequate priority and urgency by the government, who had promised a three-year-long programme of research. RORO ferries in current operation were at the same risk of capsize. The HFA believed that the government should put its energies and funds into a practical and economic solution to focus on what should be done, and not merely debate on whether or not something should be done.

Referring to the Royal Institute of Architects statement about the vulnerability of existing RORO ferries, the HFA urged that 'this body of eminent professionals cannot be ignored. Theirs is an independent and expert opinion.' The HFA further questioned Lord Brabazon's statement that, if the government believed that ferries currently in service were safe, why were they having a research programme? The HFA concluded its statement by saying 'No longer can the government say that they are not aware of the risk with these vessels. The decision is no longer a technical one, it is a moral one.'

Home

Five survivors and some relatives returned to Dover aboard a Townsend Thoresen ferry on Saturday 7 March. They were met at the Eastern Docks by a group of Red Cross nurses who were moved to tears by the stories they heard. Nurse Gwen Mackett had spoken to a man who had lost his wife, 'When I heard that I just walked away in tears. I couldn't hold it back. I have been a nurse all my life but you never get used to hearing tragic news like that.' The survivors and their relatives were driven away without commenting to the press. 'They were very shocked, dazed and tired. They just wanted to get home. Although we are Red Cross nurses and people believe we are used to this sort of thing, we feel very much for them.'

Survivor John Ward returned to his home in Orpington, Kent, on the afternoon of Saturday 7 March. His son, John Ward Jr, described the moment he arrived, 'He was wearing my old ski jacket and a pair of blood-stained jeans. My jacket was also ripped and covered in blood. He still had his wallet that is fixed to a chain and strapped to his jeans. I went over to dad as soon as I saw him. He was still shaking. I must have given him the longest hug ever.'

On Saturday, the chairman of Dover District Council, Mrs Amelia Williamson, announced the creation of a Disaster Fund to raise money for the Zeebrugge survivors, as well as the families and relatives involved, with priority being given to widows and orphans. 'It happened so suddenly, it has completely shaken us all. We have so many friends who are working on the ferries. I am devastated. All the people who live in the Dover district feel a sense of horror and deep mourning.'

A group of Belgian radio amateurs took it upon themselves to collate information about the ferry survivors. A team of twenty volunteers asked 170 survivors to write down their full names and addresses. This information was then passed onto a Belgian radio station, who then called for a radio contact in the Dover area. Radio station Kent Raynet then relayed the survivor information to the Coroner's Office in Dover and Kent Police HQ in Maidstone. The 170 names were transmitted between 1 p.m. and 7 p.m.

The Kent Red Cross had set up an emergency desk at Townsend Thoresen's crisis room in Dover within hours of the disaster. Two Kent Red Cross ambulances waited at Gatwick Airport for the Saturday evening flight from Ostend, bringing in the first survivors. Other Red Cross branches in Kent helped families who had problems getting to and from Dover or Gatwick. Kent welfare officer, Sue Robertson, spoke of the Red Cross's efforts: 'We helped where we could. Most of the time we provided transport but our members were also there to comfort families and to provide basic necessities. We established a close working relationship with the Belgian Red Cross and could not have done what we did without their support and co-operation.'

The Kent Salvation Army immediately offered its help by making a room available at its head office in Dover. Manned by two Salvation Army officers and a Church of England minister, notes were carefully made of all calls, contacts and visits. These notes would be used later by Kent social services for follow up and long-term care.

As the disaster unfolded, four Salvation Army officers and several ministers went to Zeebrugge to help the survivors, and relatives identifying bodies, and offering comfort to the bereaved.

Late on the evening of Saturday 7 March, 190 survivors arrived back in Britain aboard a British Caledonian DC-10, flight BR995, landing at Gatwick Airport. Many anxious relatives had gathered in airport lounges, not knowing if their loved ones would be amongst those on board. When the plane arrived, more than half an hour late, the *Herald* survivors were led into a private room to meet their families. Some were wrapped in yellow blankets and some had limbs in plaster.

On Saturday morning, Rosina Summerfield found out that her boyfriend, Kevin Batten, was alive and being treated at another hospital. When the family were reunited, they found that they were stranded in Belgium with no money and no passports, and they found it difficult to leave. Rosina's company flew from the UK to collect her. At first, they had been told that they could return but their journey would have to be by ferry. There was uproar from those who had survived one ferry disaster and were not prepared to step on board another boat in their lives. Then British Caledonian announced they would be flying home the survivors. Those who wanted to go, boarded coaches for the airport and were driven straight onto the tarmac to the waiting plane. 'The poor coach driver tried to convince a terrified Ryan that the aeroplane was not a boat as he wouldn't get on.'

Mrs Valerie Sherratt returned home on the Saturday evening Gatwick flight without her missing husband Norman (40). She had last seen him as she left him to visit one of the ferry's on-board shops. They had been on a day trip. Injured and in a state of severe shock, she had been in no fit state to stay in Belgium and was being comforted at home in Woodchurch, Kent, by her sister-in-law. It was Norman's half-brother, Dave Edwards, who went to Belgium to search the hospitals. The couple had three children.

When Rosina Summerfield, her son Ryan, boyfriend Kevin Batten, and friend Julie Clark arrived back at Gatwick, they were met by a gathering of Townsend Thoresen representatives. 'As they first approached us in a lounge, I remember the poor man that I was screaming at because all I had were the clothes I was stood up in. I was so angry by this time.' Their home in Park Royal was mobbed by the press, so they went to Rosina's mother's house that night.

After arriving back at London Gatwick, Miles Southgate had to break the dreadful news to Pam and Peter Spooner that their son Martin was not on the list of survivors. He recalled that this was a 'traumatic experience'.

Survivor Nick Kember of West Malling, Kent, had to return to the UK on Saturday, after failing to find his missing girlfriend, Lita Harris. After briefly meeting relatives, Nick flew back out to Belgium to continue looking for Lita on Sunday afternoon. Their neighbours had broken into their home while they were gone after they heard the couple's dog howling inside.

Brian Bunker had spent most of Saturday searching for his wife and daughter in the local hospitals. He found out later that night that the body of his wife, Diane, was one of the few that had been recovered. Her body was identified by Brian's father, who had been flown over by the British Army.

On Sunday 8 March, three children, two of them teenagers, who were all orphaned in the disaster, were flown home to England aboard the private executive jet of P&O Chairman Sir Jeffrey Sterling.

Sixteen coffins were loaded onto an unmarked grey truck and driven onto a cargo ferry at Zeebrugge, to make the final journey back to Dover on 10 March. A police escort accompanied the first of the victims who had been repatriated to Buckland Hospital, 2 miles from Dover harbour. Later that same night, another fifteen bodies arrived at the hospital. Post-mortems were to be performed, before inquests could be opened. An initial nine inquests were opened on seven men and two women, and adjourned until 19 May.

In the days following the disaster, Rosina Summerfield was appalled by the media attention. A few stories appeared in the newspapers, one of which was an entirely fanciful account of Rosina's time aboard the *Herald* during the disaster. 'I remember Anne Diamond on the breakfast TV show (TVAM) saying that I had watched my child float away when I was nowhere near him.'

Petar, Julie and Carly Zutic were reunited with their families in Dumfries, Scotland, three days after the disaster. They had been flown to Gatwick, then travelled on to Newcastle, where a friend picked them up and drove them to Dumfries. Julie's mother, Mrs Alma Jardine, said, 'It's so wonderful that they survived. We're so thankful that they're still with us.' On 15 March, the youngest *Herald* survivor, Carly Zutic, was christened in Halifax, West Yorkshire. After the service, her Yugoslav grandad, Dusan, said, 'We can't describe our relief and joy.'

Dover and District's Sunday Football League secretary, Tom Donnelly, received abusive phone calls after Chairman Colin Hall made the decision that all planned football matches had to go ahead. One club who had a player missing on the ferry wanted their game cancelled, while another team who had lost several members wanted their game to go ahead. 'The decision was, in my opinion, correct. To those people who hurled insults over the phone I wish to add that I have feelings as well and was saddened by this terrible disaster and the loss of league members. I was upset that my feelings were questioned after such a terrible thing like this.'

Stan Mason finally arrived back in his home town of Golborne, Lancashire, a day after his daughter was due to be christened there. The plan had been that Stan would begin a five-month tour of duty in Northern Ireland, while Cath and Kerry stayed at Cath's childhood home with her father. Instead, Stan slept in the room that he and Cath had shared after they were married – except now he was alone. In Golborne, Stan was surrounded by memories of his missing wife – the pub where they went when they were courting, the shops, their old haunts, family and friends.

On 18 March, three ferry victims were laid to rest. Lance Corporal Gary Thomas (23) was buried in Huyton, Merseyside, after a requiem Mass at St Aidan's Church. He had been due to marry Susan Lambert four days earlier. Among the mourners were two fellow soldiers who had been on board with Gary.

At the Guards' Chapel in Whitehall, London, the funeral for former Grenadier Guardsman Peter Martin (53) was attended by 500 mourners, including his wife, Kay, who suffered leg injuries in the disaster. She was joined by staff from Lancing College, West Sussex, where Peter was a security marshal. Policeman also paid their respects – former colleagues of Peter, who had retired from the Metropolitan Police two years before.

The funeral of 29-year-old Ann English was attended by 150 mourners, at Medway Crematorium, Chatham, Kent. Among them were many survivors of the disaster just twelve days earlier. She left a 4-year-old son, David.

Jan Willis had been on a day trip with six fellow students from Barking College. All of them survived. Jan had injured her head when being rescued from the *Herald*:

At the hospital again my 'save everyone else' nature kicked in and I was arranging for other family members of a stroke patient to have help and support. One odd thing – my permed hair went dead straight, probably with shock.

Survivor Eleanor Parker was found by her husband, Andrew, sleepwalking at their home at the top of the stairs, less than a month after the disaster. She was having a nightmare, screaming, 'hold onto the rope! Don't let go!' Eleanor put it down to feeling guilt that she had survived when others had died. She remembered all the children who had been running around when the ferry had set off. She remembered the woman in a wheelchair who had gone crashing through a window into the sea. 'I never thought it would be like this. I first thought I would be grateful that we were all OK'.

Other survivors were experiencing problems sleeping without the lights on, some had developed a terror of water and many suffered survivor guilt. They were all diagnosed with what became known as Post Traumatic Stress Disorder (PTSD).

Cheryl Taylor, the 14-year-old schoolgirl whose best friend Nicola Simpson fell from her hands as she tried to hold onto her, had kept it all inside. Her parents decided to send her to a counsellor.

On Wednesday 18 March, a requiem Mass was held at Westminster Cathedral by Cardinal Basil Hume. The Vatican City's secretary of state, Cardinal Casaroli, relayed a telegram from Pope John Paul II, which said that he had 'prayed to Almighty God, commending the souls of the victims to his ever merciful love and imploring strength and comfort upon the survivors and upon the families involved.' Another telegram arrived from Cardinal Danneels, Archbishop of Malines-Brussels, expressing his 'profound sympathy' in the name of the bishops in Belgium.

Members of the Lamy family were invited to a memorial service in central London. Among those paying their respects were Margaret Thatcher, Neil Kinnock, various MPs, members of the royal family and other famous people. As Tracy Edwards was about to go in, her baby daughter, Sarah, who had been ill all through the night, would not settle. She was playing up and screaming. People began to stare, 'looking at me as if I shouldn't be there. Yet I felt I had the biggest right.' Baby Sarah continued to scream and cry, and Tracy was torn between duty to be there and caring for her baby. Margaret Thatcher approached them and began to chat. The press followed, but were quickly dismissed by the Prime Minister. 'It was not a press opportunity and I thank her for her help and support.'

After a few really kind words, she told Tracy that her baby was more important at this moment, and that she would make a difference staying with her. 'Nothing I could do inside the church would make a difference to my family, my family needed me now to look after my child.' Mrs Thatcher arranged for Tracy and her daughter to be taken to the nearest hospital. Baby Sarah was admitted with a perforated eardrum and ear infection.

I know some people have negative thoughts about Margaret Thatcher but I truly believe she was kind and caring at that moment in time and there was no need to come and help or talk to me. This was a strong reminder that we are people that live, breathe, get sick and feel.

The general public wanted to know everything about us, what made us in some ways so special. Bad luck would be my answer. How special are we to lose four generations of a family in one go? It was the story of the century and people felt they had the right to know about you and, in effect, have a piece of you. It was on the television, newspapers, magazines and posters. Everywhere you went you saw the ferry on its side. A grave where people screamed and were killed, trapped and hurt. What a lovely symbol to keep plastering all over the media.

On a daily basis, the press would be waiting for us, outside our homes, and relatives' homes.

George Lamy decided to organise trips away, so they would be away from it all – but not until his daughter's body was found.

On Wednesday 15 April 1987, seventy-five years to the day of the *Titanic* disaster, a memorial service was held at Canterbury Cathedral. The Archbishop of Canterbury, Dr Robert Runcie addressed 1,800 mourners – among them many survivors, relatives, crew members, rescuers and others who had become involved in the disaster.

Prince Phillip bowed his head, with Princess Anne at his side. Also in attendance were Prime Minister Margaret Thatcher, Labour leader Neil Kinnock, Liberal leader David Steel and SDP (Social Democratic Party) leader Shirley Williams. Surviving crew members, Bosun Terry Ayling and Assistant Purser Stephen Homewood, carried a giant cross of golden carnations dotted with rosemary, in step, through the nave of the cathedral to the altar.

Addressing the families of the victims of the disaster, Runcie said, '… for them, the tragedy remains, and with it the numbness of loss and grief. The tragedy was so sudden, the loss so unexpected. To those who carry this burden of pain, we offer our deepest sympathy'. As Runcie spoke of the extraordinary courage of that night, sunshine suddenly flooded the cathedral:

> Even in the darkest moments at Zeebrugge, there were rays of light. I think of the passenger with spinal injuries carrying his baby to safety with his teeth. I think of the four men trapped in lower decks taking turns to hold above water the head of an elderly woman. I think of the man who acted as a human bridge to allow others to crawl across and the grandmother who tried to save someone in a falling wheelchair.

On Wednesday 29 April, the parish church of St Mary in Ilkeston, Derbyshire, was filled with 200 mourners as four ferry victims were laid to rest. Eight-year-old

Martin Hartley said goodbye for the final time to his dad Richard (31), mum Hazel (38), and paternal grandparents, Joseph and Elsie (both 65). 'I want to say goodbye. I want to be able to look into the sky and see five stars up there.' The fifth victim, family friend Patricia Hawley, had been buried recently. Martin called her 'auntie'. Several times during the service, he broke down. He was comforted by Rev. Leslie Walters, the clergyman who led the service, who said later, 'He has stood up to things very well today, but only later will we really know how he is. Time alone will tell.'

A couple who had planned to marry on Saturday 18 April, were laid to rest together in the village where they had planned to live. Beverley Taylor (26) of Swindon, Wiltshire, and her fiancé Peter Hilling (47), of Frimley Green, Surrey, were buried in Ashton Keynes, Wiltshire.

In Plymouth, sweethearts David Harris and Jacquie Wyatt, both aged 24, who had become engaged at Christmas 1986, were cremated in a joint ceremony.

After Cath Mason's body was recovered during the righting of the ferry, she was taken back home to Golborne. As she lay in the chapel of rest, Stan stood by her coffin with Kerry, holding her tight – the first and only child of Cath, who had wanted lots of children, maybe four or five. He visited her several times before the funeral, kneeling by her coffin, and talking to her. 'She's my wife, you talk to her, don't you? It's your wife and you love her. Of course you talk to her, it's normal. She gave me everything, 100 per cent, and I gave her everything I could.'

On the day of Cath's funeral, her daughter Kerry's christening dress was placed next to her body, along with a few photographs and a little rag doll. 'I just held Kerry and kept thinking about Cath, and wondering what we were going to do. Kerry's got no mother, and I've got no wife. It's going to be very different. She was the best wife that anyone could want.'

After the funeral, Stan, his sister Jean, and Cath's aunt Rita looked after Kerry on a kind of shift pattern. 'Cath's gone, but Kerry has pulled us out of the muck. I have a lot of fun with her. She's the only thing I care about, the only reason to live. There's a lot of pleasure in bringing her up.' The army gave Stan the rest of the year off in compassionate leave so that Stan could be both father and mother for their daughter.

Two months after the disaster, 'human bridge' Andrew Parker was still fighting nightmares and depression. He had still not returned to work. 'The ferry is now ruling our lives. The depression is sometimes very little, sometimes very great, without warning. Our lives are not our own anymore.'

The uncle and aunt of a crew member's wife were travelling back from Germany on the night of the disaster. They made it their business to catch that particular crossing on the off-chance that the crew member would be on duty. It was only after the disaster that the crew member discovered that his wife's aunt and uncle were both victims. He hadn't even known they were on board.

It was extremely difficult for the crew member and his wife at the funerals of the couple. 'At that time some members of the family took the view that the disaster was the crew's fault, although to be fair, there were those who made a point of making it clear that in no way did they feel the same.'

Doctor's receptionist Joan Davis (28) had saved the life of Lisa-Jo Cain (11), who was orphaned in the disaster. They called each other once a week. 'She's not too bad,' said Joan, 'She's back at school. I feel close to her, merely for the reasons that she has lost everybody … I'm here whenever she needs me.' Joan was suffering from pains in her joints, and has nightmares of 'everybody screaming out for help.'

Anthony Ray (19) of Wembley Park, London, had organised the day trip for his brother, Peter, sister, Karen (22), and Karen's fiancé, Alan Woodhall (24). Anthony and Peter survived the disaster. Their sister and future brother-in-law had died. Peter said, 'I will always cherish the memory of them walking off hand in hand. They were so happy and so in love.'

Martin Hartley returned to classes at Cotmanhay Junior School. Deputy Headmaster John Hindall said:

> Martin is a remarkable, sparkling little boy. He obviously misses his parents very much, but he's settled down into school very well. Martin epitomises the disaster. When people think of the ferry disaster, they think of him. He represents the hope of any good that might come of the tragedy.

Martin's dad, Richard Hartley, was 31 when he died aboard the *Herald*, with his parents Joseph and Elsie, both 65, and his wife Hazel (38). Family friend Patricia Hawley (40) also died. Richard and Hazel's 8-year-old son Martin was the only survivor from the group. Gillian Bowen remembers living next door to the Hartleys in Ilkeston, Derbyshire, when Richard was a little boy:

> The houses we lived in were very old terraced houses, two up, two down, with the toilet in an outhouse at the bottom of the garden. I was at school with Susan. The back gardens of our houses were separated by an old rickety gate, so I was always squeezing though to go into their yard to play with Susan. My family used to go for lots of walks around the countryside and we used to take John with us. Elsie was a really good friend to my mum. In those days people were poor so all the neighbours used to help each other out, especially with food. Elsie was a very happy-go-lucky person, always had a smile on her face. Joe was of a more serious nature.
>
> I remember one time when my mum noticed from the back garden that there was a fire in their kitchen. My mum got through the old rickety gate and ran into their kitchen and got water from their tap and kept throwing water on some towels that were on fire (they were hung up at the side of the range). Elsie was in the parlour, oblivious to what had just happened, but back in those days, neighbours looked out for each other. They were a really loving family. Our family were in total shock when we heard that three of our dear old friends had died on that ferry.

Just one week later we travelled to France on the sister ferry to the *Herald* and I was terrified of being on it and the same thing happening to us. A friend that we were travelling with went and got me a neat whisky from the bar to steady my nerves.

Post-mortems performed on the Hartleys showed that Joe and his son Richard had both drowned. Elsie had had a massive heart attack during the capsize and was probably already dead when she went into the water. The autopsy on Pat Hawley was performed by Professor Jacques Timperman on 11 March. Her body was returned to her husband, Malcolm, the following day.

Martin Hartley's aunt, Glenys Bridges, wrote two letters to the *Herald Link* about Martin's progress, after he was the only survivor of his family members on board:

I am Martin Hartley's auntie. We now have full care and control of Martin for life, thank God. We had to attend High Court at Derby and again at Nottingham. The judge put a total ban on all publicity and photographs, for which we are very grateful, because the press have been hell. After telephoning your office, I understand people are still enquiring about Martin.

Well, he is fine now, having grown two and a half inches and put six pounds on in weight. Martin has been with us since 22 May 1987. His half-brother Lance and his common-law-wife looked after Martin but asked us if we would have him. It was the least I could do, his mum Hazel being my half-sister.

We have four children, all grown up now, one married with a son aged two. So Martin fits in very well. He still attends the same school as before the disaster so has the same friends and teachers, who have been marvellous to him We still have our sad moments, which is understandable. We talk him through it, nurse him and love him and answer any questions honestly. Martin now calls us mum and dad by his own choosing. At this moment in time he is trying to throw the javelin and pole-vault with my clothes prop, having seen athletics on the TV over the last few days.

We are still receiving gifts for Martin, the last one being a tracksuit, a pair of jeans and a sweatshirt from someone in the South of France. They were posted to the mayor of Ilkeston and we had to collect them from the Town Hall. The gifts of money have been too much, really. There is over £50,000 in our local fund. We must have a magic postman for the address only has to be 'Martin Hartley, Ilkeston' and it arrives at our house.

Recovery

The vessels of three salvage and rescue companies had been on hand on the night of the disaster, rendering assistance to the rescue efforts – Smit Tak International Ocean Towage and Salvage Company, along with the Union de Remorquage et de

Sauvetage (URS) and Tijdeliijke Vereniging van Bergingswerken (TVB, also known as Norma Ltd).

An agreement was reached two days later, and a contract in principle was established with Townsend Thoresen. Smit's motto had been 'Get on with the job and think about the contracts later.' The three companies had already begun to work together at the scene of the disaster, and Smit's *Taklift 6* was put in position. The contract was signed on 14 March, on a 'No Cure, No Pay' basis, which meant that the companies would be paid upon successful completion of the salvage operations. Smit had already requisitioned and purchased equipment worth millions to commence the recovery of the *Herald*. Over 100 missing victims were thought still to be on board.

On 10 March, diving operations had to be stopped temporarily due to fumes escaping from the cargo compartment. The first four of thirty-two strongpoints were delivered, with the rest still under construction in Rotterdam. Welding and cutting equipment, generators and compressors were also delivered. A lorry trailer was found on the seabed the next day, lifted out and delivered to Zeebrugge. It had been blocking access to the submerged vehicle deck.

On 13 March, the *Herald* listed a further 5°. Pad eyes and guide rails were positioned and welded, and the first of sixteen steel pipes for piling into the seabed arrived. Pull barges were prepared. After obtaining permission from the Port Authorities, the first pipe was piled the next day, but two days later all work was stopped because the weather had worsened. *Taklift 6* left the scene because of the heavy swell, with work recommencing at 2200hrs that night.

By 18 March, the *Herald* had moved 2° to the south. The *Union 3* arrived, with five anchors from Holland which were transferred to the *Smit Orca*. The next day, all sixteen piling pipes were in position. There was further movement of the *Herald*, and over the next three days, her fore had moved 3m to the west, her midships 3m to the east, and aft 5.7m to the east. All sixteen steel pipes had been piled into the seabed by the next day.

On 26 March, a diving survey found that the *Herald*'s port side had penetrated 1m into the seabed. Another truck was discovered on the seabed a day later, but due to bad weather, was not removed until five days after.

Stormy seas on 31 March shifted the *Herald*'s position again. With listing increased to 11°, the aft of the *Herald* had moved 8.4m to the east. It was also found that the ferry had sunk another 2.5m into the seabed.

On 3 April, in order for the pull barges to have enough room to manoeuvre closer to the *Herald*, it was necessary to remove debris and looser parts of the ferry's structure, including the aft mast. The mast was then placed and secured to the starboard side of E-deck, against a set of external stairs. The first pull barges were connected to the *Herald* two days later. *Taklift 6* was positioned at the fore of the ferry with *Taklift 4* aft. Both pull barges on scene were also connected.

Taking a break
from recovering
bodies. (Courtesy
of Mike Marten)

Wrecked corridor.
(Courtesy of Mike
Marten)

Ruins of the
C-deck lounge
with the bureau
de change safe in
the foreground.
(Courtesy of
Mike Marten)

Wreckage of the vehicle deck. (Courtesy of Mike Marten)

Divers on the vehicle deck. (Courtesy of Mike Marten)

Divers on the bridge of the *Herald*. (Courtesy of Mike Marten)

Divers near the open bow doors. (Courtesy of Mike Marten)

Debris floating inside the wreck. (Courtesy of Mike Marten)

Diver Mike Marten inside the wreck.
(Courtesy of Mike Marten)

Diver Mike Marten on the wreck.
(Courtesy of Mike Marten)

Remains of the bridge. (Courtesy of Mike Marten)

Cleared C-deck lounge. (Courtesy of Mike Marten)

Remains of crew stores. (Courtesy of Mike Marten)

Row of wrecked cabins. (Courtesy of Mike Marten)

Cleared lounge. (Courtesy of Mike Marten)

Wreckage on vehicle deck. (Courtesy of Mike Marten)

Wrecked cabin. (Courtesy of Mike Marten)

Ruins of the crew messroom. (Courtesy of Mike Marten)

Remains of a cabin. (Courtesy of Mike Marten)

Remains of a corridor.
(Courtesy of Mike
Marten)

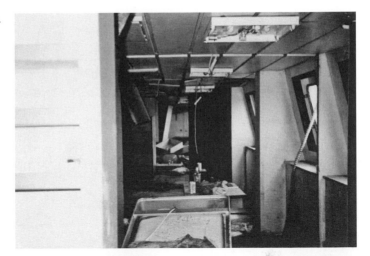

Wrecked interior.
(Courtesy of Mike
Marten)

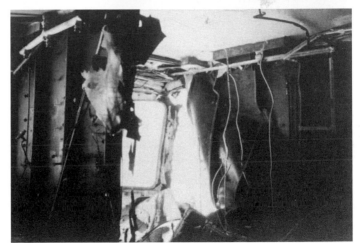

Empty lifeboat davits.
(Courtesy of Mike
Marten)

Wreckage of the B-deck outdoor seating area. (Courtesy of Mike Marten)

Mud-covered vehicles on the vehicle deck. (Courtesy of Mike Marten)

Members of the
Group 2 Fleet
Clearance Diving
Group returning
home on a Townsend
Thoresen ferry, their
body recovery work
complete. (Courtesy of
Mike Marten)

Members of the
Royal Navy and
Belgian Navy diving
teams after their body
recovery work was
complete. (Courtesy of
Mike Marten)

The *Herald* is finally
raised. (Courtesy of
Mike Marten)

This sequence of six photographs shows the *Herald*, now renamed
Flushing Range, at Vlissingen, Holland, after salvage.

The *Herald* at Vlissingen,
Holland, after salvage.
(Courtesy of Inge Desmedt)

The *Herald*, now renamed *Flushing Range*, at Las Palmas, on her way to Taiwan for scrapping. She is
accompanied by Townsend Thoresen's *Gaelic Ferry*. (Courtesy of Inge Desmedt)

At 0400hrs on 7 April 1987, 100 salvage workers were taken to the site of the *Herald of Free Enterprise* wreck in a pre-dawn mist, arriving by tug. Among them were Salvage Director Hans Walenkamp, and Technical Salvage Master Hans Van Rooy. The ferry was to be raised from the seabed so that the remaining bodies, missing after the ferry capsized a month before, could be recovered.

Townsend Thoresen had always maintained, despite contradictions from various organisations, that of the 543 people thought to have been aboard that night, 409 had been saved, sixty-one people had been killed and that seventy-three people still remained in the ferry – making 134 victims; but, the Belgian Transport Minister Herman de Croo, in conjunction with Kent Police, had calculated that there were 349 survivors, sixty-one officially deceased and that 133 victims still lay inside the wreck – making a total of 194 victims.

It seemed incredible to many that the ferry company was still insisting on their original figures. There was no official passenger list, and no one knew exactly how many people were on board, because Townsend Thoresen had no policy of counting every person on board, just the vehicle drivers and not their passengers. The company must have feared the worst. It seemed like they were in denial.

Sea conditions were ideal, with a slight south-easterly wind. At 0820hrs, two barges and three floating cranes began winching the ferry upright. There was a grinding of machinery until the 0846hrs high tide, when the actual lifting began. Directing the progress of operations from the hull of the upturned *Herald*, were two Smit Tak engineers. By 1000hrs, the ship had been raised by ½m when the port funnel broke the surface. Just over two hours later, at 1210hrs, 5m of the *Herald* was clear of the surface. At this point, the maximum strain was exerted. Within half an hour *Norma*, the floating crane, withdrew from the scene, its job done. *Norma* had been there to support the funnel area, to prevent the superstructure collapsing.

At 1430hrs, work was halted for twenty minutes, after the port side of the bridge was found to contain a considerable amount of sand. The engineers feared that the accumulation of sand could affect the stability of the ship. There was also a minor oil slick, which it was thought might cause further problems. As more of the port-side superstructure became visible above the surface, it became apparent that both the bow and stern loading doors were open – the bow doors had never been closed, the stern doors had burst open after the stern had taken the brunt of the impact with the seabed.

A body could be seen hanging from a port side window. Three more bodies were then seen floating in the water nearby.

By 1835hrs, the *Herald* was in its normal vertical position, with the entire superstructure above the waterline. The first investigations team boarded, and the body recovery operation began. Smit supplied lighting and aluminium ladders etc. The Smit vessel, *Deurloo*, which had been at the scene on the first night of the disaster, was to transport any bodies recovered back to shore.

Members of the Royal Navy's crack Group 2 Fleet Clearance Diving Group, based at HMS *Vernon*, Portsmouth, and led by their commander, Jack Birkett, were among the body recovery team sent aboard. They included Chief Petty Officer Eddie Kerr, Warrant Officer Nick Fellows, and Leading Divers Mike Marten, Paddy Doonan, Roy New and Chris 'Billy' Smart. They were with a team of twelve Belgian Navy divers, including Alfons Daems, commander of the Belgian Navy divers since 1984, and Lt Col Guido Couwenburgh, both of whom had saved dozens of lives on the night of the disaster.

Birkett and Kerr had also been on the *Herald* searching for survivors on the night of the disaster. Birkett spoke of finding the bodies of a young couple in their twenties in the ferry's cafeteria. 'They must have been husband and wife. They just had their arms round each other. The last thing they did. So young. I just felt a terrible sorrow.'

Doonan found the body of a girl aged about 11, still clutching a doll. One man was found trapped in a walk-in refrigerator – whether he had got in there deliberately, fell in there during the capsize, or his body had been washed in there afterwards, no one will ever know. Another man was found still clutching the book he had been reading before the ferry keeled over.

Marten said that, to help them overcome the smell of decaying bodies, they found unbroken bottles of perfume from the ruins of the duty-free shop and soaked their collars and drysuits with it so that the fragrance of perfume would be all they could smell. It seemed to work. The divers had to pull bodies out of the debris with their hands. There were fears that all of the bodies would be badly decomposed but a surprising number of them had been preserved in the thick black mud that had accumulated inside the ferry, particularly where it had been resting against the seabed.

When the divers returned to their bunks on the Belgian frigate, *Godetia*, 'I don't think they were crying', said Birkett, 'Some couldn't talk. The tears will come afterwards. There will be long term scarring in the minds of all of us.'

Two days later, the *Deurloo* had already transported 104 bodies back to the naval base at Zeebrugge. Body recovery was still ongoing, along with the clearing of mud and sand from the upper decks. Later in the day of 9 April, when Townsend Thoresen heard that some 123 bodies had been found on the wreck, Chairman Peter Ford said, 'The figure is somewhat higher than we estimated. In all conscience it cannot be exactly said how many people are still aboard.'

Between 10 and 13 April, 3m high waves, during a force 9 gale, battered the sides of the ferry's superstructure, shattering windows and doors. By the following day, the *Herald* had changed position again, being pushed 16m to the east and 10m forward, towards the harbour entrance. It had sunk further into the seabed, 2.5m fore and 3m aft. With the ferry listing at 15.4°, and waves continuing to sweep through broken windows and doors, the superstructure plating was becoming increasingly damaged.

On 15 April, work had resumed. Over the Easter period, *Taklift 4*, *Taklift 6* and *Takheave 32* were in position to arrange the attaching of lifting slings in readiness to tow the *Herald*. Pumps were placed in the engine rooms and G-deck vehicle deck.

Bad weather had increased the list to 15.8°, and caused the *Herald* to sink a further 20cm into the seabed. The *Deurloo* and the *Norma* were engaged in changing several of the strings and wires for the attachment to the pulling barges.

By 23 April, the pulling and lifting operations had begun, using the barges and sheerlegs. The *Herald* was pulled 29m to the west and out of the trough and the list was improved from 15° to 3°. Submersible pumps with a capacity of 3,500 tons per hour were in position.

On Friday 24 April, the salvage operation to raise the *Herald* was abandoned for the night, after water leaked back into the ferry only four hours after attempts to pump out 15,000 tons of water from the ferry's car deck. The ferry listed to 12°, which prevented Royal Navy and Belgian divers from entering to recover more bodies. They had been on standby all day.

Three days later, the *Herald* had been completely re-floated. The *Herald* was towed to Zeebrugge, and anchored in the outer harbour. Four more bodies were immediately found. The next day, the CORREX team from Germany boarded the ferry for 'preservation work', to treat the machinery and electrical systems from further corrosion. By 9 May, both of the vehicle decks had been cleared of all vehicles. Most had been severely damaged. The vehicles had been 'discharged' – meaning that they had in effect been bulldozed out of the *Herald* once it was ascertained that no bodies remained inside.

By 13 May, the *Herald* was floating without assistance, and all work aboard her had been completed. The final survey was carried out by the Salvage Association, and the towage certificate was issued. The *Herald of Free Enterprise* was handed back to Townsend Thoresen. That same day, the *Herald* left Zeebrugge forever, towed by URS (Unie van Redding – en Sleepdienst) tugs to her temporary new home at Scheldepoort Flushing at Vlissingen, Holland.

The salvage operation is estimated to have cost in excess of £4 million. On the same day as the ferry was righted, lawyers met with Townsend Thoresen in London, pressing for payments to exceed the £38,000 limit for loss of life imposed by the Athens Convention. The solicitors were urging for sums of £150,000 for dependants of wage earners. However, the talks broke up after three hours of little progress.

On the day that the *Herald of Free Enterprise* was righted, Miles Southgate returned to Belgium with his father on another ferry. He wanted to be there for when his friend Martin Spooner's body was recovered. He had many feelings of guilt, often dreaming that Martin had come back to life – 'Where've you been hiding?' Miles had asked him in his dreams.

Scrapped

After the *Herald of Free Enterprise* was towed to Vlissingen in Holland, the wreck was declared a 'total loss'. Townsend Thoresen no longer wanted her and neither did anyone else. For a few months she was a macabre tourist attraction. At one point, relatives of victims that had died in the disaster were offered a free cruise by P&O. On one such cruise, some relatives woke up one morning and opened the curtains of their cabin to find the wreck of the *Herald* outside their window.

In September 1987, the *Herald* was renamed *Flushing Range*, after the name of the port in which she was a temporary visitor (Vlissingen was the Dutch name for Flushing). On 30 September, *Flushing Range* was sold to Compania Naviera SA, of Kingstown, Saint Vincent, who had decided to sell her for scrap. Five days later, she left Vlissingen, under tow from the *Markusturm*, and accompanied by Townsend Thoresen's *Gaelic Ferry*. The *Gaelic Ferry* had been laid up at Zeebrugge since the previous year, after being used as a barge to carry obsolete link-spans from Southampton to Zeebrugge. The plan had been to construct a new double deck berth but they never left the ship. The link-spans ended up in Taiwan as scrap.

On the night of 16/17 October, the English Channel was hit by a hurricane. For twenty-four hours the two ferries were missing, until they were spotted by the French coastguard near Cape Finisterre. Two days later, they were drifting off Gijon, Spain. The journey continued after the tow was re-established.

The tow broke again on 27 December, off Port Elizabeth, South Africa, and the *Flushing Range* was towed into the port on 2 January 1988. The *Flushing Range* finally made it into Kaohsiung, Taiwan on 22 March 1988, just over a year since she had capsized with the loss of almost 200 lives.

At the scrapyard in Kaohsiung, the new owners, Jing Hung – brothers, Jerry (29) and Jonathan (31), and their father – revealed they had paid £800,000 for the wreck and £350,000 towing fees.

Almost immediately, cranes and ancient pulleys began offloading piles of scrap steel onto a fleet of battered lorries. Through the windows, a pile of lifejackets could be seen, piled near the remains of the information desk.

'It's excellent quality', enthused Jerry Wang, 'We should get a very good price. This should make very good scrap. It will not take long to break up and I think we will be very pleased with it.' The two brothers expected the *Flushing Range* to be gone in less than three weeks.

Alongside the *Flushing Range*, and also there ready for scrapping was the cruise liner *Uganda*, used as a hospital ship during the Falklands War.

According to Robin des Bois (robindebois.org), some ships which are sent for scrapping in the Far East are not scrapped at all and end up refurbished and renamed. One such ship appears to be the tanker, *Norgas Discoverer*, which started life in 1971 in Norway as the *Bow Elm*. Supposedly sold for scrap in 2004 to China, the tanker appears to have been considered excellent construction quality. It was probably converted to a general cargo carrier by removing all the gas transport equipment, and was renamed no less than three times, finally becoming the *Ling Hai* in 2006, sailing under the Panamanian flag, for the Shanghai Shuojin Shipping Company (IMO 8990328). The IMO number can be explained by the return to service of a ship previously declared demolished. The name changes are a mystery, and cannot be found in any main shipping registers (e.g. Lloyds). Robin de Bois goes on to say that a Norwegian website alleges that the Chinese owners created a 'false past' and a new official number to put the supposedly demolished ship back into service.

Is it inconceivable that the *Herald of Free Enterprise* could still be sailing amongst the islands of the Philippines, or somewhere else in the Far East? Structurally, the ferry was sound. Was it refurbished, repainted, refitted and ultimately renamed?

Identification

Ten Kent police officers were sent to Zeebrugge to help in the task of identifying the dead and collating the information about the survivors. Some bodies had already been positively identified, with the next of kin informed. However, with no official passenger list in existence, there was much confusion over some of the names that were known, and lists were still being checked. The first full list of survivors and the names of some of the victims was expected to be released late on the Saturday night.

In Zeebrugge, despite police attempts to keep spectators and journalists away from the relatives entering and leaving the sports hall mortuary, one distraught man tried to attack photographers, and a woman shouted, 'Go away! My baby is dead!'

On Saturday morning, the community sports centre in Zeebrugge was cleared to install a funeral chapel. After fitting out the hall, Civil Protection delivered sixty coffins, whilst the Red Cross, volunteers and medics brought the bodies, recovered during and after the first night, to the sports hall from the navy base. The Red Cross washed the bodies and arranged them in the coffins and generally made them presentable for the families to identify. The coffins were placed in three groups – men, women and children – to make it easier for those looking for a particular family member.

The Community House in Zeebrugge was designated for receiving the victims' families. It was here that the State Police and the Red Cross gently questioned the family, and compared their notes with the list of survivors and identified dead. If the person that the family was looking for did not appear on either of those lists, the team accompanied the family member to the funeral chapel where their loved one might be amongst those victims not yet identified. At the Community House, a field kitchen was installed and a first aid post was set up in the cellar of the building.

At Zeebrugge's new navy base, a large vehicle hangar was converted into a primary mortuary. Bodies were taken off at the landing stages, and loaded into ambulances

and navy trucks before being transported to the hangar. Police made notes and photographed each body, before the Red Cross placed them in a body bag.

Nearby, two tables had been specially installed for anatomopathological examinations. A more descriptive examination then took place. Clothing, jewellery and
other personal property were put into plastic bags and tagged with the number of
the victim. The body was then put back into the body bag, awaiting transfer to the
funeral chapel at the nearby sports hall.

Registration then followed, by an army physician and a navy officer, and later, by
the British Military Police. Women were often the most problematic victims to be
identified as they do not tend to carry identification on them or in their clothes.
Women often carry such things as purses and documents in their handbags. In the
case of the ferry disaster, many people had become separated from their belongings.

As the first group of survivors left from Ostend airport on Saturday evening,
another group of relatives arrived to identify the bodies of their loved ones. They
were taken to the holiday centre at Duinse Polders, owned by Townsend Thoresen
and featured in many of their holiday brochures.

Although the press were kept out of the funeral chapel at the sports hall, they were
congregated at the entrance and harassed relatives as they entered or left the building.
Shocked relatives, among them some survivors, were pursued by aggressive photographers, shouting questions and even climbing fences for better pictures. Some
of those who had just identified the bodies of their loved ones screamed at them to
go away. It was necessary to transport the relatives from the reception centre at the
Community House, 150m to the sports hall using ambulances and minibuses since
this seemed to be the only way to get through the throng of photographers.

Experts later identified 'Disaster Syndrome' – rescue workers who were over the
exhaustion limit refused to give up or be replaced, especially members of volunteer organisations. Everyone who had worked their normal day shift on Friday had
either gone home for the weekend, or were about to change shifts. Workers at hospitals generally changed shifts between 2000hrs and 2200hrs. The disaster occurred
at 1928hrs, with emergency services alerted shortly afterwards. The vast majority of
hospital workers volunteered to stay on until reinforcements arrived, either for the
next shift, or those who had been called in for their expertise, or the staff who rushed
to the hospital to help where they could.

The situation in the hospitals stabilised in the early hours of Saturday morning. By
Saturday evening, those who had been on duty since the previous day managed to
find rest on a bed or stretcher. Members of the Red Cross who had been drafted to
Zeebrugge from inland were accommodated at the navy base.

A Red Cross nurse spoke of her experiences during the disaster:

> At the navy base it is cold and cloudy. The sentry recognises our uniforms and points
> us to the field secretariat, which is installed in the mess. On the vessels the flag hangs

half mast. We report to the secretariat. The navy supplies great logistic help, food, blankets, sleeping accommodation, showers. As it is the weekend, this is possibly easier as a lot of [conscript] personnel are on leave, but all we ask for is arranged with a few telephone calls. We get to the hangar. We know what kind of work is waiting; it is not agreeable but it has to be done. The nurses also act as a buffer between the anatomopathologists and the volunteers, who feel more secure when their familiar medics are around. We are volunteers as they are, to help where needed. In the hangar the military police let us enter, we will work a few hours together with the old team to prepare the victims for removal to the funeral chapel. At the first victim I get a strange feeling in my stomach that lasts longer than I thought. But we are working. There is a smooth co-operation with the army [Navy Medical Service], state police, identification team, British police, judicial authorities … everybody knows his task and performs it. Our teams are relieved every two hours, without difficulties.

Later, I came to the funeral chapel [in the sports centre]. In my hospital work I am accustomed to dead patients but the rows of coffins, fifty in all, leave a very profound impression. 'Drama, tragedy' is perhaps the best description. The hall is cold and silent, until some family members come in, crying in despair. A few young volunteers can't stand it and start crying themselves. They are drawn out of the chain and brought to the base. Friends receive them with warmth, coffee and rest. It is no shame, they did more than their best. I am proud of our volunteers.

Four hundred people are saved, fifty others were given back to their families. We did nothing less than we could. But the job is not finished; there are still victims in the ferry and we will come back for the salvage. Sunday, in the evening divers begin with their first preparations.

Captain De Winne of the Gendarmerie was part of the Disaster Victim Identification (DVI) Team – unique to Belgium. The motto of the DVI is, 'To speak for the dead, to protect the living.' The DVI was set up in the wake of the Los Alfaques disaster in Spain in 1978, in which many Belgians were involved. At that time, Interpol composed a commission that was meant to standardise the forms on which personal information of the people concerned was recorded. A study group, led by Lieutenant Bruggeman, had compiled a manual – *Manual on Disaster Victim Identification* – which was released internationally in November 1986, four months before the Zeebrugge disaster.

The DVI Team first went into action on the night of the *Herald of Free Enterprise* disaster. The original organisation of the DVI Team was implemented. Led by a commander, the team consisted of a secretariat, responsible for all administration tasks and ordnance. Liaison officers were appointed to take care of contacts with foreign police and other organisations involved in the disaster. The disaster area was divided into numbered sectors, with several teams allocated to search their sectors. Bodies that were found received a number, were photographed and taken to an assembly point. Then the bodies were taken to the 'Technical Identification Zone'.

Each body was then described externally and internally by pathologists and odon-
tologists. Specific characteristics, such as tattoos, were photographed and fingerprints
were taken. Then clothing was described and subsequently laundered. Jewellery and
other personal effects were registered and photographed. After a last check, the completed forms were taken to the 'Identification Centre'.

The role of the identification centre was to compose a list of victims that would
most probably have lost their lives in the disaster. The Social Intervention Service of
the Belgian Red Cross gathered this information, both nationally and internationally.
These forms, known as 'ante-mortem forms', were entered into a central computer.
A specially designed computer program compared around fifty parameters that featured on the ante- and post-mortem forms – the greater the number of matches
between the two, the higher the probability of confirming the identity of the body.
The results of these comparisons were then passed to judicial and administrative
authorities to issue the death certificate.

The rescue team's responsibility was in three parts – they interviewed family members who had come to Zeebrugge, to collect the ante-mortem evidence about their
missing loved ones; the team also kept an eye on the mortuary after the bodies were
taken there from the Technical Identification Zone; a possible meeting with the families of the victims would follow, no doubt involving a certain degree of counselling.

Captain De Winne was the commander of the DVI Team during the *Herald of Free
Enterprise* disaster. He presented the following lecture on PTSD on 25 May 1989, at
the Central Bureau of Investigations, in Brussels. After thanking psychologist Luc
Quintyn, he said:

Although in Zeebrugge, we worked very closely with other services like the
Emergency Service and the Social Intervention Service of the Belgian Red Cross, the
Civil Defence, members of the navy and British police; and all these collaborators have
witnessed the same facts. I still cannot express their feelings and experiences, since they
have had a totally different training and they live in a completely different world.

The members of the DVI Team were all policemen from the Surveillance and
Search Brigade, who carried out judicial investigations and who have often been
confronted with corpses. So the first night, 6 March 1987, when more or less fifty
corpses had to be described, we considered the job almost as routine. After that, the
long waiting period began until the re-floating of the ship on 7 April 1987. During
this period, a lot of rumours about the things we could expect did circulate among
the people involved with the disaster.

Some foreign colleagues, like Marc Rand from the West Yorkshire Police who
witnessed the Bradford Fire, and Colonel Bordewijk from the Dutch DVI Team,
shared their experiences with us. That is why we reckoned that stress and the psychological strain would be considerable during the future stages.

Therefore, the following measures were adopted:

The creation of a work environment that would improve a peaceful atmosphere. This way, the hangar at our disposal on the naval base was divided into various appropriate working areas. The 150 men had to work there, would not have to disturb each other and if somebody entered the warehouse, he would not be immediately confronted with the corpses.

It was seen to that when tasks were distributed to the members of the DVI, those who would have to search and technically identify the corpses would not have to cope with the victims' families and vice versa. This is in order to diminish their personal involvement.

A clear briefing in which everyone was informed as well as possible about what he would have to face and what his tasks would represent in the whole operation. This is to achieve a better execution of the tasks and to enable rescuers to talk about their fear of the unknown.

The request for the presence of a psychologist and a physician to assist the members of the DVI from April 7, 1987 on, during their activities.

There followed a series of slides at the lecture, in which Captain De Winne attempted to show the workshop attendees various situations that the various members of the DVI Team were confronted with. Some images were very graphic.

On 7 April 1987, the waiting period ended and at last we could act. Around 7 p.m., we were taken on board the ship by helicopters. For most of us, the 'lift' was a first stressing situation. On board the *Herald* we saw chaos. Mud, pieces of wreckage and among them, the corpses. Immediately, the lighting equipment was installed and everybody got to work.

On 8 April, around 3 a.m., the first corpses were taken away to the hangar and stored in cold storage containers. At 8 a.m., while on the ship, corpses were still being recovered, the technical identification and the description of clothes and jewels started. The embalming was also carried out on the spot. It must be said that the bodies were very well preserved. The same could not be said of the corpses that were washed ashore, or that were discovered in the water.

The most difficult moments were those when children were discovered. Those who worked in the identification centre also get their share of emotions to deal with, when they found family pictures of the victims, while comparing ante-mortem and post-mortem data. The task of those who had to take care of the family members, and were in charge of the morgue, was also very painful. Luckily, they were helped by the social workers of the Social Intervention Service of Danny de Beukelaer.

Finally, our work ended completely on 20 May 1987, when the *Herald of Free Enterprise* was towed out of the harbour of Zeebrugge. The job was finished and this thanks to teamwork and a near collaboration with other services.

Before I finish this speech, I wish to name the chaplain of the naval base, Jean Seruys. He was constantly busy at taking care of the small and big material and moral problems we all had to face. I can easily say that he has done a good job, together with Luc Quintyn.

To conclude, I have to mention that the psychological follow-up of the members of the DVI team has never happened. This is not due to Luc, who still has some individual contacts. The cause of it all is rather that at that moment the Gendarmerie was not sufficiently aware of the fact that stress stemming from such circumstances should be diminished and treated professionally. Talking about your experiences with others without appropriate assistance can help, but is not sufficient for everybody. Therefore, we hope that this workshop will contribute to the creation of a national PTSD team.

Rising Toll

On 9 March, two more bodies were recovered. They were believed to be those of soldiers. On the same day, one of the injured survivors died in hospital. Fifty-three people were now officially dead.

On 22 March, two weeks after the disaster, the bodies of three women were found washed up on a beach in Holland, some 12 miles from Zeebrugge.

Townsend Thoresen were still maintaining that 409 people had been saved and 134 were dead or missing. But the Belgian transport minister, Herman de Croo, knew that many more had died. He insisted that up to 194 people had died. Kent Police agreed with the Belgians – sixty-one bodies recovered and 133 people unaccounted for.

As far as it could be determined, 193 people aboard the *Herald of Free Enterprise* lost their lives – 155 passengers and thirty-eight crew members. According to the DVI Team in Belgium, 188 bodies were recovered and identified, one person died two months later in hospital and four victims were never found.

Between the times of the ferry capsize and the day before the ferry was raised, known to Belgian authorities as Phases 1 and 2, a total of sixty-one bodies were recovered, identified and returned to their families. These included the three women who were found washed up on a Dutch beach, and one man washed up on a beach near Ostend.

During Phase 3, which was the period when the ferry was righted, a further 117 bodies were found and taken ashore, and preparations made for families to identify them at a temporary mortuary at St Jan's Hospital, Bruges. When the ferry was stable, known as Phase 4, the remaining water inside was pumped out, and the ferry was then refloated and towed back into the harbour at Zeebrugge. Salvage workers found another nine bodies in the lower decks of the ferry, bringing the total of recovered bodies to 188.

With the death of a woman who had broken her neck during the capsize, in a London hospital two months after the disaster, and with a further four people known to have been aboard and whose bodies have never been recovered, the official death toll was 193. This figure is based on the evidence gathered over the months following the disaster by British and Belgian civil authorities.

However, there may be more victims that may never be known, owing to the system operated by Townsend Thoresen at the time. Enquiries came from around the world for information about people who were thought to have been on board, as they had not been in touch with concerned families back home. In mid-April, a letter from a solicitor in Portland, Oregon, enquired about a Samuel Friedman, a Canadian citizen, who was missing from the NATO base at St Stevens Woluwe on the outskirts of Brussels. The letter asked 'Have you found his body?'

Missing

Four victims of the *Herald of Free Enterprise* disaster were never recovered.

Nine-month-old Nadine Bunker had been with her parents, army captain Brian and Diane. Brian Bunker had left his wife and baby daughter in the C-deck lounge of the ferry whilst he had gone to the cafeteria, one deck above, to get them all some food. After he was rescued, Brian had spent four hours on the hull of the ferry helping pull survivors out. His family were not amongst them.

Bombardier John Graham Gaylard (36), of the Royal Artillery, was travelling from Dortmund to meet his brother in St Albans.

The widow of RAF Corporal Alan Stedman, of Watford, wrote to the *Herald Link* in a plea for information about her missing husband:

> I would like to know if anyone saw my late husband Alan. He was 31-years-old, 5ft 10in tall, slim build with dark brown hair. He was travelling in a dark blue Daihatsu Charade car, which was full of household items. He had travelled from Berlin and was in the RAF (although he was wearing civilian clothing at the time), dark blue trousers and jumper and possibly a dark grey suede jacket. Alan's body has never been found. It would help me so much if anyone saw Alan at all. He was always a helpful man, so I'm sure he would, if he could, have helped somebody.

Writing at the time of their tenth wedding anniversary:

> Yet another hurdle to get over. Is there any end to the pain we have to suffer? I'm finding the strength to get through these sad lonely days. I have two beautiful little girls aged 7 and 4 years. For them I'm working hard at being a good mother and father. There are so many of you out there like me. It might help you to know that I know what you're going through.

Help

The *Herald* Assistance Unit (HAU) was established a few weeks after the Zeebrugge disaster by Kent County Council's Social Services department. Two teams were formed – the 'Home Team' and the 'Away Team'. Crew survivors and the bereaved, mainly in south-east Kent, were taken care of by the 'Home Team', while the 'Away Team' looked after the passenger survivors and bereaved across the rest of the country.

The 'Away Team' consisted of nine health professionals – four full-time social workers; one part-time social worker based in the Midlands; and one part-time psychologist and three part-time nurses with counselling and loss related issues based in London. The brief that the teams were given was unprecedented in Britain – an outreach service in the response to a disaster to an entire nation. The teams were faced with the fear that because so many people involved were located across the whole of the country, many would not come forward for help and would suffer in isolation. Therefore a proactive approach was applied, where victims were contacted first rather than having to request help.

A computerised database of the victims, the survivors and next of kin was set up. Around 350 people had survived the disaster – forty-two were crew members. The armed services had elected to take care of their own, leaving 263 passenger survivors. The map of survivors was then divided into sectors, with each worker being allocated a region. There was a large concentration of victims and survivors in the Greater London area.

Personal letters were then sent out to each contact on the list, along with a leaflet – 'Coping with a Major Personal Crisis'. This leaflet was originally created in Australia, in the aftermath of the Ash Wednesday Bushfires four years previously. It had also been used in the aftermath of the Bradford Football Club fire in May 1985. The leaflet proved to be very useful as many of those who received it took it with them wherever they went. The letter gave details of the HAU and of its intention to visit.

June Thomason, co-ordinator of the twelve-strong *Herald* Assistance Unit, believed efforts to minimise the long-term emotional effects couldn't really begin until the ship was righted and all bodies recovered. 'We can give advice on practical things like money, insurance claims etc. But our major concern is the effect of all this on people's long-term health – mental and physical. It is impossible to underestimate how much some people will suffer.'

A twenty-four hour telephone line was in operation at the unit. Some people made immediate contact, many of them distressed and asking for help. These were deemed as a priority, along with those survivors who it was felt had more immediate unrecognised needs than the bereaved.

Four months later, as the inquests approached, the focus of the team's help was turned to the bereaved. After the initial letter, a follow-up letter advised the victims that they would be visited on a particular day at a particular time. If a visit was not wanted they were asked to let the unit know.

The uptake on the visits was relatively high – 85 per cent of the bereaved, 72 per cent of survivors, and 82 per cent of the bereaved survivors chose to accept a visit. Of the other percentage who were not visited – 12 per cent were not contactable and 13 per cent felt their existing support was adequate, the remaining 75 per cent declined the visit that was offered. Overall, just 15 per cent of all those that were offered a visit declined.

A total of 205 visits were made. An unspecified number of visits were made to the families of seventy-four victims who had died whilst travelling alone, and to twenty-nine families who had lost one or more members – totalling eighty-one of the deceased victims.

The intention had been to visit victims on a one-off basis. Those who were deemed to be most 'at risk' received a second visit – in total, 25 per cent. This risk factor was based on a structured interview concentrating on the relating of the story of the capsize and the aftermath. They were asked to elaborate on their thoughts and feelings both at the time of the disaster, and at the present time. The teams also tried to identify previous life events which may have been compounding the victims' current feelings, and actions which may be taken to mitigate these feelings.

In effect, the visits that the victims received from the teams amounted to a 'Critical Incident Stress Debriefing'. For many of those involved it was the most thorough recounting of events they had gone through. The teams had been prepared to offer to put people in touch with local counselling services, and some were already receiving professional help, but the majority of those visited declined the offer of counselling.

Almost all of those that were visited said that they found the visits useful, despite being initially wary. Generally speaking, they said it was easier to talk to the teams because, aside from fellow victims, the HAU most closely 'understood'.

Those who had been contacted about visits but had not been visited after six months decided that it was 'too late'. It was around this time that victims were beginning to organise themselves, forming such groups as the '*Herald* Families Association'.

When the inquests came around in September 1987, for many it was the first time that the bereaved had understood how their loved ones had died. Post-mortem details had answered questions such as whether they had been unconscious when they drowned, and witness statements had shed light on what they were doing and where they were when they had died. During the inquests, the requests for contact with the HAU rose notably, particularly from the bereaved, but by Christmas 1987 the teams found that it was very quiet. It was almost as if the victims were avoiding contact with the outside world.

'We just sat tight, hoping it would pass quickly', some later said.

In February 1988, the 'Away Team' wound up its work, after nine months of visiting those affected by the disaster. The 'Home Team', concentrating their efforts in south-east Kent with the crew survivors and bereaved, continued their work.

In the weeks leading up to the first anniversary in March 1988, the lines again were very quiet. On 6 March 1988, the 'Away Team' divided their time between the memorial sailing to Zeebrugge and the memorial service in Dover. The team offered support where it could. Those who had not taken up the offer of visits from the unit said, 'I just couldn't come before.' The anniversary to some, it seemed, was just the start of the journey to the resolution of grief, instead of a conclusion.

The 'Away Team' disbanded in March 1988, and the 'Home Team' finished their work three months later. It had been hoped that the work of the unit could have been extended to eighteen months and even beyond, but economic restraints came into play. Kent County Council had financed the support network across the whole of the UK. The first full year of the HAU had cost the council almost £300,000.

As the Zeebrugge disaster faded from the headlines, it became apparent that the victims' suffering was becoming overlooked, and new problems were being created. There were many lessons to be learned from the work and experience of the HAU, in terms of psychological support:

1   A leading agency was needed to co-ordinate support, with close liaison with other involved agencies, both statutory and voluntary, to avoid competitive rivalry and 'convergence' on victims.
2   A minimum period of eighteen months must be given to offer support.
3   A team dedicated to, and working solely for, the disaster has high credibility and acceptability to victims.
4   Maximising service uptake could be achieved using a proactive outreach, using many different modes of contact (written material, visits, telephone crisis supports etc.).
5   The classification of 'victim' must be applied broadly, with help being offered to all involved, not only the primary victims
6   Face to face contact to be established quickly after the disaster, with lessons to be learned from the six month cut-off for survivors, who tend to believe that by then it is 'too late' to make a visit and offers of help are then frequently denied.
7   Key points must be heavily supported and those affected should be engaged on occasions such as inquiries, inquests and first anniversary memorials.
8   Training and considerable support must be given to those working long term with the psychological support of victims as the nature of this work is extremely demanding.
9   Central financial support, presumably from the government, must be given to local authorities and health service facilities in the event of disaster support work.

The HAU identified the three 'at risk' groups:

The Bereaved	The Survivors	Rescuers/Carers
Multiple and singly bereaved The other two *Herald* crews Townsend Thoresen The Dover community Crew who had changed shifts	Passengers Passengers who did not get on ferry	Immediate rescue, triage, support Body recovery and ID teams Long term carers

The HAU was phased out fifteen months after the disaster, but the *Herald Link* was born. It was a newsletter that was produced by an editorial group of survivors and bereaved. Aside from being a continuation of support for those visited by the HAU, it was designed to distribute news – but its most important feature was its forum for letters and poems sharing feelings and experiences. It was a channel for people to make contact, and place requests for information, particularly for those bereaved still asking about the last movements of their loved ones. The *Herald Link* proved very effective for those victims who were geographically dispersed. Less than 2 per cent of all of those affected asked *not* to receive further copies.

Mandy Smith, of Hither Green, south-east London, lost her two elder brothers in the disaster. She was one of the handful of people who attended the meeting of the editorial board of the *Herald Link* at the *Herald* Assistance Unit in Dover on 4 September 1987. '… I realised that everyone involved seemed to feel the same sense of, not only immense grief, but of severe isolation too … although I have the rest of my family, who are all suffering terribly, we just can't understand each other's grief. It is so different for a wife, husband, mother, father, etc.'

Also at the meeting was survivor Robert O'Neill, of Hendon, north London:

> I found that talking about my experience in the disaster with other people most helpful, and helped me come to terms with what had happened. And now, through this [*Herald Link*], I hope everyone involved in the disaster could write in and share the experiences and express any views they may have about the disaster. I hope you will take the time to write in as it will not only help you but others as well.

Richard McKenny, another survivor, of St Leonards-on-Sea, East Sussex, found the meeting:

> … very fruitful and very friendly … I found a warmth of friends that were eager to get rid of their frustration and anxieties at this meeting, together with discussions on how to carry on with the publication of the *Herald Link*, to bring home the message of everyone out there who was either involved or related to the disaster … I feel that if we all keep together on this issue to try and get rid of this trauma that we are suffering either from the loss of someone dear to us or the symptoms of being a survivor, we shall succeed in time to come.

Mrs C. Brian of Burnley, Lancashire, wrote to the *Herald Link*:

> You are the only people willing to help us apart from the Methodist minister, the Reverend Mervyn Appleby, who lives in Dover. You may even know him, he's been fantastic. If there is anything our family could do to help anyone, please do not hesitate to contact us. Even though we live so far away, we know exactly what people are going through, if not more. We not only lost our father on the *Herald* but we lost our youngest brother John, aged 23 years, in a road accident in Greece at Christmas just twelve weeks before my dad died. So unlike most people, we have had two tragic losses.

The Sprules family of Dover wrote about the loss of their son Stephen, a crewman on the *Herald*:

> We have all lost someone very dear. I lost my son who I loved very much. I know I am not alone as my husband lost his son, and my daughter lost her brother. But our grieving is so different. We all think and feel for others at times like this, but the hurt and pain for our loved ones is ours alone. I hope you, like us, have family and friends that are a great help. But the pain is still there. We know ours will be for a long time, probably forever.

Addressing the survivors, the Sprules said, 'Although you survived, you may be grieving for loved ones you lost, along with the memories of that terrible night. This must be dreadful. We can only imagine what it must be like.' To everyone involved:

> There have been so many things to do that must have been very unpleasant. I am sure you must have all been affected in some way. We send heartfelt sympathy to everyone. Our thanks to all involved. The love of Stephen has broken our hearts, which I am sure will never mend, although we are told the pain will ease as time passes.

The Social Services team of south-east Kent provided counselling support for bereaved relatives and survivors locally and nationally. Team leader Colin Weaver spoke of the aftermath of the disaster in the 'Summer 1987' edition of the *Civil Protection* magazine:

> Dover is a small town and it was thrown into panic and confusion by news of the ferry accident. Most of the Townsend Thoresen crew – three shifts of 80 – live in and around Dover. Few townspeople here did not have someone close to them – a friend, a relative or a neighbour – who was caught up in the tragedy … losing someone close to you in a disaster like Zeebrugge has a greater impact than ordinary bereavement. There are all sorts of complicated feelings to come to terms with, such as guilt, fear and helplessness.

European Ferries 1981

TOWNSEND THORESEN

Zie Engeland met uw eigen auto

De snelste autoveerdienst over het Kanaal
Slechts 75 minuten Calais-Dover

(Reproduced by kind permission of P&O Heritage)

Make 1983 your Blue Riband Year!

Sail with Townsend Thoresen's Blue Riband fleet in 1983 and you're on course for a great holiday. Choose from thousands of sailings, day and night, on 7 great routes to the continent. Plus the shortest crossing between N. Ireland and Scotland.

Enjoy the outstanding facilities and supreme comfort of fine, modern ships that include the Blue Riband record breakers between Dover and Calais. Rely on the special brand of Townsend Thoresen service.

And we can offer you lots of exciting holiday ideas, too - coach tours, inclusive motoring holidays, special mini-break fares, and day trips for all the family. All at a price that's right. For all the details, get your copy of the 1983 Townsend Thoresen Brochure from the Automobile Association or by writing to Townsend Thoresen, Brochure Department, 1 Camden Crescent, Dover, Kent CT16 1LD.

This year, give yourself the Blue Riband treatment. You can't beat it.

The European Ferries

TOWNSEND THORESEN

The fleet you can't beat

Dover-Calais only 75 minutes

Blue Riband RECORD BREAKERS

TOWNSEND THORESEN

(Reproduced by kind permission of P&O Heritage)

(Reproduced by kind permission of P&O Heritage)

(Reproduced by kind permission of P&O Heritage)

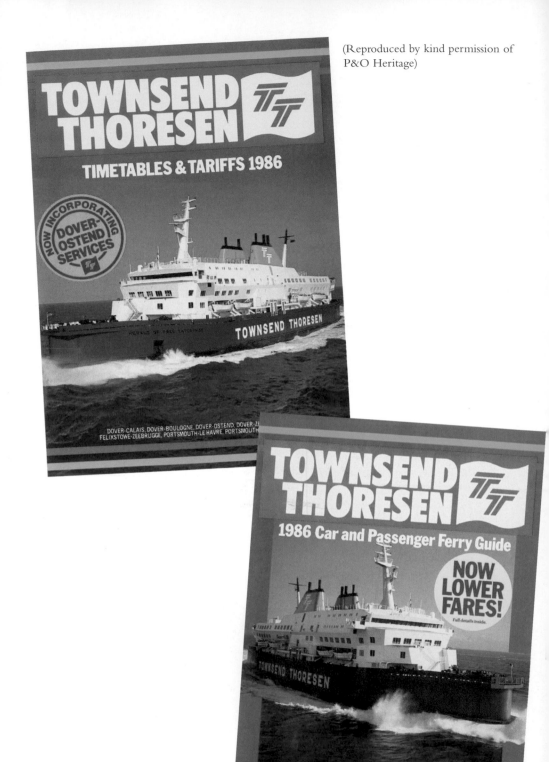

(Reproduced by kind permission of
P&O Heritage)

(Reproduced by kind permission of
P&O Heritage)

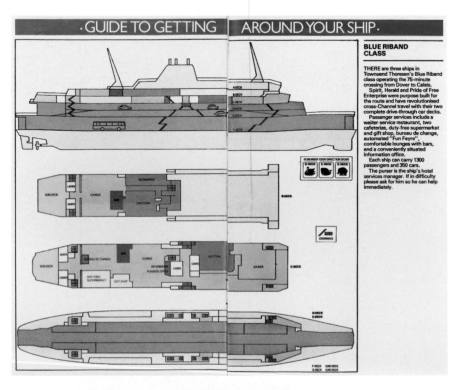

(Reproduced by kind permission of P&O Heritage)

Advertising literature featuring the three sister ships of the Spirit Class. (Reproduced by kind permission of P&O Heritage)

Routes you can't beat

Blue Riband

DOVER ━━━━━ **CALAIS**

Three beautiful, big new ships: *Spirit*, *Herald* and *Pride of Free Enterprise*. Holders of the coveted Blue Riband award for the fastest Channel crossing by ship with a car.

They offer you a winning combination of speed and reliability, spacious luxury and traditional Townsend Thoresen courtesy.

They also offer you all those facilities which travellers find invaluable. For instance, when you get to France, why waste precious driving time? On board, we offer you an excellent choice of reasonably-priced meals: the senior-service Blue Riband restaurants, the comfortable cafeteria, and during the summer months, the Salad Bowl.

Even at the busiest time of year, you'll find there's lots of space on these big ships. The famous white cliffs of Dover have long

Sold England's half and herself to seafarers. Today, Dover is easily the most popular car ferry port in the world, now fed by fast roads such as the M2 (which includes the new Canterbury By-Pass) and the M20 from London, the M25 and M26 from points west, and with good access from the east through the Dartford Tunnel.

At peak times, Townsend Thoresen ships sail every 90 minutes, so you have lots of choice. Why not go overnight? With quieter roads you can get away in a really good start.

At Calais, the premier car-ferry port of France, you'll find a superb new terminal and can quickly get on to the newly opened section of the A26 and so open the way to the entire Continent.

Go the Blue Riband way. You can't beat it.

ROUND THE CLOCK SAILINGS

The fastest ships to the Continent - Just 75 minutes

SHIPMATE

the newsletter of Townsend Thoresen's Junior Sailors Club

JOG OF A LIFETIME

Putting their best feet forward in a record-breaking bid to jog around the world – and raise money for charity – are runners Henry Weston (right) and Simon Westcott.

The two athletes – part of the four-strong British Transglobal team attempting the mammoth 16,000 mile jog in aid of the World Wildlife Fund – are pictured arriving in Dover ready to board the Townsend Thoresen ship Pride of Free Enterprise before sailing to Calais.

The journey, which began at London's Tower Bridge, will take the team through Europe to Istanbul, North Africa, Pakistan, and on through the Far East to Australia. The final section sees the joggers running through Mexico and the United States on their way back to Tower Bridge.

Altogether the journey is expected to take the team up to two years to complete. And they have a long way to run before breaking the world record. At the moment it is held by an American who ran 10,500 miles.

ALL AT SEA WITH KENNY

Changing roles from master of comedy to master of ship was all done in the best possible taste by TV's loony laugh-raiser Kenny Everett.

Kenny – who was once a DJ aboard a pirate radio ship in the North Sea – couldn't wait to get up to the bridge during a Dover-Calais crossing aboard the Townsend Thoresen Blue Riband ship Pride of Free Enterprise.

And joining in the fun, the ship's master Captain Chris Double lent Kenny a prop to make him feel just the part – his smart Captain's hat!

FERRY RUN

Townsend Thoresen will be transporting thousands of European athletes across the Channel to compete against British participants in the "Roads of Freedom" Women's Road Race Series, due to be held at Crystal Palace, London, on 14 October.

Any Junior Sailors Club member who would like to join in the excitement of the event will be given free admittance at the gate on production of their JSC membership card.

★★★★★★★★★★★★★★

DID YOU KNOW?

The largest barn in Britain is at Frindsbury, Kent, measuring 219ft in length

DID YOU KNOW?

The longest single unbroken apple peel on record is 172ft 4ins, peeled by a woman in America

COULD YOU BE A SUPERSTAR?

Response to the Townsend Thoresen Young Superstars Award Scheme has been overwhelming – with more than 1.5 million participants signed up in the first three months.

The Scheme – launched last February and aimed at encouraging young people to develop and enjoy their sporting abilties in a wide range of disciplines – was adopted by 16,000 schools and colleges throughout the UK soon after the details were announced.

Letters poured in by the sackful from teachers, sports organisations and the young people themselves all wanting to hear more about the Scheme and how they could take part.

One school enrolled its entire register of 2,000 pupils. And within weeks, participants up and down the land had achieved success at bronze, silver and even gold levels!

Junior Sailors who may have missed hearing about the Scheme can ask their sports teacher to send off for details today.

Designed to be organised during school games lessons or out of school hours, the Scheme – which is backed by top British sports personalities including Olympic Gold Medallist Lynn Davies and coach and TV commentator Ron Pickering – encourages boys and girls between the ages of eight and eighteen to try for standards in up to 21 sports.

Participants work at their own speed, gradually building up their skills to bronze, silver or gold level.

So even those who thought they were not sporty, stand a good chance of achieving success.

All participants receive a special pack containing a Personal Record Chart, button badge and stickers.

And every youngster who achieves a standard receives a certificate and may obtain a special cloth badge.

This year every Senior achieving a gold award qualifies for the prestigious Victor and Victrix Ludorum scheme – which is seen as the ultimate test in all-round sporting ability.

All enquiries about the scheme should be made to: The Townsend Thoresen Young Superstars Badge Award Scheme, Enterprise House, Avebury Avenue, Tonbridge, Kent TN9 1TH.

SHIPMATE, an on-board children's magazine of the Junior Sailors Club. This issue features Kenny Everett, pictured on the bridge of the *Pride of Free Enterprise*. (Reproduced by kind permission of P&O Heritage)

Number Eight   SPRING 1984

SHIPMATE

the newsletter of Townsend Thoresen's Junior Sailors Club

YOU'RE NEVER TOO YOUNG!

Our picture of two-and-a-half-year-old Christopher Griffiths in the number seven issue of Shipmate (Picture Yourself) started a tidal wave of letters from our very youngest readers — or at least their mums, dads, brothers, sisters, grans and grandads!

For when we asked if pint-sized Christopher could be the youngest shipmate, practically a whole crew of you wrote back to say you knew someone younger still.

We had letters from all ranks — from Able Seaman to Captain — and everyone was younger than Christopher. A lot of you have made almost more crossings than you've had hot dinners!

Among the youngest was five-month-old Tim Tattle, pictured here getting his ship's log stamped for his Petty Officer's badge, with his dad, Colin. Tim, of Bushey, in Hertfordshire, was snapped aboard Herald of Free Enterprise, while making his second crossing.

But even Tim was outdone by heaps of even younger members — which goes to show that you can never be too small to go to sea! If you think you know a sailor even younger than Tim, don't tell us — tell the Guinness Book of Records!

CASE DISMISSED

It was a case of "bin and gone" for Wokingham Junior Sailors Nathan and Timothy Parry before their return from a holiday in France last summer.

For the brothers — both Petty Officers — left their cases outside their holiday home at Bay Sur Aube in Dijon, France, ready to be

loaded into the family car.

But when the Parrys were ready to leave, the cases couldn't be seen for dust. For over-zealous dustmen had mistaken the bags for rubbish, and scooped them up into the dustcart.

While neighbours tried in vain to recover the bags, Nathan, 14, and Timothy, 13, could only mourn the loss of their carefully packed Junior Sailors Club membership cards.

The family returned to France at Christmas. "But this time we all kept our hands on everything!", said Mrs Parry.

And the Junior Sailors Club was able to issue the brothers with new membership cards.

It's Superstars time

Superstars champ Brian Hooper and Townsend Thoresen's Bryan Thompson

Sporting Junior Sailors can follow in the tracks of their favourite sports personalities with the new £300,000 Townsend Thoresen Young Superstars Badge Award Scheme.

The Scheme — which is now operating in schools and colleges throughout Britain — is aimed at encouraging all youngsters to enjoy their games lessons, however sporty or non-sporty they may be.

Boys and girls aged between eight and 18 can try for bronze, silver and gold standards in up to 21 sports ranging from football to fencing! Special certificates and badges will be awarded as each standard is achieved.

Would-be Superstars can get details of the Scheme from their school sports teachers. The Scheme is designed to be run during normal school games lessons or out of school hours. In this way, participants can utilise school facilities and gain the support and encouragement from their teacher.

Chance to excel

Sports-minded or not, the Townsend Thoresen Young Superstars Badge Award Scheme encourages every young person to take an active interest in physical activity — and gives even those with special ability the chance to excel in new sports.

Olympic gold medallist Lynn Davies, coach and TV commentator Ron Pickering and

a host of Britain's other top sports personalities are backing the Scheme, which aims to make sporting activities fun and accessible to all youngsters.

Participants work at their own speed, gradually building up the level of skill required to win an award.

The Townsend Thoresen Young Superstars Award Scheme is split into six sections, including Target Skills, Power and Strength, Games Skills, Obstacle, Speed and Endurance and an Open section, which recognises achievements already gained in other sports.

Nationwide scheme

Participants of all ages between eight and 18 must choose at least one activity from each discipline in order to qualify for an award. Altogether there are 29 skills throughout the disciplines for youngsters to choose from — like darts, weight lifting, squash, water polo and golf.

Judo expert Brian Jacks, Superstars winner, in action

Everyone who takes part in the Scheme will receive their own Pack which contains a Personal Record Card, button badge and stickers. Display charts, showing details of all the events and how to score, will be given to teachers.

Every youngster who meets the bronze, silver or gold standard for his or her age group will receive a certificate and may obtain a cloth badge.

Seniors who have achieved a gold award will be able to enter a nationwide Victor and Victrix Ludorum scheme, which is recognised as being the ultimate test of all-round sports ability.

This edition of *SHIPMATE* features a toddler getting his ship's log stamped at the Information Office aboard the *Herald of Free Enterprise*. (Reproduced by kind permission of P&O Heritage)

A SPECIAL SAVING
JUST FOR YOU

When you entered the recent Channel 4 Tour de France Competition perhaps you didn't realise that you were sure to be a winner. But we're pleased to say – you are! Because we've awarded every entrant a generous £5 saving prize to give you the chance of going on your very own Tour de France – with your car. You can use your saving on any return ticket on Townsend Thoresen car ferries when you take your car to the Continent. The offer is valid until 31st March 1987.

Over the page, we list all the special low fare bargain breaks we're offering this Autumn to our valued customers. Add to that the £5 saving and you can travel over to France or Belgium for next to nothing – especially when you consider the savings you make on those duty free purchases.

You've got to agree it's the ideal chance to nip across just for the day – or a little longer – to do some bargain and unusual Christmas shopping at a giant hypermarket. Or even to treat yourself to a second holiday. We've some irresistible little packages in a wide variety of easy-to-get-to places from sophisticated hotels in Paris to enchanting little country auberges.

But read all about it – decide on what suits you – and present this leaflet when you pay to get your £5 saving. Oh, and by the way, if you haven't travelled with us before – you're in for a nice surprise. On all our smooth, smart modern ships there is the friendliest welcome afloat anywhere. We haven't gained the No. 1 Car Ferry Award for the last seven years for nothing!

IT'S EASY GOING
TOWNSEND THORESEN

(Reproduced by kind permission of P&O Heritage)

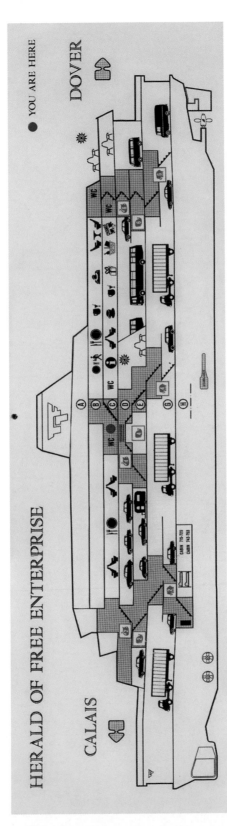

The 'You Are Here' whereabouts board, located on the starboard side of the *Herald*, and recovered from the wreck after the ferry was raised.

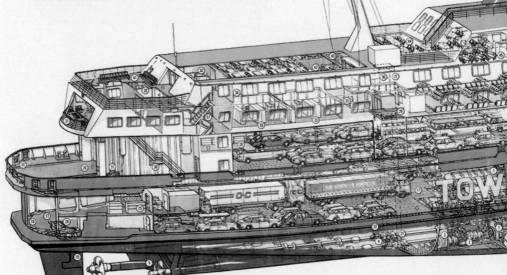

Spirit of Free Enterprise is one of three new 8,200-ton car ferries of the 'Blue Riband' class introduced by Townsend Thoresen on its Dover routes during 1980. The others are Herald of Free Enterprise and Pride of Free Enterprise.

They are the largest ever built for cross-Channel service and with a service speed of 22 knots - at least three knots faster than current vessels operating between Britain and France - will make the crossing from Dover to Calais in 75 minutes, although record crossings have been made in just over 50 minutes.

'Blue Riband' ships are the first to have two complete "drive-through" vehicle decks. They can each carry up to 1,300 passengers and 350 cars and with all three in operation up to 30 crossings a day are possible giving a total capacity of 40,000 passengers and 10,000 cars in one day.

Features of the new ferries include a de-luxe restaurant, self-service restaurant and a cold buffet cafeteria. The duty-free supermarket is double the size of those of Townsend Thoresen's previous ships and is sited alongside perfume and gift shops and a bureau de change.

PRINCIPAL PARTICULARS

		Capacities:		
Length, o.a.	131.90 m	Passengers		1 300
Length, b.p.	126.10 m	Cars		350
Breadth, o.a.	23.15 m	Freight	60 x 12 m trailers + 60 cars	
Breadth, moulded	22.70 m	Propulsion	3 x CCM-Sulzer 12ZV40/48	
Depth, to main deck	7.30 m	Output, c.s.r.	3 x 8 000 bhp at 530 rev/min	
Depth, to upper vehicle deck	12.70 m	Trials speed (wind force seven)		23.75 knots
Depth, to lounge deck	18.05 m	Blue riband speed (average)		23.90 knots
Gross register	8 200 tons	Service speed		22.00 knots
Deadweight (approximate)	2 000 tonnes			

Key

1 Three Sulzer ZV40/48 medium-speed mai
2 Transmission coupling and gearbox
3 Shaft alternators (port and starboard shafts
4 Propeller pitch controls
5 High skew c.p. propellers
6 Fin stabilisers (port and starboard)
7 Service pumps
8 Three A.P.E.-Allen diesel-driven NEBB alter
9 Electrically-powered bow thrusters (port an
10 Electrically-powered bow propeller and mo
11 Bow rudder
12 Fresh-water tanks
13 Sewage treatment plant
14 Fuel oil tanks
15 Stern rudder

The 'Spirit of Free Enterprise' 3D cutaway plans proposed for the three sisters in Townsend Thoresen's Spirit series, as appeared in *The Motor Ship* magazine. (Courtesy of Mercator Media)

ENTERPRISE"

6 Stern clam-shell vehicle loading doors
7 Main vehicle deck
8 Bow clam-shell vehicle loading doors
8 Anchor (port and starboard)
0 "H" deck accommodation, showers and toilets
1 Service lift "B" to "H" deck
2 Elevator "G" to "H" deck
3 Service lift "B" to "H" deck
4 Steering gear
5 Auxiliary services ("F" deck) port and starboard
6 Upper vehicle deck ("E" deck)
7 Upper vehicle deck door (open position)
8 Hostable car decks port and starboard ("D" deck position)
9 Hostable car decks (stowed under "C" deck)
0 Escape stairway "C" to "E" deck

31 Foot passenger accesses at terminals
32 Toilets
33 Duty-free shops
34 Bureau de change (port side)
35 Gift shop
36 Passenger saloon and bar ("C" deck)
37 Passenger saloon and information desk ("C" deck)
38 Cafeteria
39 Cafeteria saloon ("C" deck)
40 Passenger saloon
41 Passenger after deck
42 Passenger saloon and bar
43 Passenger-saloon and coffee bar
44 Dining saloon
45 Cafeteria and saloon

46 Ship's personnel mess and cabins
47 Wheelhouse, also port and starboard wing control stands
48 Captain's and officers' quarters and radio room
49 Crew's quarters (port and starboard)
50 Radar mast
51 Anchor-handling and mooring equipment
52 Lifeboat stations
53 Inflatable liferafts
54 Rope ladders
55 RFD marine escape system stowage
56 Access to RFD escape chute
57 Main passenger staircases

St Danaas church, Zeebrugge, focal point of the Zeebrugge Disaster commemorations.

The memorial to the disaster within the Rose Garden in Zeebrugge.

The Rose Garden in Zeebrugge, close to the marine base where much of the activity took place on the night of the disaster.

A memorial window at Ealing Abbey dedicated to the memory of a young Polish couple who died in the disaster.

IN MEMORY OF
MAŁGOSIA AND PITEK
WHO LOVED AND
CARED FOR CHILDREN
AND ALL THOSE WHO
PERISHED IN THE
ZEEBRUGGE FERRY DISASTER
6TH MARCH 1987

The plaque next to the memorial window in Ealing Abbey.

Life After

Eleven weeks after the disaster, on 25 May, 14-year-old Nicola Simpson and her father, Tony, both survivors of the *Herald*, returned to Belgium aboard the Townsend Thoresen ferry *Free Enterprise VI*. It was their first ferry trip since Nicola almost died and her mother Patricia was killed. They were in Belgium to thank the divers who pulled her from the freezing waters inside the ferry, and the doctors and nurses who brought her back from the dead.

After an official ceremony to honour the rescuers in Brussels, Tony and Nicola had a private meeting with the King and Queen of Belgium. Nicola said, 'I still think about mum, but I don't think about what happened as much as I used to lying in hospital. It happened – so you have to come to terms with it, really.'

On his twins' fourth birthday, three months after the disaster, survivor Alan Rogers tried to kill himself. He spent two weeks in hospital after his wife, Sue, found him unconscious from an overdose.

Larry O'Brien escaped by clinging to a fire hose, but not before he helped rescue thirty, and maybe as many as fifty people, by pulling them up on a rope. O'Brien was very humble about his actions that night, 'I never saw myself as a hero and I still don't. What happened that night was that, for fifteen minutes, I was fully convinced I was going to die.' Despite Larry's modesty he was rewarded by Goodyear Tyres, in their first 'European Highway Hero' programme, in front of 150,000 spectators at the Nascar Daytona 500 stock car race in Florida, in February 1988. He was awarded with a $5,000 cheque by the chairman of Goodyear, Robert Mercer. Larry and his wife, Cindy, were in Florida on holiday paid for by Goodyear.

Tracy Edwards had lost her mother, grandmother, sister and baby nephew in the disaster. Her father George Lamy had survived. She said:

> Smit Tak began to raise the ferry during the first week of April, right next to the Easter holidays. Kim's body was found in the ladies' toilets. Her son Stevie would have celebrated his first birthday on 19 April. The date of the large family farewell was arranged for 21 April. This was a time of mourning and I feel should never be described or discussed. I thank everyone who attended.

That same night, Tracy, her husband and daughter flew to Tenerife. The rest of the family later went to Menorca. Whilst in Tenerife, Tracy had cause to complain to their holiday rep about their accommodation. Despite changing apartments, they were still not happy but were continually fobbed off by their rep that they were 'trying, the powers that be', and 'the fault of the accommodation provider'. After five days, their rep told them, 'That's what you get with last minute package holidays. It's like being in prison. You're stuck with it until your plane leaves.' Enraged, Tracy decided to use the press to their advantage and calmly went to speak to some of the reporters that had been following them. The story appeared in the newspapers the next day and Tracy and her family were upgraded to the apartment that the Labour party leader Neil Kinnock had just vacated.

On 6 May, the family arrived back in England. It was Tracy's birthday, but she had nothing to celebrate. 'I realised that if you run away from something it is always there when you get back, usually bigger than before and harder to deal with.'

The Austrian Postal Service, who had heard of the Lamys' treatment after the disaster, were appalled and invited them to stay in the holiday village of Bad Ischl, near Salzburg. An aide from the British Post Office accompanied the Lamys and another bereaved family to Austria. They had almost missed the plane, as George couldn't find his passport, remembering just in time that he had given it to the aide. Next, they were stopped at Austrian customs after officials discovered they were carrying white powder. It was baby Sarah's soya-based baby formula, as she was allergic to milk. George Lamy took exception to the authorities' treatment of his family:

My dad became impatient and, not being able to understand the armed guards, was getting irritated by their behaviour towards me. They started to push him with a machine gun. He pushed it back. The officer then pushed him harder. Then, like a scene from 'Dirty Harry', my dad put his finger down the end of the barrel and said 'Do it, do you feel lucky?' I really laugh about this, but analysing this is a psychological way, my dad had lost all hope and life itself. He really didn't care anymore.

Tracy handed baby Sarah to her father, which snapped him out of it and they finally cleared customs.

When the family returned to England, Tracy was put on sick leave by her employers, the local government authority. She didn't feel ill, but felt that her bosses were protecting her.

Tracy returned to work after all the hype over money had settled down. However, new care legislation had been implemented, and the care home she had been working in closed down. She was redeployed to an office processing change reports – the Social Service's way of keeping records up to date. One day, as she was leafing through the 100 or so reports they received every day, Tracy came across the name 'Victoria Lamy', the nan she had lost in the disaster. Victoria had lived in warden-controlled accommodation, and the report was informing the Social Services of a change of circumstances. 'This really affected me. Silly things still do.'

The first anniversary approached really quickly. The Lamys once again found themselves in the news, and television was producing special programmes with clips of the events of 6 and 7 March 1987.

Tracy gave up work soon after the anniversary. She could not cope with work and being recognised. She became Mrs Edwards, rather than Mrs Lamy-Edwards, in effect to hide away from the world.

Later on in 1987, Jane Hind moved out of the family home in Beckenham. One day, she returned to visit her brother to find him living there alone with a candle for lighting, no heating and no hot water. 'Just what he needed after he had lost the main part of his family.' Her stepfather had moved out to live with another woman. 'We then had another struggle as my name was on the mortgage and my stepfather tried to say that I had paid nothing towards the house so was due nothing. A situation I could really have done without when I was still trying to come to terms with the loss of people I had loved so much.'

The husbands of Margaret Pelling and her daughter Shirley Lopez received counselling and compensation after the disaster, but the rest of the family did not. Jane revealed that neither she, nor her brother, was asked if they needed any support. Any compensation that was paid went directly to her stepfather and brother-in-law as next of kin:

> We didn't see any of this money at all and both lost contact with us very shortly after the disaster. Sadly they were not as affected as we were by the loss of our loved ones as we found out afterwards they had both been seeing other people.
>
> My brother is two years older than me and he was the only boy so we all spoiled him. I think when my mum died I took over from her and have mothered him ever since. I love him so very much and my only wish is for his happiness but mum dying just destroyed him really. I suppose to be honest it destroyed all of us in our own ways.

Jane recalled:

> I fully understand that disasters such as this have to be in the media. But when they are showing dead bodies, whether they are covered or not, I feel that this is just not right. I remember sitting there and the only contact I really had with the disaster was to watch the media, but every time I saw a body I found myself thinking 'is that my mum or my sister or my uncle?' I sometimes feel that the families the disaster affects are not thought of at all. I still find it heart-rending to see the picture of the ferry on its side and to think that my family were on it.

Moira Peach, of Rugeley, Staffordshire, lost her lorry driver husband in the disaster:

> I lost my husband Tom … I almost lost my mind on 6 March and my daughters almost lost a mother. I wrapped myself up in my own grief and shunned my two girls. Luckily for all of us I have got lovely caring children and my eldest girl, Lisa, was so strong that she dragged me out of my own miserable semi-coma of grief long enough to see their heartache and to do something to help them.
>
> Six months on in the aftermath, I felt lost and lonely. My world is so, so different now. My home has no male in it, no male smells or 'mess'. I miss my husband so much for so many different reasons, some so small, but painful nevertheless.

I must know, did anyone see my husband Tom? About 6ft tall of solid muscle, black hair, greying at the sides, aged 42, dressed in jeans, a jumper and a dark blue body warmer, as far as I know. He was a very friendly person, a truck driver. Someone must have seen him, please, if anyone can tell me exactly what happened to Tom.

Let me add, I understand how survivors of the horror feel. I don't begrudge anyone their lives. I am only sad that more people never survived it. As far as I know, Tom was helping people out of the cafeteria when he died but all I hope is that if he saved just one person, then the loss of his life wasn't such a dreadful waste.

Mark McGurk, of Ipswich, wrote to the *Herald Link* of his family's experiences following the death of John Rogers, a crew member:

Since the death of my stepfather John Rogers, a motorman on the *Herald*, I think all my family's life has changed. The thing seems like a very prolonged recovery from a very severe bang on the head. We all feel so much for my mum, who previous to this tragedy had so many other personal tragedies. Speaking personally, I feel there is nothing I can do to help my mum through such a terrible time in her life. I feel helpless and also at times feel so bitter that the man my mum so loved, and at last found so much happiness with, should be lost in such a way. Like so many, I wish I could find a reason for all this, but what possible reason could be attributed to this? … Time is going to be the healer but it's going to take a long time, so patience must also be required.

Gillian Baddeley (16) and her two stepbrothers Mark (18), and Colin (14), returned to Wallasey after identifying the bodies of her mother and stepfather. The body of their uncle, Derek Whitworth, was washed up on a beach near Ostend a month later. Her eldest stepbrother, Ian (20), became guardian of the teenagers, and Gillian took it upon herself to be the homemaker. She was offered no counselling or therapy. After Gillian made an appeal in a national newspaper, her father, Alan Marrion, was reunited with the daughter he hadn't seen since she was aged 4. 'I'd planned to find him when I was older,' she says. 'It wasn't the happy reunion I'd imagined. But to feel fatherly arms around me was a great comfort.'

For survivor Jan Willis, the aftermath was lonely:

No one from the ferry company wanted to know. Six months later a lone social worker turned up but really showed no interest. For me, returning to work was difficult. I hated the job and now in hindsight I was probably suffering from stress and PTSD, not recognised at the time. My GP said just be grateful you are alive. He probably did not realise how damaging those words were. It felt like you are nothing, it took years to realise I am something.

Jan had no counselling at the time. 'I had no brothers or sisters and a small family, and I'm not really sure how they coped as I rarely talked about it. My childhood sweetheart relationship failed soon after, as I felt he didn't do enough. Looking back what did I think a 21-year-old engineering student could do? That was a sad time, especially when you are so young.' Jan struggled to find a support group and very quickly she and her friends all fell apart. 'I have not seen Karen [Watson] since June 1987, very sad.'

Although Jan had returned to work as a bank clerk three weeks after the disaster, she never settled back in. She had hated the job before but now she wanted out. She left at the end of the year. 'I genuinely wanted to change the world and I was looking for ways to do it. I had always loved the police and tried to apply for a cadet. A year after Zeebrugge I was accepted into the Metropolitan Police.'

Susan Teare wrote to the *Herald Link* from Germany:

I've had what can only be described as a weird year. Firstly I became engaged, then Andy and I were survivors of the *Herald*. Soon afterwards, Andy went to a new posting in Germany and I was left to recover from my injuries, come to terms with what I had been convinced was my death, as I happened to be under water and would still be there if Andy had not come back for me. I was also trying to arrange for our wedding in October and from June, to get back to work, difficult for all of us I know, but as I was due to leave in September it was impossible and I failed. We then got married and I left family, friends, job, home, lifestyle in England to come back to a new home, husband, life, country, language etc. Soon after, Andy was off on an exercise but I was so busy I had no time even to take breath. He returned just before Christmas and we never seemed to be in. Now it's all over it is time to take breath, no plans to be made, only time to reflect. I am not complaining, we have been so lucky and are very happy. But now it's beginning to hit home. I seem to be spending more time thinking about what has happened and crying about it a lot more than I have done. I am not unhappy or depressed, just still trying to sort out what happened and why we have been so lucky. I do feel increasingly isolated from all of you. Our friends (with the best of intentions) either want to know all the gory details or are bored of it – it's old news, whereas to me it's more vivid than ever ... but we do have *Herald Link*, we can read how other people are getting on, what they are doing, what happened to them and it really does ease the feeling of isolation ...

In the New Year's Honours list, thank goodness, many heroic feats were recognised. But what about the passengers that showed great courage? Only one was remembered. I would not be here if my husband had not dived down into the boat as she was going over to get me out. Then he left me at the bottom of a rope and went back into the ship to find other people. He was not looking for anybody in particular, just anybody he could help. He repeatedly went back into the boat until he was made to leave the boat at midnight, suffering from shock, exhaustion and hypothermia. I did not know where he was until midday Saturday, the last I had seen of him was him climbing back down into the boat. Many, many other passengers behaved in the same selfless way as highlighted in the last issue of *Herald Link*. Surely ensuring these people are properly recognised is one way to thank them and to help them come to terms with the event. My husband's reaction was, even after saving twenty lives, 'I obviously didn't do enough' and he is now going through self-doubt and guilty feelings.

Kent survivor Sonia Saunders wrote to the *Herald Link* about the loss of her husband Mick:

It is nearly Christmas and it is going to be jolly lonely without my jolly husband Mick, always the life and soul of the party. He always liked to make other people laugh. He used to dress up as Father Christmas and go around knocking on people's doors on Christmas Day. The kids loved him. Now he's gone – whoever thought the day we went over to Zeebrugge would be our last day together? I will never forget that night. I think I could write a book. I am trying to adjust my life and to start anew. It's quite hard at 54. I find I cannot stay indoors or concentrate on anything for long. It's so hard, I even talk to him knowing he cannot hear me.

Irene Blanchard of Hullbridge, Essex, wrote to the *Herald Link* at Christmas 1987:

I expect when this goes to print, Christmas will be behind us. I, just like you all, am dreading it. I am a survivor of the *Herald*. I lost my darling husband Norman, our daughter Sharon and three-week old granddaughter Rebecca (Sharon's baby). I just feel my life is over, like theirs. So one night after waking at three in the morning (yet again) I put my thoughts on paper. I hope it is of some help to someone.

The day after this terrible 6 March, my daughter Debbie lost her home in a fire. They have a pub, and while waiting at Dover to hear news of us, was told they had lost the pub. Lots of people who saw her at Dover have asked about her baby she was expecting. I'm happy to say that on 12 September she had a little girl, Victoria. How she coped through this all has kept me going. I love my children dearly but feel so alone many times.

I have met the young lad, Gary Barnett, who saved my life. You see, I can't swim. John Quinn [*Herald* Assistance Unit] arranged all of this – thank you once again, John and Gary.

Barry Ducker, of Swaffham, Norfolk, the lorry driver who was rescued from the sea after dropping out of the vehicle deck, was later reunited with his rescuers, Andre Vermoote and Aime Moens. Months later, Barry's wife said, 'Barry still has sleepless nights as he relives the tragedy and sees those people he could do nothing to help.'

At the end of November 1987, the Duckers went to Knokke-Heist to stay with Aime and Gabby Moens. Whilst there, they visited the hospital where Barry was treated after his rescue. Mrs Ducker wrote to the *Herald Link* on behalf of her husband's rescuers to enquire about another survivor who they had picked up from the sea and put on a tug. 'They say her name is Eileen or Irene and that she was young and was swimming in the water.' This mystery girl was the one who told Aime and Andre that Barry was still on the ship. 'It's the only good thing to come out of that dreadful night, their friendship.'

Heather Crocker of Bermondsey, south London, lost her brother, Colin Virtue, and sister-in-law Jackie. She wrote to the *Herald Link* of her loss:

> The letters in *Herald Link* are more of a comfort to me than going to see my doctor or going to Guy's Hospital to see a psychologist. I just felt that nobody could help me. I've been suffering from panic attacks and I hardly go shopping anymore – I am frightened to drive and cannot even get in the bath without anybody in the house, and my brother had a terrible fear of boats when we were very young, and that day I was thinking of Colin and his wife Jackie all day. They were so loving, so caring – everything a brother and sister-in-law should be – I couldn't have wished for better. They were my life, always there when I needed them and now I feel so lost. They were with two friends, Stephen and Janet [Turner], all found on C-deck.

Mrs Oriana Gomez, of London, was on board with her son Jonathan (12), and friends Andrew and Eleanor Parker and their 12-year-old daughter, Janice. All of them survived. Oriana wrote to the *Herald Link* offering her thanks to God that they all got out alive:

> When I read about how the bereaved families are still suffering and feel how lucky my son and I were, my little pain seems nothing compared to other families'. But we must always pray and ask God for strength for the future. One thing I would like to ask. On the night of the disaster, there was a young man calling for Sue. My son and I always wonder if he found his Sue – he was between the bar lounge and the cafeteria.

In the Christmas 1987 issue of *Herald Link*, Mrs Rita Smith of Bromley wrote about the loss of her two sons, Steve Smith and Chris Moy:

> It is eight months now since that tragic night when our lives were thrown into complete turmoil, never to be the same again. But I thought it might help others to know how I have coped, at first there seemed no point, no future, and certainly no reason to live (I've even contemplated suicide). I lost two sons on that ferry – and I miss them so much, but when I feel at my lowest, instead of looking forward to

all that I have missed, I look back over the years that we had. Steve (the eldest), was my constant companion – we had something very special, Steve and I, right from the day he was born. He was 33 when he died. Chris and I had been separated for several years – owing to my having a breakdown. He was fostered out (we didn't have the help that the youngsters have now and sadly the squeeze was put on us and he was adopted). I tried for years to trace him – and finally four years ago we were reunited. He came to me at his own free will and from that moment we were all as a family, became complete again. Steve and Chris hit it off from the start, that is why they were together on 6 March and sadly they died together.

But I had so much love and completeness in those four years just watching them together, also my two daughters, Wendy and Mandy. Steve and Chris's laughter will be with me forever and I know that this is not the end – we will meet again. Four years was not enough, Chris, I want more! God bless both my boys.

Chris Moy left a wife, Janet, and a 1-year-old son, Chris, from a previous relationship. Steve left a wife, Julie, who was on board with the two brothers.

The mother of Nicola Payne, lost on the *Herald*, wrote about those left behind:

We lost our lovely daughter Nicky on the *Herald*. Her husband [Darren Perkins] also died. They were both only 20 years old and the heartbreak we feel is too painful to describe, but my husband and I have found the strength together to go on as we must for the sake of the two little children they left behind. Timmy was 3½ and Jodie-Ann was 20 months when their parents died, and it is not easy to turn the clock back and start again. Our youngest daughter is now 16 and suddenly new found freedom has disappeared and 6 a.m. rising is now a way of life. I thank God for these little children, our daughter and son-in-law will live on through them but the biggest pain of all is when little voices say 'where's my mummy and daddy gone?'

Soldier's wife Angela Wilson, of Germany, wrote to thank her rescuer:

I have just celebrated my birthday and it is due to a man called Harry that I was here to celebrate. All that I know about Harry is that he lived in Liverpool although he wasn't born there. Harry saved my life that night, he dragged me out of the water and onto a ledge and kept me safe until we were rescued. I would also like to thank whoever carried my son, Steven, whose sixth birthday it was that night, out of the boat at the end of a rope. Steven is frightened of his birthday coming up again in case something else happens to him. And to everyone who spent their first Christmas without a loved one, you were in my thoughts and still are.

In August 1987, survivor Richard Smith, of Hove, East Sussex, received a message on his answer phone. A lady had seen him on television riding in an exhibition cycle race during an athletics meeting at Crystal Palace. As his answer phone only allowed for a thirty-second message, she only had time to say that she had lost her son on the *Herald*. Richard wanted to call her back as she sounded very upset, but the message cut off and she didn't have time to leave her name or number.

The Conway family of Milton Keynes, Buckinghamshire, wrote:

Please send our understanding to all survivors and the offer of any help we can give. We have all suffered in many different ways, but the fact that we went through the ordeal brings us together and we must feel close to one another. We were only a family of three on 6 March 1987 – Chris, Debbie and 2-year-old Matthew. Four weeks after that awful day, Paul was born. At that time several survivors and relatives made contact with us and said that they found comfort in the fact that something good has come out of something so terrible.

Richard McKenny lost his wife, Sheila, in the disaster. 'It has been a long rocky road to tread on, but like people say, time heals a lot of wounds. Maybe that's true but a lot of water has still got to run under the bridge, but there is one thing I have learned and that is to come to terms with oneself and just carry on.'

Richard's stepdaughter, Lynette Carvley, and Lynette's daughter, Becky, struggled with life after the disaster. Becky only just managed to complete her BTEC course in Graphic Design at Hastings College, but cut herself off from her friends and became reclusive. She shut herself in her bedroom, suffering from depression and rarely left the family flat. The Channel Disaster Fund, set up to help the victims, bought her a Tibetan terrier dog. She called him Bilbo. This finally got her out of the flat, taking him for walks. Seven months after the disaster, Becky was diagnosed with PTSD.

Lorry driver John Wickham survived the disaster. His wife Judy, of Guildford, wrote about her husband's experiences:

He had just had a meal and then went to have a drink with his friend to wet his coming baby's head – he was so thrilled at the prospect of becoming a father, but sadly he died that night and never saw the beautiful little girl he had a week later.

We have made new and lasting friends that night, bound together by a tragedy we hope will never happen again.

The parents of waiter Clayton Dyer, wrote to the *Herald Link* appealing for information about the last moments of their son:

Please could anyone give us any information about our son Clayton? He was a crew member working as a steward in the restaurant on B-deck on 6 March. He was only one of two crew to have been brought off dead that night. If anyone remembers anything about Clayton, we would be very grateful. Clayton would have been 19 on 13 March. He was wearing black trousers, blue crew shirt and dickie-bow. We all miss him so much – life will never be the same again.

Mrs Barbara Fisher of Northamptonshire wrote to the *Herald Link* to look for a fellow survivor who helped her after they were both rescued:

> I would like to make contact with a young man I met on the night of the disaster. If I remember, he had been with a group of friends and had been separated from them. They came from in or around the Birmingham area. I met him on the tug that brought us in. I was petrified of being parted from my daughter, who I was sure had perished until she was found to be in the arms of another survivor who was in the tug. This young man and a lorry driver sat on the bridge of the tug with me offering comfort as I babbled on in a panic. The young man offered to carry my daughter for me in the ambulance with us. On arrival, he offered to go to the children's ward with her while I received treatment. That was the last I saw or heard of him. I would very much like to take the chance that he may see this in *Herald Link*, and make contact.

Crew member Max Potterton of Herne Bay, Kent, recalled the night of the disaster:

> I would like to contact the lady who I travelled with in the ambulance. She was on a stretcher and another man also travelled with us. She told me her name three times but I forgot it as soon as I got out of the ambulance. We met again briefly at the church service at Canterbury, and I didn't realise it was her until she disappeared into the crowd. I would also like to say a great big thank you to the lady on the *Sea Horse* who gave me her pink cardigan.

Speaking to the *Daily Mirror* ten years after the disaster, Alan Rogers told how his family had been torn apart. 'We haven't been able to put it behind us. It's torn us apart. We are just five people living in the same house'. All five family members were diagnosed with PTSD. Alan lost his thriving business after being registered disabled from injuring his vertebrae. The three children were all referred to child psychiatrists. All have trouble sleeping, and son William told his father, 'I wish I'd died, daddy.' In the aftermath of the disaster, William's paintings at play group were all completely black.

The family had to return to the Continent on a ferry shortly afterwards to identify their belongings. 'It was horrible. Sue and the kids were crying and I was sick.'

A group of survivors returned to Zeebrugge on the first anniversary. 'It was very frightening passing over the actual spot.' Later, Emma Rogers was with the Sea Cadets, but whenever she saw a ferry they had to cover her head to bring her back to shore.

Assistant Steward Clive Bush, reflecting on the time that had elapsed since the disaster, said:

> Although the passing of years has made dreams and nightmares less frequent, I still experience them from time to time. I think maybe I'm more concerned than I used to be about the welfare of my fellow man. Also the gain of material wealth has no importance to me.
>
> I feel that, certainly for me, 6 March 1987 is lodged somewhere in my brain and will never be totally eradicated. I cannot speak for any other crew member but when that date arrives each year, I have to admit to being somewhat apprehensive and a little depressed and I reflect more than usual on how lucky I am and to remember some wonderful colleagues who are no longer here both from the night and who have died since. Of course, it is important to think of all the passengers who perished but the crew members were my other 'family'.

Tracy Edwards lost her mother, grandmother, sister and baby nephew at Zeebrugge. Her father, George Lamy, was the only survivor from the family outing. In 1991, Tracy's daughter, Sarah, started at the same primary school that Tracy herself had attended. All the other mothers dropping off their children knew her, her family and about the disaster. 'This is when I had to face up to the past, and decided that I should be proud of my family and not hide from what had happened. The family were victims of this disaster by birth and not by choice.' Tracy's younger children, born in 1988 and 1990, knew nothing of what had happened.

George Lamy couldn't bear to stay in London, and spent half of his time in Tenerife and the other half in Lincolnshire. He died in 2002, and was buried with the family as he requested.

After the 7/7 London bombings of 2005, Tracy and her family decided to live permanently in Lincolnshire, where they always felt comfortable. It is where they would come to run away. She said:

> I was in Debenhams last week and a mannequin dressed in 80's clothes set off a reaction that I haven't had in at least fifteen years. I think it is best described as a mild panic attack. The model reminded me of my sister so much. I just grabbed hold of my daughter for help. She is studying to be a social worker and mentioned it to her tutor. The tutor explained that the suppressed memories must have resurfaced recently and I would be fine.

Survivor Richard Davies became a tutor for Cricket without Borders (CWB), after its founding in 2005 in the UK. CWB is a charity dedicated to cricket development and HIV/AIDS awareness in Africa. CWB has three main goals – to spread cricket through coaching to children and teaching adults how to coach; to link the sport to

HIV/AIDS awareness and incorporate these messages into coaching sessions; and to bring together and empower local communities through cricket. CWB is run almost entirely by the dedication and enthusiasm of its volunteers.

Explaining his role within the charity on the CWB website, Richard writes, 'My job … is to make sure all of the volunteers stand in the sun all day having great fun with the kids, whilst I supervise from the shade of the nearest large tree.' His experience and enthusiasm for the sport went back to the age of 7, going on to work as a cricket professional at Worksop, Nottinghamshire and Lancing College, West Sussex for twenty-eight years. 'Each time is different, seeing new towns and kids in each country through the eyes of all the new volunteers. It's been a great journey, watching the charity evolve and flourish with a superb group of volunteers taking on management tasks within the charity.' Looking back on his life-changing experience of surviving the disaster, his motto is, 'Enjoy every minute of life and give something back.'

Lorry driver Brian Gibbons threw himself into his work following the disaster, sometimes working eighteen hours a day. 'It helped me, though I don't think it helped my family.' However, Brian's hard work meant he could provide a standard of life for his family that he had never enjoyed, growing up in poverty in Birmingham.

He was haunted by nightmares for years. He met families who often asked him if he had seen their loved ones; he had to tell them no. 'You have feelings of guilt because you survived and others didn't. You shouldn't, but you do.'

In January 2012, Brian watched the TV coverage of the capsize of the *Costa Concordia*, off Tuscany in Italy, in which thirty-two people died. He wanted to pick up the telephone and tell them not to stop looking, that there would be people on board who would be trapped in air pockets. 'I didn't think something like this could happen again.'

These days, Brian's job as a haulage contractor, and his six children and nine grandchildren keep him busy. 'It's the grandchildren who have helped me most, they're the ones who help overcome the psychological problems. When they smile, everyone else melts away.'

On 3 December 1987, the Christmas special for the popular ITV programme 'Surprise! Surprise!' was filmed at the Saaihalle, Bruges. The Bennett family – Michael, wife Maureen and daughter, Theresa Gander – were reunited with their rescuers, St Jan's Hospital Director Mr Van Oyen and Nursing Director Nadine de Gendt, by presenter Cilla Black. Although bemused by the concept of the programme, and having no idea who Cilla Black was, Nadine was nevertheless happy to meet with the Bennetts again, and spent time with the family on their tour of Bruges, which included Cilla singing on one of the city's tourist canal barges. The programme aired on British television at 8.15 p.m. on Sunday 27 December. As well as the sequences filmed in Bruges, the Bennetts were reunited, in the studio, with Robert O'Neill, who had spent time in the water inside the *Herald* with Theresa and her boyfriend, Mark Webb. While they were waiting for rescue, the three of them had shared a bar of Toblerone to keep their spirits up.

On Monday 8 May 1988, Nadine de Gendt, nursing director of St Jan's who was awarded an MBE, was invited to Margate, Kent. She officially opened the Thanet Hospital Healthcare Exhibition, which displayed photography commissioned by the *Sunday Times*, to best describe the humanity of the NHS in the 1980s. In 1988, the newspaper ran a 'Best of Health' competition, which was open to all 194 UK health authorities.

Rosina Summerfield, her son, boyfriend and housemate had all survived the disaster, but it had ultimately led to the break-up of the family. Although she attended counselling sessions, it didn't help, as she was not open to it at the time. Years later, when Rosina had her second child, the echoing sound of crying in the hospital took her back to that hour trapped in the ferry, listening to the sounds of people dying on the other side of the wall. She couldn't stand it. Rosina believes she coped well in the aftermath of the disaster but she admits that 'my friends and family might have different opinions,' as she still suffers panic attacks. She believes counselling may be beneficial these days.

In an interview with *Truck* magazine in January 1996, Ian Rycroft, who had been the Managing Director of EC Transport (Wimborne) Ltd in Dorset, and whose company had been blamed for carrying cyanide on board the *Herald*, spoke of life for the company after the disaster. In February 1992, Rycroft's friend and co-director of EC Transport at the time of the *Herald* disaster, Colin Phillips, was convicted of conspiracy to break the arms embargo on Iraq, which had been in force in the late 1980s. EC's role in the affair was to ship five containers loaded with equipment and components for making munitions fuses. The consignments were sent from the UK to Jordan, which was covertly being used by Iraq to get around the arms embargo. Ordtec (Ordnance Technology) were also convicted at Reading Crown Court. The case was considered as serious as the 'Supergun Affair' for which Matrix Churchill and the subsequent Scott Inquiry became infamous, for the re-arming of Saddam Hussein prior to the invasion of Kuwait in August 1990. Ordtec and its directors went bankrupt. EC Transport came close to collapse but survived.

In 1995, all of the convictions were overturned, after it was revealed that the defence counsel were deprived of documents that could have been used to argue that the government knew what was going on and had turned a blind eye. After the bad press and wrongful convictions that EC Transport had experienced, it turned its attention to Bosnia in order to survive. Specifically, 500 tonnes of surplus cargo rations from the British Army of the Rhine in Germany was transported to the war-torn country. Rycroft then won another, larger contract, working for the United Nations High Commission for Refugees (UNHCR), to run convoys of desperately needed supplies to mainly Muslims within Bosnia.

EC Transport (Wimborne) Ltd, which had existed since 1974, was dissolved in 2003. After several more years of an eventful and varied life, Rycroft, its controversial Managing Director, died in Spain in 2011.

Steward Henry Graham was transferred to the *Vortigen* with the majority of his surviving colleagues, but quit the ferries shortly afterwards. He moved, with his family, back to Cumbria but found that commuting to Dover was too 'knackering', driving the length of the country all the time. They looked at buying a three bedroom semi-detached house on the south coast but quickly realised it was too expensive. Someone told them about living in France, so they thought they would give it a six-month trial. They moved to a hamlet in northern France in 2000, and have been there ever since.

Although the Graham family make regular visits to see family in the UK, Henry said they wouldn't ever go back to living in the 'rat-race' that the UK had become. Henry admits that he is not fluent in French but knows the basics and anything he gets stuck with, his wife Sue, or his daughters step in.

Henry is disappointed that some passengers sold stories to the newspapers of drinking amongst the crew and says that the experience has allowed him to 'take with a pinch of salt' the stories of Captain Francesco Schettino's alleged activities on the night that his ship, the *Costa Concordia*, crashed into rocks off the Italian island of Giglio in January 2012, with the loss of thirty-two lives.

David Gudgeon had lost his wife, Eileen, in the disaster while Irene Blanchard had lost her husband, Norman, as well as her daughter and granddaughter. David and Irene met at a support group organised by the *Herald* Families Association – they married in August 1989, and now live in Norfolk.

On the tenth anniversary of the disaster, Miles Southgate returned to Zeebrugge aboard a freight ferry which stopped at the scene of the disaster. He dropped a couple of wreaths over the side in memory of the friend he lost on the *Herald*, Martin Spooner.

Speaking to the *Northants Evening Telegraph* on the twentieth anniversary of the disaster, Paul Fisher relived the experiences of that night aboard the *Herald*, and what had happened to his family, all of whom had survived. They had returned to their home in Kettering amid a 'media frenzy', and had tried to get back to normal. Paul and Barbara eventually separated and subsequently divorced. 'It's not something I want to dwell on. I just want to get on with my life.'

Compensation

Several weeks after the disaster, EC Transport (Wimborne) Ltd of Shaftesbury, Dorset, received a letter from Townsend Thoresen's lawyers in Belgium, threatening a writ and asking representatives from the haulage company to attend a hearing at a commercial court in Belgium. The ferry company had accused EC Transport of transporting chemicals banned under international maritime law from being carried on passenger ferries.

EC Transport managing director, Ian Rycroft, said that he had warned Townsend Thoresen in a telex that his lorry contained hazardous goods. 'I was very surprised that the shipping company put our lorry on the *Herald of Free Enterprise*. I expected it to travel on a freight-only ferry later the same evening.' He went on to say that the shipper, a government organisation in Western Europe (later revealed as West Germany), had supplied comprehensive documentation. EC Transport was insured to carry dangerous loads at sea and on the road but could not always be sure what the load contained. 'We are not chemists: we have to rely on the sender.'

On 15 April, *The Times* featured the chemical story, under the headline 'Disaster Ferry Carried Banned Chemical Cargo'. The report said, 'Some of EC Transport's lucrative business is carrying explosives for the Ministry of Defence. All its staff, including Mr Broomfield (Roger Broomfield, *Herald* survivor), have been vetted by security forces.' The report went on to claim that suspect chemicals, including cyanide, were aboard the lorry that was driven aboard the *Herald*. The firm regularly carried explosives and radioactive and other hazardous materials. Rycroft and his firm had been fined £1,600 at Bournemouth Crown Court, in July 1986, for passing off hazardous explosives as being less dangerous than they really were, and for exposing people to unnecessary risks.

The Times report followed reports that alleged illegal cargo was discovered washed up on beaches in Belgium and the Netherlands. Five hauliers, including EC Transport, were identified as carrying loads only allowed on freight ferries. Several drums of illegal chemicals exploded, injuring five Belgian salvage workers, all of whom were treated in hospital.

In September 1987, Ian Rycroft accused Townsend Thoresen of holding up legal proceedings in Belgium and threatened to sue. EC Transport's legal representation in Belgium confirmed that no writs had been issued by the ferry company. Rycroft claimed that press reports shortly after the disaster, which accused his company of transporting illegal chemicals, had attracted adverse publicity to his company and he accused Townsend Thoresen of 'building a corral around itself to protect it from its own legal problems. If nothing happens within this month, there is a good chance we could sue Townsend Thoresen for slander.' In November, Rycroft was told to collect his cargo, which was being held in Belgium, and told to dispose of it in England.

Larry O'Brien lost his Ford Transcontinental cab in the disaster, which was not insured for marine loss. His truck was officially covered by the Athens Convention, and by the Hague-Visby rules (a set of rules for the international carriage of goods by sea, passed in 1964), which pay out £2,900 for the loss of such a vehicle. P&O eventually offered £5,900, due to the circumstances of the disaster, but his truck was worth £15,000 and the loss of personal belongings in the cab, amounting to £2,500 and his loss of earnings wasn't taken into account. P&O said they would pay the £5,900 and release the truck free of charge and pay the ferry to Dover.

'Townsend Thoresen was proved negligent in the inquiry, so I think they should pay more. If it were an Act of God, it would be different. I'd accept it – but it wasn't.' The trailer that Larry was transporting belonged to Transcontinental of Rosslare. They pursued a separate claim for compensation.

After the disaster, Larry worked for Transcontinental as a staff driver, having lost his cab and therefore his job as an independent. Over a year after the disaster, Larry said, 'I sometimes used to worry about things but I don't anymore, after living through that.'

Lynette Lee (formerly Carvley), had lost her mother in the disaster. 'The ferry company were a waste of space. I went to the tribunal as a test case for compensation. I was awarded some, which was up to the time of the tribunal. This included payment to give the Inland Revenue for the sick absence up to the tribunal, which I paid to them.' Lynette and her daughter, Becky, put their compensation money together and invested it in a new house in Hastings. 'It really helped moving house. There were too many memories at the flat', Becky said.

George Lamy had lost his wife, mother, daughter and baby grandson. The compensation he received personally was enough to buy some land. He decided to build a house and ended up building two in the end, one for himself and one for his other daughter, Tracy and her family, so they could be close. As he had lost his car in the disaster, he bought a new one. Tracy said 'He had to buy a new car, he really loved the car he lost in the ferry, a Rover SD1 2.8i. He had customised it and it looked really lovely.' At the hearing, the decision on how much compensation was to be paid for each victim was revealed. 'How much is life worth? Well, according to maritime law, £2,000.'

The names and occupations were read out:

This is how they decided. One long list of names, occupations and ages, so cold and calculated with no feeling or composure, like an auctioneer:

Victoria Lamy (75), pensioner. £2,000.
Kim Lamy (20), mother, not working. £2,000.
Stevie Lamy, 11-month-old baby. £2,000.
Frances Lamy (42), worker. £15,000.

Mum had to be valued by our solicitor, by her status and job. My dad's car was worth more than the others put together, by the time they paid for the contents. It seemed to get really petty. Amounts were awarded for the loss of Christmas presents and housework. They awarded my daughter £2,000 for the loss of Christmas presents, but she has never received any lump sum. We were never sure what happened to it. I was never interested in this side of things, so I don't really know.

The first lorry to be recovered was an Iveco Turbotech, owned by W.A. Stallard of Upton-on-Severn, Worcestershire. It should have been on a previous sailing, but had been delayed because it was carrying hazardous cargo and ended up being the last vehicle to be loaded, on the outside of the top vehicle deck. When the *Herald* capsized, the truck fell out of the open bow doors, still attached to its trailer. During the salvage operation, the vehicle had to be removed to gain access to the vehicle deck. Salvage workers had to cut off the trailer to remove the truck's cab. Photographs of the lorry being craned out of the sea dominated the front pages of most of the national newspapers.

Roy Stallard, owner of the truck, was given free passage to Zeebrugge to retrieve what was left of his vehicle. He took a tractor unit and low loader across and found his truck simply dumped on the quayside. Eventually the truck was rebuilt by Stallard. His son, Mark, drove the truck back to the Continent later. The original driver of the truck, Mike Jenkins, survived the disaster but gave up driving. 'The trauma was just too much for him', said his ex-boss, Roy Stallard.

In June 1987, Belgian company, Langlois, in Ghent, announced that they would be handling the sale of an estimated 100 tonnes of damaged passenger cars that had been salvaged from the wreck of the *Herald*. Known as 'Lot 1', the cars were described as 'so damaged that they are unsalvageable'. Most of the cars were expected to be sold for scrap. A month later, Langlois announced that the damaged lorries from the salvaged ferry would be available for inspection, before being offered for sale by sealed tender at the end of July. Known as 'Lot 2', these vehicles were described as being in a better condition than the passenger cars offered for sale earlier.

Philippa and Graham Edmonds, of Edmonds Transport, Norfolk, were asked to go to Zeebrugge to identify their lorry, which was the second vehicle to be recovered from the ferry. At first, Townsend Thoresen demanded the £170 fare but, after the couple refused to pay, the ferry company issued free tickets.

In July 1987, Edmonds Transport was still experiencing difficulties in receiving financial settlements for their lorry, a Ford Transcontinental, lost in the disaster. The insurer paid out £27,000, but refused to take into consideration salvage costs, a £25,000 reefer unit carrying £25,000 worth of resins, and a recent engine rebuild. The Channel Disaster Fund also couldn't help, as a credit ratings check on the Edmonds showed they were still creditworthy. The company also lost £1,000 per week during the six weeks it took for them to replace their truck.

By October 1987, the insurance firm Commercial Union had paid out to four hauliers the full cost of their lost vehicles. Other insurance companies had done the same. Commercial Union, annoyed that Townsend Thoresen had claimed that it is only obliged to pay scrap value of each vehicle by law, urged hauliers and other insurers to team up and use one solicitor to pursue full reimbursement from the ferry company. By using one solicitor, costs would be shared. One of Commercial Union's clients who was compensated in full for the loss of his vehicle was Ian Rycroft of EC Transport.

The following letter was published in the *Guardian* on 15 August 1987, sent by Mrs Ann Biggins and Mr John Waters, who lost their parents, Alan and Molly Waters, on the *Herald*:

On the matter of compensation, we think that £10,000 or whatever is left after the application of inheritance tax, a paltry amount (even if it is above the legal minimum) to set against the slaughter of our parents and horrors of these last months and the ever continuing ache of loss.

Of course, such things cannot be quantified in terms of cash but a warped justice applies where a man can have his life snuffed out for £10,000 while another is awarded £500,000 for damage to his reputation.

We believe Townsend Thoresen's expenses will be met from their insurance. While such companies can operate with such laxness and incompetence as to not only endanger but take life and do so with virtual impunity, what price British justice?

The Rogers family of Cheltenham were awarded £26,000 in interim compensation payments from P&O. 'I want a lot more', Alan said, 'I feel very bitter about what it's done to my family. It's ruined our family.'

Ann English left a 4-year-old son, David, who was brought up by his mother's partner, whom he called dad. David English was awarded compensation of £55,000, to be put into a trust fund until he reached the age of 18. By the time David had become of age, the interest earned on the original compensation had boosted the fund to £126,000. Not having any guidance or counselling as to how to invest the money wisely, David bought a house and quit his job. Turning to drink and drugs, he lost everything over the next seven months. He went from homeowner to bedsit. 'The money goes to your head. It was blood money. I'd rather have had one of the company directors take me out to lunch and given me an apology for everything that had happened.'

Survivor Jan Willis said:

The ferry company ignored me like I was an embarrassment, it was disgusting. Compensation was minimal. I was intimidated by the lawyers … who said because I had joined the police and had done well for myself, I would lose in court. I know different now but I was only 19.

Brian Bunker was offered £5,000 by the London firm of solicitors representing P&O – that was essentially £2,500 for the loss of his wife, Diane (29), and £2,500 for the life of their 9-month-old daughter, Nadine. Not surprisingly, Brian rejected it, until most of the survivors and the families of the victims were left with no choice. With the compensation he decided to set up a fund as part of the Gurkha Welfare Trust to help the special needs children of Gurkha soldiers.

No money could compensate for the magnitude of his loss, but Brian felt that to be offered such a paltry sum showed exactly how the company regarded the relatives that had been bereaved. He referred to the case of Jeffrey Archer, former deputy chairman of the Conservative Party under Margaret Thatcher. In July 1987, when compensation claims were being settled for the Zeebrugge disaster victims, Archer won damages of £500,000 against the *Daily Star* newspaper for libel. The newspaper had accused him of paying a prostitute for sex. Brian had been offered just 1 per cent of what Archer had been awarded for an alleged lie in a newspaper, for the loss of his wife and daughter.

Honours

In an unprecedented gesture to foreign nationals in peacetime, eleven Belgians were honoured by the Queen at a special investiture ceremony at Buckingham Palace on 8 March 1988. They were among twenty-seven people who were awarded medals for their part in their efforts, during and after the Zeebrugge disaster. Belgian ambassador Jean-Paul van Bellingham said, 'the whole of Belgium is delighted by the invitation to Buckingham Palace. We Belgians are usually subdued but today, as a nation, we shall live intensely through the pleasure and pride of being honoured by your Queen.'

Right: A medal struck by P&O and given to surviving members of the crew.

Below: St Jan's Director of Nursing, Nadine de Gendt-Bruylandt, who received an MBE in 1988.

This commemorative medal was struck by
P & O
in appreciation of
the unique assistance rendered at Zeebrugge
on the night of March 6th 1987

The Peninsular and Oriental Steam Navigation Company

The Belgians

KBE (Knight Commander of the Order of the British Empire) (Honorary)

Olivier Vanneste, Governor of West Flanders, took charge of operations on behalf of the Belgian Government. He recalled a human chain of people from Zeebrugge, to move more than 300 survivors from the harbour wall to hospital. 'I am thankful to her Majesty that I received this award but I receive it for the whole group of people involved. I was in overall command but there were so many who were courageous.'

OBE (Order of the British Empire)

Captain Marc Claus, nautical director (pilotage) of Zeebrugge port authority. Claus co-ordinated the rescue operation at sea. 'What comes back to me now, asleep and awake, is the sound of the radio messages and the telephone ringing in the control tower. I am still haunted by what I could have done and what I might have done. My reward has come as a great surprise but it is an award for everyone that worked that night.'

MBE (Member of the British Empire)

Director of Nursing, Sister Agnes von Loo, St Lucas, Bruges (twelve survivors). She had never been forthcoming about her part in the rescue. 'It is a great honour for me but I see this not for myself, it is an accolade for all of my nurses who worked so hard that night with such devotion.'

Dr Daniel den Dooven, Queen Fabiola Hospital, Blankenberge, accompanied by his wife Aime (33) and daughter Amelie (5). He had been on call at home and recalled that his 150-bed hospital had to prepare to receive sixty-five survivors. 'I am deeply grateful for this honour but I was most grateful for the time we had to organise the reception of survivors. My job on the night was that of a doctor, and was nothing compared to the fear and the trauma suffered in the disaster by the passengers. I shall never forget what I saw in human suffering.'

Harbour Master Rene van Havere, chief harbour master, Zeebrugge. Although pleased and proud to be given the award, he said, 'I would rather not be pleased, in fact, I would rather the tragedy had never happened. I see it as an honour bestowed upon the harbour service, and the port authority as a whole, not me.'

Dr Geert Fransen. St Jan's cardiologist and head surgeon saved the life of 14-year-old Nicola Simpson. Speaking of his award he said, 'I am surprised to have been chosen among the many people who worked at the hospital that night. I was simply doing my job as a surgeon. My reward was seeing Nicola regain consciousness.'

Mrs Nadine de Gendt-Bruylandt, director of nursing at St Jan's Hospital.

Queen's Gallantry Medal
Lt Commander Guido Couwenbergh, Belgian Navy Diver, who saved forty people single-handed.

Lt Commander Alfons Daems, Belgian Navy Diver.

Piet Lagast, Tijdelikje Vereniging Bergingswerken, civilian diver.

Dirk van Mullen, Tijdelikje Vereniging Bergingswerken, civilian diver

All eleven Belgians attended a flower-laying ceremony at a memorial service on an embankment erected by the Belgian Government to thank Great Britain for taking in 360,000 Belgian refugees between 1914 and 1918.

Secretary of State for Transport's Award of Plate (awarded by Paul Channon)
Captain Henri Vermeersch, *Burgemeester Vandamme* (Belgian tug).

Captain Andre Pape, of the *Sea Horse* (Belgian tug). Captain Pape was awarded a commemorative plate from Britain's Transport Secretary, presented at the British Embassy in Brussels. 'I do not know what this means,' he said, 'but I am very happy with the honour. I think so much about that night. The good thing is that we did manage to rescue so many. The bad is that so many others died.'

The British

George Medal (for acts of great bravery)
Andrew Parker, *Herald* passenger, a bank official from Herne Hill, south London. His family, and eighteen others used his body as a bridge to escape. Speaking of his medal, 'I hold it not just for the other people who were brave but for the 193 who died a year ago last Sunday.'

Michael Skippen, *Herald* head waiter. Posthumously awarded to widow, Lynda (24), at a private investiture in the Palace's Blue Drawing Room, before the main ceremony. 'I shall never forget why I'm here, alone in this place. I have lost an awful lot, for Michael can never be replaced.'

OBE (Order of the British Empire)
Commander John (Jack) Birkett, Royal Navy, Mine-warfare and Clearing Diving Officer (MCDO). Superintendent of Diving during the operation to rescue passengers and recover bodies from ferry.

MBE (Member of the British Empire)

Chief Officer Malcolm Shakesby, *Duke of Anglia*, on scene commander of operations.

Miss Barbara Taylor, British Red Cross co-ordinator, for support and comfort for relatives in Zeebrugge.

Mrs Christine Spetch. A social worker with the Soldiers, Sailors and Airmen Families Association, she was flown to Zeebrugge on 6 March 1987 from Rheindden Base, Germany. Mrs Spetch also worked for Bradford Social Services during the fire disaster in 1985. She spent five weeks in Zeebrugge, completing a list of the missing, and tracking down survivors. 'It was a particularly harrowing and distressing time for those who had lost members of their families. Most survivors were in a state of shock. Some just wanted a friendly listener. Others became intensely frustrated and angry at not being able to trace their relatives.'

Dr Bill Moses

Queen's Gallantry Medal

Stephen Homewood, *Herald* Assistant Purser. 'This honour is for the people who cannot be here today and I regard this award as being for those who died, too – who knows what the people who perished did?'

Leigh Cornelius, *Herald* deckhand.

William Walker, *Herald* deckhand.

Thomas Wilson, *Herald* quartermaster.

Able Seaman Eamon Fullen, Royal Navy. He worked in the water for five hours without a lifeline, trying to free lorry drivers trapped in an air pocket.

Lt Simon Bound, Royal Navy, diver.

Queen's Commendation for Brave Conduct

Chief Petty Officer Edward Kerr, Royal Navy.

Chief Petty Officer Peter Still, Royal Navy.

Michael Fellows, Royal Navy, clearance diver.

Secretary of State for Transport's Award of Plate (awarded by Paul Channon)
Captain Billy Budd, in charge of coaster *River Tamar* from Whitby Shipping, Sheerness. About to sail from Zeebrugge when the *Herald* capsized, he went alongside and put his three crew aboard *Herald* to lead the rescue.

The award, which takes the form of an inscribed nautical instrument, such as a barometer, clock or binoculars, is rarely handed out. It has been presented since 1854 for saving lives at sea.

Other Honours
Lorry driver Alan Hawkes (54) from Peterlee, County Durham, was presented with the Transport and General Worker's Gold medal, known as the 'workers' Victoria Cross'. He had been aboard with his stepson, Stephen Scott (15). Alan was credited with saving three girls from the freezing water.

At the British Academy of Film and Television Awards (BAFTA) in 1988, the winner of the 'Television/News or Outside Broadcast Coverage' was the 'Special Edition of Channel 4 News: Coverage of the Zeebrugge Disaster'. The BAFTA award was presented to the Channel 4 News editor, Stewart Purvis, who had persuaded his bosses to air a special thirty-minute programme focusing on the disaster and its immediate aftermath. The special programme was up against the BBC and ITN's News at Ten in the same category.

P&O struck a medal for the surviving members of the *Herald* crew. Some of them were simply posted through their recipient's letterboxes, with no ceremony at all.

Lessons Learned

On the night of the disaster, Kent's County Emergency Planning Officer (CEPO), Eric Willcock, said that his team's role was mainly accomplished well in advance of the disaster. In the 'Summer 1987' edition of the *Civil Protection* magazine, he said:

> It's our job to help all the various organisations that may be involved in a ferry disaster to draw up detailed plans. As Kent CEPO, I have an overview of these emergency plans and make sure, as far as possible, that everyone is talking in the same terms and that the plans all dovetail.

The callout system operated on a cascade or pyramid system, much like the plan in Belgium, although the one main difference being that the Kent CEPO believed it was essential that *some* information is relayed onto each contact. In Belgium, no one was allowed to ask anything about the emergency situation in order to save time. 'How else are they to know the type of emergency, and whether it is major or minor?'

On 25 and 26 May 1989, a workshop – 'The Zeebrugge Disaster: Two Years On, Lessons for the Prevention of Psychological Trauma' – took place at the Military Hospital in Brussels. The workshop focused on Post Traumatic Stress Disorder (PTSD) which had only been formally recognised as a psychological disorder in 1980. Throughout the 1980s, progress was made in diagnosis, prevention and therapy.

The Heysel Stadium Disaster in 1985, and the Zeebrugge Disaster in 1987 had highlighted the shortcomings of psychological help for victims, families and helpers and problems with the organisation and delivery of these services.

The aim of the workshop was to seek possible solutions to problems in the development of treatments for PTSD and how to organise PTSD teams. It was headed by Peter Hodgkinson, clinical psychologist, of Gravesend's Centre for Crisis Psychology, and Luc Quintyn, clinical psychologist of the military hospital's Department of Clinical Psychology. Many people who had been involved in the disaster and its aftermath were invited to participate. Speakers included Hodgkinson and Quintyn, Dany de Beukelaer of the Red Cross, Captain Joan De Winne of the Disaster Victim Identification (DVI) Team, Bert Pijnenburg, Ignaas Lindemans MD, Medical Colonel de Backer (disaster planning) and Dr C. Hendrix (PTSD in Industry).

In the aftermath of the disaster, the nursing director of St Jan's Hospital in Bruges, Nadine de Gendt-Bruylandt, made an assessment of the hospital's capabilities, and offered a list of recommendations from the 'lessons learned'. The characteristics of the disaster were listed:

Accident at sea
Darkness
Great number of persons involved
Large number of survivors
Low number of seriously injured
Time of the disaster: favourable as to render assistance
Large number of hospital beds in the region
Presence of medical emergency teams in the region
Other regions: helped by additional emergency teams
Presence of casual relief workers
Language
International interest
Spread of the survivors
Spread of the injured
Mostly short stay at hospital
Injured arrived at the hospital over a long period of time
Late admittance: Saturday and Sunday

Late arrival of family members
Long period of disaster sphere
All deceased concentrated at one hospital
Remaining missing persons, objects

The first phase was classified as 6, 7 and 8 March. During this phase, the communications with the following were evaluated – families, crisis centre, police, embassies, hospitals, hotels, the press and television. The needs of the patients were also assessed.

The second phase, classified as 9–25 March, was called the aftermath. During this phase, the care of the non-identified deceased was a priority, and included the installation of facilities for a mortuary, autopsies, embalming and layout. The identification team was also installed at the hospital. Support was offered for families and relatives.

The third phase was the period between 26 March and 18 May. Information on the righting of the ferry, and the organisation of the second mortuary dominated this time.

From 19 May, the hospitals that had collaborated to assist the victims of the disaster evaluated their effectiveness, along with the police. Disaster plans had to be adjusted. Contacts had to be established and maintained with rescuers, survivors and families. Documentation, reports and lectures had to be prepared.

After assessing in full the experiences of all concerned, the following lessons for the future were identified:

To believe only official information centres.
Stay calm in order to gain confidence and to increase efficiency.
Be prepared to receive the media before they disorganise your organisation.
Pay attention to non-wounded victims.
Co-ordinate the activities of volunteers.
Pay extra attention to people who may have responsibilities in the accident.
Organise a continuity of responsible staff authorised to take decisions.
Try to involve persons who were not involved in the first hours with responsibilities in a later phase.
Pay attention to the rescuers – debriefings.
Evaluate your own feelings, emotions and the way you and others have been functioning.

On 22 June 1993, Nadine de Gendt-Bruylandt MBE, presented a further workshop on disaster planning in Belgium. Called '*Herald of Free Enterprise* – Lessons Learned', and as before, the disaster was split into four phases:

Phase 1 – 6, 7 and 8 March 1987, the day of the disaster and following weekend. Communications with families, crisis centres, police, embassies, hospitals, hotels, media, victims' needs.

Phase 2 – 9–23 March 1987. The care of the non-identified deceased, autopsy, embalming, layout, installation of the identification team at the hospital and support of families and relatives.

Phase 3 – 26 March to 18 May. Debriefings, contact with rescuers, helpers and the organisation of mass mortuary.

Phase 4 – 19 May until the time of the workshop. Evaluation with other hospitals, adjustments of disaster plans, documentation, lectures, contact with rescuers, survivors and families.

Several key lessons for the future were identified:

Only believe official information centres
Pay attention to non-wounded victims
Co-ordinate the activities of volunteers
Pay extra attention to people who may have responsibilities in the accident
Organise a continuity of responsible staff authorised to take decisions
Involve persons who were not involved in the first hours with responsibilities in a later phase
Pay attention to the rescuers: debriefings
Evaluate your own feelings, emotions and the way you and others have been functioning

In response to press criticism of Kent police's handling of information, Chief Constable Frank Jordan conceded that it was impossible to fulfil public demand for information in such chaotic circumstances, particularly as in some cases there was no information available. The casualty bureau was set up along tried and tested lines using experiences staff.

The policy of giving information only to immediate relatives was proven correct by experience. Sadly, and extraordinarily, the system was further burdened by bogus and obscene calls and even journalists testing response times! Instances of fraud required officers to be constantly on alert. The Belgian authorities who shouldered onerous responsibility for identification in Zeebrugge were faced with a massively difficult task and delays were understandable.

The Chief Constable said there would be a review of procedures to learn from the disaster.

In 1993, V.G. Vandermoere presented an evaluation of the aftermath of the *Herald of Free Enterprise* tragedy and Belgium's preparations for potential further disaster:

The follow-up period of the disaster in Belgium was identified as the time between 7 March and 13 May, the day the *Herald of Free Enterprise* left Zeebrugge forever. On 7 March, the day after the disaster, arrangements had been made for a funeral parlour and a steady supply of coffins. Vehicles were begun to be salvaged from the sea around the ferry, as well as the recovery of barrels that had broken loose from the trucks which had been carried aboard. Primarily to allow access for the rescue workers and to minimise the dangers of shifting vehicles, there were also environmental aspects to consider. Family members of survivors and those still missing also began to arrive in Zeebrugge. More British families continued to arrive on 8 March. A reception centre was set up for them. The next day, 9 March, the deceased were begun to be identified. At the same time, salvage efforts began to raise the *Herald*. More than 120 victims still lay within the hull of the ferry. On 24 April, the righted ferry was attempted to be towed into the harbour but it failed because of poor weather. On 13 May, the ferry finally left Zeebrugge. This follow-up period was classified as forty days.

Four key aspects of the forty day follow-up period were identified – the reception of relatives; identification of the victims, and the performance of all the formalities required for repatriation to the country of origin; care for environmental problems, public health, precautionary measures for aid workers; and getting the *Herald* afloat and into port.

The reception of relatives – hotel reservations had to be made, and transport to hospitals and reception centres arranged, and additional phone lines were installed. There was a permanent effort to secure the victims' and families' privacy against onlookers and, even more so, the media. This included the formal announcement and enforcement of a restricted area 500m around and above the wreck. Emotional and practical help was given to the relatives who had come to Belgium to view the bodies of their loved ones. This task was carried out by the Red Cross, many of them volunteer teenagers with special social skills and fluent in other languages, mostly English. A gendarmerie officer was also available. A medical team was also on standby should the relatives need any medical assistance. Special private rooms were reserved for those who wanted to talk.

Identification and repatriation of the dead – the identification of the victims was carried out by the Disaster and Victim Identification (DVI) team, under the authority of the examining magistrate and according to the Interpol manual. There was an organised inventory of all objects and [parts of] bodies found at the scene.

These were then taken to an identification centre where everything was treated and described on the basis of Interpol standard forms and procedures, and catalogued onto computers. In the meantime, ante-mortem data was collected from relatives and friends, and entered onto the computers. Then, comparing both sets of data, a conclusion was drawn as to the identity of the victim, with supporting evidence from police, dentists and medical experts. A group of British undertakers was on hand to ensure compliance with the particular customs and traditions. A fast supply of a large number of coffins, meeting international standards, was also needed.

Authorities anticipated that bodies would not only be recovered from the wreck but also in the sea around the wreck, as well as washed ashore in Belgium, Holland and France. Once jewellery and other personal effects and clothes had been cleaned, they would have to be bagged and labelled with the identity of the victim. The necessary cold storage would have to be reserved before the bodies' actual repatriation back to the UK.

Care for the environment, public health and precautionary measures for aid workers – there were a large number of barrels, which had spilled from the lorries aboard. (Though much commented on in the media, about the detrimental effects of pollution from barrels which had released their contents, some barrels were attributed to actually saving a number of lives.) All public services were made ready, including daily measurements by a special ship with a laboratory to analyse readings. This ship belonged to the Ministry of Public Health. Other boats and navy helicopters were also utilised to monitor the ongoing situation. The rescue workers were issued with special instructions regarding clothing, the use of masks and precautions about entering into the wreck.

Getting the wreck afloat and into port –the whole operation proved to be a technical *tour de force*. The recovery of the remaining victims was under scrutiny of the world's press. Although only doing their job, they sometimes got in the way of recovery workers and were at times intrusive to the victims' families.

The first helicopter was flying over the wreck 25 minutes after the disaster occurred. Despite criticism from some quarters about the noise of the helicopters causing communication problems for the rescue workers, it was concluded that the noise gave hope to passengers still trapped in the wreck of the *Herald*, still clinging onto anything they could to save themselves going under the icy water in complete darkness. They had been discovered and help was on its way.

The Emergency Committee meets when the difference between life and death is settled. In the case of the *Herald* disaster, this was after 2200hrs. Governor Vanneste co-ordinated the meetings, assisted by members of the Emergency Committee – the nautical director of the pilot service, chief of police, gendarmerie officer, senior firemen and the head of civil defence. There were also permanent contacts between the Chief of Police and the people in charge at sea, in the port and in the hinterland.

The efforts of all the participants in the rescue could not have been bettered and their discipline was described as 'outstanding'. It was feared, however, that the official services and other organisations may have tried to compete and tried to show their work to their best advantage.

Between one and two hours after the disaster, 'all' telephone lines were blocked, due to the amount of calls being made in Belgium and the amount of cross-Channel telephone traffic, from the worried relatives and the British press. However, the secret 'WINTEX' line, which had been used for the NATO exercise nearby, remained available. Communications were mainly through portable radio sets, connected with their headquarters, 100 and 101.

The press were sometimes described as being 'arrogant'. Indeed, there were many complaints about bad behaviour portrayed by the press. Survivor Rosina Summerfield was tricked into giving an interview to a BBC reporter as she made attempts to call her mother to let her know she was safe. Her words were broadcast on a late night BBC news bulletin on the same night of the disaster, when all she wanted to do was let her mother know she was safe. The press also tried to trick their way into the Novotel, where uninjured survivors had been taken. More often than not, they were thrown out.

After the disaster, it was concluded that the press should not have direct access to the crisis centre. It proved necessary to appoint a contact through which all news could be channelled. In the case of the *Herald*, this was, unfortunately, realised too late. It was an error to establish a press centre in the same building as the crisis committee. The staffing level of the press centre was high – maintaining communications, computers, and telephones as well as the drafting and translating of press releases.

Later, it was decided that all future registration of the victims, including survivors, was to be carried out by the gendarmerie. During the disaster, difficulties were experienced in registering names. Casualty figures were inaccurate – one of the reasons was that many people were in a state of shock. Some people were counted twice, others not at all. Survivor George Lamy, searching for his missing family, said that lists of survivors and missing were inaccurate, since the list of survivors did not even include himself.

An additional North Sea Disaster Plan would be needed to co-ordinate an overall command. There had been a problem of overall command in territorial waters and the open sea. A further crisis centre needed to be established for Northern West Flanders on the North Sea, due to its proximity to one of the world's busiest waterways. The crisis centre was to have equipment ready for use, including 'secret' telephone lines so that the crisis committee could start working immediately.

The Zeebrugge Disaster Plan – originally drawn up for the harbour and implemented during the *Herald of Free Enterprise* disaster – was subsequently adjusted, drawing on conclusions made from the disaster. On 11 March 1988, a new plan was approved by the Council of Ministers in Belgium, arising from a necessity to plan and co-ordinate relief operations because of the number of departments involved.

The plan is designed to give a solution to incidents involving the loss of vessels and their cargo, passengers and crew, shipping traffic, access to the harbour if blocked and any environmental problems that may occur. The plan extended to Belgian territorial waters, the continental shelf, the areas as determined in the Bonn Agreement regarding sea water pollution, and an area within a 75 nautical mile radius from Ostend, for aid and assistance at sea.

The North Sea Disaster Plan, based in Ostend, works because it is permanently operational, both in its readiness to deal with the disaster at sea and the care of the victims involved on land. Although expenses are usually met by each department involved, they may be recovered from those who have caused the accident or disaster.

A General Provincial Disaster Plan was drafted in the province of West Flanders, where a plan for a specific type of disaster is not in place. Where there is a disaster with more than ten victims, the disaster is handled at provincial level; where the number of victims is below ten, the community is the first authority to act.

The most important aspect of the plan is to deliver fast and efficient aid. To achieve the best results for this, the province of West Flanders was divided into eight areas, with each area having a Medical Emergency Group (MEG), which would be ready day and night. Additional quick response assistance is also provided by the 100 Centre in Bruges and Kortrijk. Within each MEG zone, the interaction type is determined by the number of victims – Type 1 is 10–30 victims, Type 2 is 30–100 victims, and Type 3 deals with more than 100 victims.

An MEG consists of a vehicle, with resuscitation equipment aboard for adults and children; a physician with specific experience in resuscitation and urgent medical aid techniques; and a second physician with the same experience, or a nurse experienced in urgent medical aid. The purpose of these MEG units is to rush to the scene of a disaster involving multiple victims, in order to establish a triage, making fast diagnoses and deciding where the victims should be taken for appropriate treatment.

In conclusion, V.G. Vandermoere writes:

… There are, however, no universal remedies giving absolute certainty. The whole process of coping with disaster rests on a number of persons in charge and relief workers who have the will, the courage, solidarity, creativity and perseverance to develop the necessary assistance and bring it to a successful conclusion. The latter consideration can hardly be provided for in a law or a disaster plan, but it is to the credit of society.

Memorials

A new memorial window was unveiled to *Herald* victims, Margaret Wieliczko (22) and her fiancé Peter Swietochowski (33), in the St Boniface Chapel at Benedictine

Abbey Church (Ealing Abbey), Ealing, west London. Designed by Mrs Isabella Blauth Muszkouska, the abbot blessed the window at a special service on 17 October 1987.

In the winter of 1987, P&O purchased a site off the A2 at Whitfield, near Dover. A small memorial wood was planted in the memory of the victims. Called 'The *Herald* Wood', part of the annual memorial service is held here every year.

The Rose Garden near the Zeebrugge seafront is a permanent memorial to the victims of the disaster. Located a short walk from the marine base where many of the survivors were brought ashore in a flotilla of boats, and opposite St Danaas Church, the garden is the focal point of commemorative services held every year, and is visited by relatives who come to Zeebrugge to remember their loved ones.

In the spring of 1988, a *Herald* memorial window was dedicated at St Mary the Virgin Church in Biggin Street, Dover. Unfortunately, when someone pointed out that the stained glass window depicted not the *Herald of Free Enterprise*, but instead the new ferry *Pride of Dover* (which hadn't even gone into service at the time of the disaster), the window had to be hastily remade.

Ruth Buckley wrote to the *Herald Link* on behalf of her husband, whose father, Paddy, mother Carole and little sister, Nicki, all died on the ferry, along with their 17-year-old neighbour, Stuart. She referred to a report in the *Dover Extra* about a memorial suggested by Mr Ottley of Folkestone:

> We think such a memorial is a wonderful idea but surely, oh surely, if such an amount of £100,000 could be raised would it not be better spent helping a hospital or similar. People, adults and children alike, die because of lack of facilities or beds. Great Ormond Street is crying out for funds. Surely such a sum could be put to a memorial ward or something in a hospital ... So if we can use money to help save lives is that not something for us to be proud of? Cannot those who lost so much take comfort from knowing that their loved ones, through their deaths, are giving life to others?

On Sunday 9 March 1997, at St Mary's, Dover, a memorial service was held as 'an act of remembrance to commemorate those lost at sea in the *Herald of Free Enterprise*' ten years before. The service was conducted by the Rev. Graham Batten of the Royal Navy and the vicar of St Mary's. The minister told the congregation:

> We have come together, families and friends, survivors and crew, representatives of all our communities, to remember before God all those who lost their lives during the disaster of the 6 March 1987. We pray for those who continue to mourn and ask our heavenly Father to wipe away every fear and bring healing to our souls. In our sadness, we also remember happier moments and give thanks for the help and assistance we have received over many years from so many people and from so many organisations.

It was followed by a reading from Maurice de Rohan, chairman of the *Herald* Families Association.

On the twenty-fifth anniversary of the Zeebrugge disaster, a memorial service was held at St Mary's as it has been every year since the ferry capsized. Silver stars were handed out to families and friends amongst the congregation, who then recorded their feelings. The messages were then transcribed into the book of remembrance that was kept in the church for visitors to sign.

A permanent outdoor memorial was established for the twenty-fifth anniversary. Organised by St Mary's vicar, the Reverend David Ridley, the first rose, part of a new garden, was planted on the Dover seafront, after flowers were cast into the sea from the Prince of Wales Pier. Rev. Ridley said:

> It will be a place outside, somewhere quiet and still if people want to reflect with their thoughts and remember their loved ones. That's something we haven't got in Dover, we have several memorials in churches but nothing actually outside, and this will be on the seafront in quite an appropriate place.

Anniversary memorials are also held every year at St Danaas in Zeebrugge. The Rose Garden there has been the focal point for commemorating the victims and survivors, but also everyone who was involved in the rescue operation and the care given to the bereaved in the aftermath.

5

ANSWERS

Inquiry

The formal investigation opened at Church House, Westminster, on 27 April 1987 and lasted for twenty-nine days (until 29 June 1987), before the Honourable Lord Justice Sir Barry Sheen, who served as the admiralty judge of the High Court 1978–1993.

Sheen had been appointed by Transport Minister John Moore, and the investigation opened just seven weeks after the disaster. Despite the huge amount of work involved, it was felt desirable to start at the earliest opportunity in the interests of all parties. For example, eyewitnesses should give their evidence before their memories faded, with the court making allowances for witnesses who might still be affected by injury, shock or emotion. Also, if the results of the investigation showed that there were lessons to be learned, then those lessons could be put into practice much sooner. The court also wished to put an end to rumours and speculation, as well providing answers for those who had been bereaved to help them in their grieving process.

On the opening day of the Zeebrugge Disaster Inquiry, Wreck Commissioner Mr David Steel QC, representing the Department of Transport, condemned Townsend Thoresen, after he had outlined the story of the disaster in 'unbearable detail' for two hours:

> These procedures were manifestly and inherently dangerous. They were procedures which the master had no business to operate ... a disease of sloppy systems and sloppy practices infecting not just those on the ship but well into the body corporate of Townsend Thoresen Car Ferries.

Steel outlined the facts of the disaster, using a scale model of the *Herald of Free Enterprise*. Steel told Sheen, and four assessors, that the inquiry would probably conclude that the ferry capsized because 'large quantities of water made their way on to the car deck. ... We think you will also conclude that the immediate cause of that was that the doors were open.' He also commented that the ferry crew broke no laws when they left port with the doors open, but concurred that it was not common practice to do so. Steel said that the story of the disaster was 'cloaked in anguish because we can all imagine ourselves and our children trying to cope with the cold and the dark and the fear.'

The legal teams were as follows:

Anthony Clarke QC	counsel for Townsend Thoresen
David Steel QC	Wreck Commissioner
Charles Haddon-Cave	representing passengers
Stephen Millar	representing Mark Stanley
Belinda Bucknell	representing David Lewry and Leslie Sabel
Richard Stone QC	Department of Transport

The Zeebrugge Disaster Inquiry hoped to answer the following:

Why the watertight bow doors were open when the *Herald* sailed.

Why, and how, did water enter the car deck, which was usually 8ft above sea level?

Was water still being emptied from ballast tanks when the ferry left Zeebrugge?

Why did Leslie Sabel go to the bridge without ensuring that the doors were closed?

Was Mark Stanley in his cabin, 'unwell'?

Why were Lewry, the first and second officers, and the bosun all on the bridge, and unsure that the doors were closed? Were there no warning lights or safety checks?

Why did the ferry capsize in ninety seconds?

Was 15 knots too fast, and did it create a bow wave which initiated the car deck flooding?

Should passengers have been made aware of emergency procedures at the start of a journey? Were there any adequate escape routes and why did the lights go out?

Were Jock Calderwood's claims true that crew members were seen banging the bow doors with sledgehammers as the ferry set sail?

Should the vehicles have been tied down to prevent the momentum of a list?

Why did Townsend Thoresen not know previously how many people were on board? And why did the ferry company persist with inaccurate casualty figures long after it became obvious that they were underestimated?

Were Department of Transport regulations for the annual overhaul of ferries enough?

Open vehicle decks are inherently dangerous. Had commercial considerations come before safety?

Had any design faults for the *Herald* been repeated on the new 'super ferries' which were due to come into service later in 1987?

Steel detailed the six major failings which he claimed led to the disaster:

No attempt was made to shut the bow doors. The man usually responsible was in his cabin.

No warning lights to show whether the doors were open had been installed on the bridge, despite requests by three different ferry masters.

The captain, David Lewry, was required by the owners to assume that all was well unless he was told otherwise.

Readings were never taken to see how low the ferry lay in the water. The draughts were never read, only calculated.

Nothing was done when Captain Lewry had warned six months before that the *Herald* had an 'alarming tendency' to dip bows-first into the water when increasing speed. A previous captain gave the same warning five years before.

No emergency plans were laid for a disaster.

At this time, Lewry had also mentioned that the *Herald* had a permanent list to port. This defect inadvertently may have saved hundreds of lives because the ferry had swung round, capsized and come to rest on a sandbank, facing the direction from which she had travelled. Had these circumstances not occurred, the ferry would have capsized, sunk and been completely submerged and most, if not everyone, on board would have been killed.

On day two, in response to Steel's comments that no laws had been broken, Richard Stone QC, for the Department of Transport, said he did not agree that no offence against the Merchant Shipping Act had been committed. He said he would consult legal experts.

Steel said, 'Quartermaster John Hobbs remained at the wheel as long as possible, and in the process lost his life.' Head waiter, Michael Skippen was praised too, for making every possible effort without any regard to himself to calm people in the restaurant when it was already under several feet of water.

On the second day of the inquiry, 28 April 1987, Mr Anthony Clarke QC told the court, 'The answer to the question, who is to blame, is Townsend Car Ferries.' He went on to tell the crew, 'We are lost in admiration for the very many acts of heroism on that night.'

Belinda Bucknell, representing Captain Lewry and Leslie Sabel, defended her clients, highlighting the fact that First Officer Sabel's duties were written, requiring him to be in two places at once – checking the doors on the vehicle deck *and* being present on the bridge:

I don't accept that personal blame attaches to them in any material respect. They were doing their best at all times with the equipment and manpower available to them. There was nothing about it [the reporting system] being particularly undesirable or calling for action. It doesn't appear that any other masters or their chief officers ever regarded that aspect of the ship's operations as being inherently unsafe.

Everybody on board that ship was aware of the dangers of sailing with the doors open.

She spoke of one time when a sailing was aborted after it was found that the stern doors were open. 'On the very rare occasions when there was a problem, the system worked. The problem was reported to the bridge and the sailing was stopped and the doors dealt with.'

On day three of the inquiry, Bosun Terry Ayling gave evidence for the second time. He strongly disagreed with lorry driver Jock Calderwood's testimony that crewmen were seen using sledge hammers on the bow door mechanism, prior to the sailing. He said that if anything like that had happened, the ship would never have sailed. Then Ayling told of how he had left the car deck. 'I could not have stood down there, otherwise I would have been in trouble for not being where I should have been. It had never been part of my duties to close the doors or make sure anyone else closed the doors.'

Ayling added:

Passengers were scrambling over each other to get out. One stewardess was knocked off a rope by a male passenger. There was considerable confusion, but we shouted not to panic and 'she's settled – she's not going any further down'. Many more passengers started to assist. Captain Lewry was injured and could not stand unaided. He wanted to stay with the ship but I told two crew members to put him onto a tug.

After Ayling had given evidence about how he and fellow crew members had saved passengers and led Captain Lewry to the safety of a tug, Wreck Commissioner David Steel QC told him, 'Many people would want to express their great appreciation of your efforts in controlling your men and rescuing so many people in dire distress.'

Day three also saw crew members Martin Barnes, John Jackson, David Matthews, Charles Smith and William (Billy) Walker give evidence about their experiences during and after the capsize.

Crew member Billy Walker (23), of Deal, escaped from the crew mess room, pulled himself through the door above and sat on the jamb, joined by Leigh Cornelius and four or five others. They all assisted to help their remaining eight colleagues still stuck trapped in the room below. A wave crashed along the corridor, carrying the body of an unconscious woman. Walker said:

We pulled her out and I cleared her airways. I gave her mouth to mouth and she was all right. Me and Leigh took turns to hold her out of the water, which was up to our chests. We took turns to get out of the water onto a locker for ten minutes at a time to keep warm. The water was so cold, you were numb. A hose pipe was lowered and let down into the mess room. Everyone got out.

Walker had returned to Deal at 10 p.m. on Saturday with a dislocated shoulder, cuts and bruises.

On the night of 6 March, the Townsend Thoresen reception office in Russell Street released a list of twelve crew survivors, including 'W. Walker' to Billy's parents. Mrs Christine Walker said, 'It relieved us completely, even though it was a common name. It was a spark of hope.' Confirmation was received at 2 a.m. and again at 6 a.m. on Saturday. Walker's mother commented on the false reports that everyone had survived, 'We felt overjoyed but bloody mad after some of those reports, and we're sorry for the other people because we know what they're going through.'

Passenger survivors also attended the third day of the inquiry – including Andrew and Eleanor Parker. Eleanor forced herself to go. 'It has been a nightmare and I need to be here to believe it was really true. I need to hear the whole story.' It was some of the evidence given by a crew member about a woman in a wheelchair that shook her. 'That lady is in my nightmares.'

On 6 May, day seven of the inquiry, Captain David Lewry said that the policy of 'negative reporting' was his idea – where he assumed the bow doors were closed unless he heard to the contrary. The counsel for the passengers, Haddon-Cave, told Lewry:

> The safety of lives at sea is the most important matter of all. It is the prime responsibility, and when one is concerned with a passenger ferry it's a heavy responsibility. It's the master's duty to be 100 per cent sure regarding the safety of his vessel and his passengers. It is particularly the case when one is dealing with a roll-on/roll-off passenger ferry because they are vulnerable to water on G-deck.

'Only if the doors are left open,' Lewry replied.

'It was plainly obvious to anyone that the system which you were operating was highly dangerous, and that an accident of some sort was inevitable, would you agree?' Haddon-Cave asked him.

'Yes,' Lewry replied. After admitting this, he added 'After the event – obviously it was a very dangerous situation, a very dangerous system.'

'It was a system that no sensible master could operate?' Lewry was asked by Mr David Steel QC, representing the Transport Secretary.

'No,' Lewry replied, 'It was the system that was operated by all five masters on the ship.'

Steel asked Lewry, 'All five masters assumed that the bow doors were closed unless they heard to the contrary?'

'That's correct,' Lewry replied. 'It was such an obvious thing. We all assumed it was almost impossible to go to sea with the bow doors open. The bow doors had to be closed before the ship proceeds to sea. Because I heard nothing to the contrary, I assumed the doors were closed.'

'You had fallen into a practice of thoroughly bad seamanship in this respect?'

'We had not foreseen this occurrence. No.' said Lewry.

Sheen criticised Townsend Thoresen's masters' reliance on negative reporting systems (the absence of any reports at sailing time satisfying the master that the ship is ready for the sea):

> That was of course a very dangerous assumption. Captain Lewry was entitled to assume the assistant bosun and the chief officer were qualified to perform their respective duties. But he should not have assumed they had done so. He should have insisted upon receiving a report to that effect.

In mitigation, Sheen pointed out that this system was operated by all of the *Herald*'s masters, and that the company orders made no reference to the door-closing procedures.

On the subject of drinking amongst the crew, Lewry confirmed that crewmen were allowed to drink during their twenty-four-hour stints aboard. A staff 'chit' system allowed each crew member half a bottle of spirits or a case of beer per week. 'There have been odd occurrences of excess drinking – three, four or half a dozen. The crew could drink, but obviously within moderation. I don't think there was any rule of thumb.'

'Is it the position that crew are regarded fit for duty unless they are drunk?' Steel asked Lewry.

'Well, yes,' Lewry replied. At this point he admitted he had once had to sack a steward for drunkenness.

On day four of the inquiry, crew member Max Potterton, who was Assistant Bosun Mark Stanley's deputy, told the inquiry that sometimes who closed the bow doors would depend upon which of the two wanted a cup of tea. Mr Robert Owen, representing the crew, asked him, 'In what circumstances would that happen?'

Potterton replied, 'I might want a cup of tea and he'll shut the doors, or he might want a cup of tea and I'll shut the doors. We're both capable of doing it.'

The Court of Inquiry then heard how the *Herald* went down. The ferry went to sea with the inner and outer bow doors open. Sheen suggested that Lewry's decision to set the ship combinators at level 6 as he left port would have increased the speed rapidly from 14 knots to possibly an ultimate speed of 18 knots:

> Towards the end of the acceleration, the combination of dynamic sinkage, or squat, and an increase of bow wave height caused water to enter over the spade and flow aft into G-deck. The court is satisfied the rate of inflow of water had increased progressively as the ship dug the bow spade deeper into the water and decreased

the freeboard forward. A large quantity of water entered onto G-deck and caused an initial lurch to port due to free surface instability which was extremely rapid and reached perhaps 30 per cent. The water collected in the port wing of the vehicle deck and the ship became stable again at a large angle of loll. Water in large quantities continued to flood through the open bow doors aperture. Thereafter the *Herald* capsized to port rather more slowly until eventually she was more than 90 per cent. It is not possible to say whether the ship reached more than 90 per cent whilst still floating or whether this was only when she reached the sea bed. There is some reason for thinking the ship floated more or less on her stern ends for about a minute before finally resting on the sea bed.

Draught Readings

In 1982, Captain Bob Blowers had sent a 'most useful and helpful memo' to Wallace Ayres, Naval Architect and Townsend Thoresen director. Blowers said that draughts were difficult to read and often 'guesstimated'. He suggested fitting automatic draught recorders, with a readout in the wheelhouse. Ayres did not answer the memo.

In a sworn deposition in May 1987, Ayres said he was aware of draught reading, probably since 1984, and had considered fitting remote and reading draught indicators. He said that the equipment manufactured at the time was not accurate enough.

The inquiry found, 'Mr Ayres may be a competent naval architect, but the court formed the view that he did not carry out his managerial duties, whatever they may have been, he appeared to be incapable of expressing his thoughts with clarity.'

Overloading

The *Herald* was overloaded significantly at the time of the disaster, but this did not contribute to the capsize. This was discovered in full-scale tests of the *Herald*'s sister ship, the *Pride of Free Enterprise* in June 1987. There were 115 extra tonnes, which were a combination of overweight vehicles and modifications over the years. At the end of the experiment, 105 vehicles weighed at Dover were found to be 13 per cent overweight on average, compared to the weights they were allegedly carrying.

The *Herald* was well under passenger capacity, but the inquiry heard of many occasions when the limit was exceeded. Management had taken little or no notice of no fewer than seven captains.

Blowers sent another memo in 1982 to operations director, Anthony Young, referring to several occasions over a two-week period when the *Pride* carried too many passengers. The capacity was 1,305. He detailed occasions, including 28 July 1982, when it was found that 250 extra passengers were aboard.

In October 1982, Captain Pearson of the *Spirit of Free Enterprise* sent a memo to Young, detailing other occasions. He said that one reason for the excess was that lorry drivers are not included in the count.

In December 1982, the matter was discussed at a meeting between senior masters and shore management. Different counting systems were considered. However, by 1983 and 1984, masters were still expressing concern.

In 1986, Captain Tony de Ste Croix, master of the *Pride*, wrote to Young detailing a sailing where he believed 1,687 passengers were carried – nearly 400 over the limit. He wrote, 'The total is way over the lifesaving capacity of the vessel. The fine on the master for the offence is £50,000, and probably confiscation of his certificate. May I please know what steps the company intend to take to protect my career from the mistakes of this nature?'

There were other captains with similar memos – Captain Stoker of the *Pride*, and Captain Martin, senior master of the *Spirit*, who found there were 1,550 aboard. Martin wrote, 'The number of passengers over and above our certified number … can only be described as a blatant and flagrant disregard of the system, and backs up other complaints from masters of this and other fleet vessels.'

Young wrote back to Stoker, 'Whatever system is operated, there will always be the possibility of human error.' There were further overloading memos to Young in September and October 1986. One reply was, 'some stray tickets had to be put into the system somewhere', and Young said that figures had been added to one sailing, giving a false reading.

Their complaints were backed up by Jeffrey Develin, company director, who said the matter was serious and needed a meeting. Young did not invite Develin to the meeting because he said it was a 'marine matter'. Develin was therefore deliberately excluded.

In November 1986, Captain Hartwell complained that he had carried 1,342 passengers and 100 crew on the *Pride*. Young replied that he was unwilling to accept the figures given to him by seven masters.

The Court of Inquiry said:

> The court reluctantly concluded that Mr Young made no proper or sincere effort to resolve the problem. The court takes a most serious view of the fact that so many of the company's ferries were carrying an excessive number of passengers on so many occasions. Not only was it illegal for the excess passengers to have been carried but it was also dangerous. It should not have been beyond the wit of the managers to devise a system which would have ensured that no more than the permitted number of passengers are carried.

The court considered the possibility of a boarding card system, in which every passenger had a card and the number of cards issued would not exceed legal capacity.

Indicator Lights

In June 1985, Captain Bob Blowers had written to Director Jeffrey Develin, suggesting that detector lights were installed on the bridge to show if the bow and stern doors were open or closed. The suggestion followed two incidents in 1984 when the *Pride* had put to sea to Zeebrugge with the doors open, after job and rank changes from the Calais run. Develin passed on the memo to other managers for comments.

The Court of Inquiry said, 'It was a serious memorandum which merited serious thought and attention and called for a considered reply.'

However, it seemed management did not take it so seriously. The comments came back:

Deputy Chief Superintendent John Alcindor – 'Do they need an indicator to tell them whether the deck storekeeper is awake and sober? My goodness!'
Marine Superintendent Ronald Ellison – 'Assume the guy who shut the doors tells the bridge if there is a problem.'
D.R. Hamilton – 'Nice.'
Assistant Marine Superintendent Anthony Reynolds – 'Nice, but don't we already pay someone?'

The Court of Inquiry concluded that '… the comment of Mr Alcindor on the deck storekeeper was either ominously prescient or showed an awareness of this type of incident in the past.'

In 1986, indicator lights were again brought up by two captains, one of whom was Tony de Ste Croix, who was told to submit his request to the marine department. Then Alcindor asked for a preliminary specification for pricing. There was a misunderstanding over what was needed, and Alcindor suggested the request not be proceeded with.

The Court of Inquiry said, 'It is only with the benefit of hindsight that it can now be seen that if, in 1986, the matter had been treated with urgency, it would probably have prevented this disaster.'

Sheen said that the replies from management 'displayed an absence of any sense of responsibility. Simplicity of such lights proved that just days after the disaster, other fleet vessels were fitted with them.'

Many factors were found to have contributed to the capsize. The Court of Inquiry found that there were:

Unstable working relationships, through poor shift patterns and the high turnover of officers.
Ambiguous work tasks and poor job descriptions.

Commercial pressures to sail early.

Negative reporting systems (reports filed only if things go wrong).

Five previous occurrences of the doors being left open and ignoring recommendations of previous enquiries.

Engineering requests for warning lights and pumps being cynically dismissed.

Inherent ship design faults.

No meetings between shore and ship management for two and a half years.

Passenger overloading (although not on the night of disaster).

Irresponsible management of P&O Ferries.

Full investigation leads to conclusion that underlying faults lie higher up in the Company. The Board of Directors did not appreciate their responsibility for safe management of their ships. The Directors did not comprehend what their duties were.

Mr Justice Sheen asked for a list of those who contributed to the rescue, saying that their courage must be recognised. This may have paved the way for the thirty-one recipients of awards in the Queen's New Year's Honours list at the end of 1987.

During the summing up at the Zeebrugge Inquiry, on 24 July 1987, Mr Justice Sheen said, 'There is no reason to think that there was any fault that could have prevented the doors being closed hydraulically.' He discounted Jock Calderwood's eyewitness testimony that he had seen two crew members 'banging furiously' at the door mechanism with hammers. Sheen told the court that he was not convinced that Calderwood had an 'accurate recollection.'

On the subject of written instruction that the loading officer should ensure that the bow doors were closed, Sheen said, 'It was not clearly worded but, whatever the meaning, it was not enforced. If it had been enforced this disaster would not have occurred.'

Mark Stanley had eventually got on board a tug and had seen the injured being taken off the ferry. Speaking during a BBC interview, he said:

There were kids being held by women who were saying 'I am not their mother'. There were mothers and fathers looking for their children, husbands looking for their wives, wives looking for their husbands. There were people asking 'How did it happen?' I knew what had happened but I didn't say anything then. As I said, whatever my responsibilities were it was my responsibility to shut the doors.

Stanley's solicitor, John Bridge, said, 'He returned to work shortly after the tragedy and joined a vessel in dry dock. He was going to sail on that, but later decided not to. He is putting on a brave face, but he is very up and down and I don't know if he will ever return to sea.' Bridge added that Stanley now plans to rebuild his life by helping other survivors, playing a key role in counselling sessions and group therapy sessions for those involved in the disaster.

On 24 July 1987, Justice Sheen released a report into the findings of the inquiry. Known as 'The Sheen Report', and officially titled, 'Report of Court No. 8074 Formal Investigation', it summed up twenty-nine days of evidence, costing £600,000 in legal costs. Townsend Thoresen spent £750,000 in the wake of the disaster and on legal proceedings. Sheen said he would reserve a decision on awarding costs, and adjourned the hearing without setting a date.

Sheen and the court concluded that the capsizing of the *Herald of Free Enterprise* was partly caused, or contributed to, by serious negligence in the discharge of their duties by Captain David Lewry (master), Mr Leslie Sabel (chief officer) and Mr Mark Victor Stanley (assistant bosun) and partly caused, or contributed to, by Townsend Car Ferries Limited (the owners).

Lewry's Master's Certificate was ordered to be suspended for one year. By law, a medical examination was not needed, but Sheen advised, 'He would be wise to do so,' because he was obviously suffering from shock. Sheen said, 'The court is aware of the mental and emotional burden resulting from this disaster which has been and will be borne by Captain Lewry. But the court would be failing in its duty if it did not suspend his certificate of competency.'

Sabel's First Officer's Certificate was suspended for two years. He would, by law, have to undergo a medical examination on 24 March 1989 before his suspension could be lifted.

Townsend Car Ferries was found to be 'at fault at all levels, from the board of directors to the managers, to the marine department, down to the junior superintendents'.

Senior *Herald* master, Captain John Kirby, was in court supporting Patricia Lewry. Mark Stanley was in court with support from friends and his lawyer, Stephen Miller.

Townsend Chairman Peter Ford, also in court, sat in the well behind Lewry. Mrs Lewry stood in tears, holding a friend's hand.

'The court sees no reason why the *Herald* could not have departed [from Zeebrugge] with the number of officers it had, if proper thought had been given to organising their duties.' Sheen pointed out that the only difference at Zeebrugge had been that the crew had to operate the ballast tanks to allow the loading ramp to reach one of the car decks. Sheen criticised the lack of information policy for such loading operations, saying orders should have been issued to cover all operations, not just Calais, but Zeebrugge as well. 'This has not been done. The standing orders displayed a lack of proper thought.'

The loading procedures were questioned, but not because of overloading. 'From the outset, Mark Victor Stanley has accepted it was his responsibility and that he failed to carry out this duty. Mr Stanley has fully recognised his failure to turn up for duty, and he will no doubt suffer remorse for some considerable time.' Sheen added that it was up to the company if Stanley was to be disciplined.

Bosun Terry Ayling was the last known person to leave the car deck on E-deck. When he was asked during the inquiry why he didn't close the doors, he replied that it was not one of his duties. 'He took a narrow view of his duties and it is most unfortunate that he took this attitude. It has to be said that his behaviour after the capsize was exemplary.'

Sheen referred to written instructions stating that the loading officer should ensure the doors were closed. These instructions were 'regularly flouted'. The instructions are not clearly worded but, whatever the meaning, it was not enforced. If it had been enforced, the disaster would not have occurred.

Sabel had told the court that he thought he saw Mark Stanley arrive on G-deck to close the doors, a mystery man wearing orange overalls. Sheen confirmed that the court had reached the conclusion that Sabel may have 'muddled one occasion with another' in trying to remember what had happened before the sailing. Sabel was '... seriously negligent. This court cannot condone such irresponsible conduct.' Sheen said that the captain should not have assumed that everything was in order, and should have insisted that there was a report.

Sheen said there were at least five other occasions where ferries had left port with their bow doors open – and that management knew about them:

> ... [Kirby] must bear his share of responsibility for the disaster ... Kirby failed to enforce orders and failed to issue clear orders about closing the doors.
>
> The board of directors did not appreciate their responsibility for safety on their ships. The directors did not have a proper comprehension of what their duties were. Guilt was with all concerned in management. From top to bottom, the body corporate was affected by the disease of sloppiness.

Sheen spoke of criticism in his report for the company, but praised the new chairman, Peter Ford, and the measures being introduced.

The court was told that the Department of Transport did not intend to prosecute anyone found to be responsible. Sheen was implicit in the suggestion that a statutory offence may have been committed, but added that neither master nor officers had been able to speak 'in their own defence' other than in general. 'Accordingly it would be quite unacceptable for this court to express the view that a statutory offence was committed.' If the court was clear that no such offence had been committed, 'then Parliament ought to enact the appropriate legislation', if it was the view of Parliament that a RORO ferry taking to sea with its bow doors open ought to be regarded as a criminal offence.

Sheen told the court that, on the night of the disaster, floating lifejackets impeded some survivors and prevented others from getting to the surface. He spoke of the need to be able to communicate with the helicopters during the rescue attempts; the helicopter lights blinded the rescuers and the rescued and the noise caused communication problems.

For the future of ferry safety, some matters would have to be implemented only when international agreement was reached. Other safety measures could be implemented unilaterally by Great Britain and in a comparatively inexpensive way.

For the immediate safety, three categories were to be considered:

The safety of the ship.
Loading and stability.
The saving of life.

The Court of Inquiry felt that all RORO ferries should be fitted with mechanical or pneumatic draught indicators, approved by the Department of Transport.

On the subject of lifesaving, accounts from the survivors highlighted four main problems:

The lack of illumination – the emergency lighting on the *Herald* came on only for a few seconds before failing when the circuits were submerged in the capsize. The lack of illumination added to the low morale of the survivors, and the practicalities of rescue. An expert surveyor recommended the future use of 'self-contained maintained light', which used Ni-Cad batteries and a continuous charge, illuminating a bulb at all times. The advantage of the lighting being illuminated the whole time is that it can be seen to be working, instilling confidence in those that may need it during a potential incident. It was also ruled essential that the lighting should be watertight.

The difficulty with lifejackets – survivors could not don lifejackets in the water due to tangled straps, the unfamiliarity with how to use them, and the onset of hypothermia, which rendered tying and undoing straps difficult, if not impossible. Further consideration was recommended by the court.

The lack of apertures from which to escape – toughened glass was in use on the external windows of the *Herald*. It was easier to break than laminated glass, which at the time of the disaster was being pushed for by the Department of Transport for its fire-resistant properties. The court said, 'In this respect there is clearly a need for a good standardised industry approach to escape windows. They should be reliable and uncomplicated and opened from either side. It is a matter of concern that passengers should be able to recognise escape routes and doors. This would include the prominent labelling of exits and lifejacket stores.

The difficulty climbing up to such apertures – the court wished to discourage the design of slab-sided vessels, as the only exits are usually at the front or rear of the otherwise enclosed deck. After the capsize, what were once corridors from one side of the ship to the other had become deep vertical shafts half filled with water. When the court asked the Department of Transport, it replied that it was not really practicable. The court did not agree, and suggested self-supporting hinged panels as an example.

'There may be better methods, but some such simple device should be developed and made a requirement.' The court also suggested that footholds be incorporated into walls to make it easier for people to climb when the walls became vertical.

'It is apparent that the top management has taken to heart the gravity of this catastrophe, and the company has shown a determination to put its house in order.' Sheen seemed confident that the new company would implement changes. These included:

Clear and concise orders.
Strict discipline.
Attention at all times to all matters affecting ship safety and the safety of those on board.
No 'cutting of corners'.
Maintenance of proper channels of communication between the ship and shore for the receipt and dissemination of information.
Clear and firm management and command structure.
Lifeboats should also be reviewed.

The false entries made in logbooks was also addressed. The draught of the *Herald of Free Enterprise* was not read before sailing and 'fictitious entries were made in her official logbook'.

The Court of Inquiry made a number of recommendations:

Door sills inside the ship to be higher.
Port berths to be improved.
Boarding passes to keep record of the number of passengers.
Passenger awareness of escape routes.
Lifejackets to be improved.
Ramps to ships to be fitted with weighbridges to avoid overloading (a spot check showed 13 per cent of lorries were overloaded).
Mechanical draught indicators.
Weekly inspections by the ship's electrical officer.
Review of all existing ferries to reassess stability.
Alteration to the glass in upper windows to allow for emergency exit.
Emergency exits on passenger decks operable from either side.
High capacity ballast pump.
Closed circuit TV cameras (CCTV) to monitor doors, cargo and vehicle decks.
Slab-sided ship design to be discouraged due to lack of escape routes to open decks.
Watertight self-contained lighting system.
Indicator lights on bridge.
Positive reporting from door crew to bridge – 'yes, the doors are shut.'

On 29 July, Townsend Thoresen was ordered to pay £400,000 towards the cost of the inquiry, on top of the £750,000 the company had spent on legal representation. £350,000 went to the Secretary of State for Transport and £50,000 to the National Union of Seamen (NUS), which represented surviving crew members and victims' families.

David Steel QC, representing the transport secretary, told Sheen, 'the court had to consider whether to administer some mark of public admonishment by way of an order of costs against the owners, so that the world will know the court thinks that, on the face of it, a further financial penalty should be imposed, even though we are told that they are insured against that.'

Mark Stanley received £39,675 towards his legal costs, and £25,000 went towards Lewry's and Sabel's costs. Sheen also ordered the secretary of state to pay £10,000 towards the legal costs of surviving passengers and the next of kin of the dead.

On 31 July, Justice Sheen ruled that no statutory offence had been committed by the operators. Victims' relatives and MPs had protested about the blanket immunity from prosecution of the company management. Sheen named Ports Operations Director Tony Young, and Technical Director Jim Ayres (now retired) – 'The court was singularly unimpressed with both these gentlemen. The failure on part of the shore management to give proper and clear directions was a contributory cause of the disaster.'

As of 31 July, the Channel Ferry Disaster Fund had reached £4,523,000. Up until then, over £1,100,000 had been paid out by the trustees, and payment of much of the remainder was to start in September 1987. On that day, a large cheque was expected to be presented by the army, from worldwide donations.

Reactions

Captain David Lewry, with his wife Patricia at his side, said, 'My deepest sympathy goes to all those people who lost family and friends on the *Herald of Free Enterprise* that night. Obviously a lot of the crew were my friends as well and we had sailed together for several years.'

Belinda Bucknell, representing Lewry and Sabel, said, 'Not only have they been prevented from carrying out their professions for the period of suspension, but the publicity which attended this inquiry must unfortunately have the effect of making them marked men for the future.'

Peter Ford, who became chairman of P&O shortly after the disaster, said:

[Sheen] was right to make ... Tough and pungent comments about management of the company and the individuals involved. We have reconstituted the management. We have instituted completely new operational safety procedures in the fleet, including new ship to shore reporting and management systems. We are taking part in a technical inquiry into roll-on/roll-off ships in conjunction with the Transport Department, Lloyds Register and the General Council of British Shipping.

Mark Stanley said:

> All these stories came out, she could have hit the breakwater on the way out or a big rock in the Channel – that wasn't a glimmer of hope to me at all, because I knew all the time it was the doors ... everyone was asking each other what had happened, but I wasn't going to tell anyone down there. I was hoping everyone would get off. When I got on the tug, I saw people coming in injured and I realised there would be loss of life. I shall always carry guilt ... whatever the other responsibilities were, I knew it was my responsibility to shut the doors and I didn't shut the doors. It's as simple as that. It's not up to me to blame anyone else and I'm not going to.

Stanley thought his world had ended, 'You thought, how can I ever live with this? You can, in the end.' Having met survivors and relatives, he said, 'Saying sorry just isn't enough'.

The officers' union, National Union of Marine, Aviation and Shipping Transport Officers (NUMAST), and the National Union of Seamen (NUS) were angry at the report's findings. Eric Nevin, the general secretary of NUMAST, said:

> The scapegoat system is not what I recognise as British justice. Why should two officers be selected for punishment when there is a complex chain of responsibility for the disaster? Only in terms of attention to duty, in a rushed situation caused by the failure of those august bodies, did two officers plus one ranking have involvement in that complex chain. Why then, should those two individual officers be singled out as scapegoats? Apparently to purge the guilt of a whole community that failed.

The NUS was disappointed that no legal action was to be taken against Townsend Thoresen. Also, it was unhappy that no reference was made to the Department of Transport's ineffectiveness as an enforcement agency.

Paul Channon, the transport secretary, pledged £1 million towards an enhanced research programme into RORO ferry stability and additional bulkhead implications.

Peter Snape, Labour's transport secretary, said the *Herald* was 'a latter day Titanic, wrecked on an iceberg of Department of Transport indifference, managerial incompetence, working methods designed apparently only in the interest of shortening turnaround times, regardless of the risk to passengers and crew!' He added that the suspension of the two crew was deplorable. The Labour party's John Prescott said the report was an indictment of sloppy practices that had gone on for years.

The Conservative party's Harry Bellingham said, 'Many people will be dismayed that this company is still sailing. It is not good enough to say there were new mangers. The management is obviously rotten to the core and people expect tough action by ministers.'

Survivor Richard Smith, of Hove, expressed his concerns that the disaster could be repeated:

The result of the inquiry and the recommendations which it made, suggests to me that nothing more will be done to rectify the fundamental instability of these ferries, other than the installation of red lights and video monitors.

It seems absolutely dreadful to me as one who has experienced the effect of water flooding onto the car deck, that given the many potential scenarios, other than open doors, in which this could happen i.e. collision or terrorist attack, financial consideration should rule and deem that nothing should be done.

Given the history of RORO ferries and the warnings that have been given from many experts for years, I think it is a scandal that ferries are still operating without bulkhead doors. However, in the face of the ferry company's greed and government complacency, I feel helpless and very angry that a similar, totally avoidable, disaster could so easily happen again.

I feel strongly that had those in a position to change things been aboard the *Herald* with their families that night and survived, things would have been done to prevent these ships rolling over in the way everybody now knows they do – and those whose business it is to know have known for a long time – as soon as water enters the car deck.

I wonder if anyone can suggest a way in which my small voice could be joined with others who have experienced the horrors, which have resulted from this case of safety being sacrificed to financial expediency, to at least try to make sure it doesn't happen again.

Mrs Ann Biggins and Mr John Waters, who lost their parents Alan and Molly Waters on the *Herald*, wrote to the *Guardian* on 15 August 1987:

Through the cumulative effect of years of incompetence and negligence came the horrific deaths of 188 people. The company whose laxness caused the tragedy is not even to be prosecuted. This is supposed to encourage other companies to take basic safety precautions? The Russian example of Chernobyl – hard labour for perpetrators and contributors – is more likely to achieve that result … We have seen it reported that the Belgian authorities are considering prosecuting Townsend Thoresen – we, and others of the survivors and relatives pray that they do. The Belgians, Police and Civil, have from the first been the most competent in this affair. Now, as with the Heysel Stadium salvaging, it seems they are the only help of bringing justice to this country's shame.

We believe Townsend Thoresen's expenses will be met from their insurance. While such companies can operate with such laxness and incompetence as to not only endanger but take life and do so with virtual impunity, what price British justice?

Survivor Robert O'Neill, writing in response to the Sheen Inquiry into the disaster and the verdict, wrote:

I would like to say something about the inquiry and the verdict. I feel that Townsend Thoresen got off very lightly indeed. I can't see why the British Government can't take Townsend Thoresen to court to face charges of manslaughter. I read in the papers that the Belgians may take Townsend Thoresen to court to face criminal proceedings. I believe that we now live in a society where the courts look after big business rather than the individual. Townsend Thoresen was guilty of gross negligence and manslaughter. All the survivors and the bereaved families should get together and take Townsend Thoresen to court. They literally got away with murder.

Inquest

On 6 March 1987, the day of the disaster, PC Bill Maddocks contacted east Kent coroner, Richard Sturt, and the first arrangements for an inquest were made. The Dover incident room was set up under the command of Inspector Bob Fautley and PC Michael Kearney. All three had been involved from the start.

Another incident room was set up at Maidstone Police HQ, and both centres had dealt with 7,500 calls in the first forty-eight hours.

In due course 1,500 statements were taken, 500 witness notifications sent, 100 firms of solicitors were informed of the inquest dates and 15,000 pages of evidence were typed up, with at least sixteen pages in each of 188 files.

PC Maddocks had given evidence at the first inquest, opening on 10 March, four days after the disaster. The end of the inquest completed more than seven months of continuous work on the disaster by the coroner's officer, PC Maddocks and others in the Dover incident room.

The first nine inquests were opened at Dover Town Hall on 10 March, four days after the disaster. and were opened and adjourned until 19 May – Alan Firbank, Peter Martin, Mrs Catherine Howard, Miss Ann English, Miss Karen Ray, Miss Irene Dowie, Mrs Kiran Parsons, Miss Maureen Edwards and Mrs Eileen Baddeley. A day later, the second batch of inquests were opened, including that of 4-year-old Emily Pierce. More inquests followed on 12 March.

On 30 July, advertisements appeared in the *East Kent Mercury* for experienced shorthand writers and secretarial staff to help take notes at an inquest starting in September.

Britain's biggest inquest opened on Monday, 7 September 1987, at Connaught Hall, Dover Town Hall, into the deaths of 188 people in the Zeebrugge Disaster. The 189th victim came under West German jurisdiction (a child whose body was returned to Germany). The inquest talked of 'at least' 193 victims. The bodies of four people were never recovered.

Coincidentally, that day would have been the second wedding anniversary of victims, Francis and Alison Gaillard. Alison's parents, Maurice and Margaret de Rohan, were there for the opening day and every day of the inquest. The inquest was an opportunity for the bereaved to hear about how their loved ones had died, and also for the survivors to share their stories by giving evidence.

East Kent coroner, Richard Sturt, relayed to the jury of eight men and three women the details of the verdicts that were available to them. These included 'accidental', 'open' and 'unlawful killing' (including 'manslaughter'). If the jury decided that the victims had died due to manslaughter, then no individual should be named and held responsible. Sturt further told the jury that if they decided on a verdict of unlawful killing, they needed to be satisfied beyond all reasonable doubt that the act, or omission, of an individual caused substantially one or more of the deaths, and that individual was guilty of gross negligence. He added 'by this, I mean that he did or omitted to do something which created an obvious and serious risk of physical injury, and that this was done without having given any thought to the possibility of the risk; or, that he recognised the risk and nevertheless decided to take it.' Sturt warned the jury not to add together separate acts of neglect.

'Although it is possible for several people to be guilty individually of manslaughter, it is not permissible to aggregate several acts of neglect by different people, so as to have gross negligence by a process of aggregation.' He informed the jury it was their duty to find out in what way, or how, each person died, in the hope of contributing to future safety, and not to go into the history preceding the capsize – which Mr Justice Sheen's inquiry had, in any case, investigated.

The jury did not have the authority to imply any criminal or civil liability, and was forbidden to comment on any matters other than these four questions – who, when, where and how? Theirs was a totally different set of questions to those the Sheen Inquiry had considered.

'This has been one of the most poignant and moving tragedies of modern times.' Sturt spoke about the burden that the jury had to face – 'During the next few weeks you are going to hear some of the most harrowing tales ever told in a British court.' Sturt discussed with the jury why it was necessary to have an inquest at all just to relive the tragic facts all over again, after so many inquiries have already taken place into the same event. Sturt assured the jury that this was the legal process but, more importantly, families and loved ones would be unable to come to terms with their grief and suffering until all the facts were brought out into the open and discussed in an objective and rational manner. He drew observations on how, at smaller and less public inquests, relatives often appeared much more at ease after hearing the facts of a fatal accident than they were at the outset, despite the distress of giving evidence.

During his opening speech, Sturt paid tribute and gave his thanks time and again to the people of Belgium and those from Great Britain, who worked bravely and tirelessly in the immediate rescue and aftermath. Thirty-two vessels were mentioned in the Sheen Inquiry. Sturt told the jury that they would hear from two of those involved – Captain Malcolm Shakesby, chief officer of the *Duke of Anglia*, on a voyage from Chatham, Kent, to Zeebrugge, who responded to the 'Mayday' call and took charge of the rescue and boarded the *Herald* on the night of the disaster; and Chief Officer Elias Van Maren of the *Sanderus*, the dredger that raised the alarm.

Sturt also reserved thanks for Captain Joan De Winne, head of the Belgian Disaster Victim Identification team, and also the staff of St Jan's Hospital, Bruges. Sturt also thanked Arthur d'Hoest, the *judge d'instruction* of West Flanders. He also thanked the more than 100 Red Cross members in Kent, and several hundred members of the Belgian Red Cross, including many teenage girls who helped carry the bodies to and from the mortuary tables based at Zeebrugge Naval Station, working non-stop in harrowing circumstances without ever flinching.

Thanks was also due to the Salvation Army and the Royal Military Police special investigation branch, as well as the navy divers who were on the scene that night, and the divers who were involved in the recovery of bodies after the *Herald* had been raised.

The clergy of all denominations were also thanked for travelling to Zeebrugge to help comfort the bereaved and survivors, and who conducted the funerals of almost all of the 193 victims. Thanks also went to the *Herald* Assistance Unit and the staff of Townsend Thoresen for counselling the bereaved. Sturt also mentioned the fine work of the British Consulate in Brussels and Kent Police, and also the NUS for helping their members cope with the disaster and its aftermath.

The inquest was due to sit every day from 10.15 a.m. to 4.15 p.m., with a lunch break between 12.30 p.m. and 2.00 p.m. A model of the ferry stood at the front of the hall.

Sturt said the inquest was 'an immensely complicated and difficult case' and that 'everything will be done to relieve any distress.' He gave the highest praise to Kent Police, who received 7,000 telephone calls relating to 3,600 possible missing persons in the first few days.

A special room with five telephones was available for twenty members of the press. Extra staff were taken on and evidence was to be gathered on three tape recorders. Computers and hi-tech printers were also used. Staff members of the *Herald* Assistance Unit and Red Cross were on hand for those distressed.

The legal representation was as follows:

Alistair Forrest barrister representing 109 victims
Alan Cooper QC   representing Townsend Thoresen/P&O

Christopher Erving   representing the NUS and the majority of the crew victims

David Osborne   representing the officers' union NUMAST

Passengers

The first relative to give evidence was George Dockrill, on six members of his family – his wife, Patricia Dockrill (41) (they had been married for 21 years in September 1986), daughter Emma Dockrill (17), and son Andrew Dockrill (8), Graham Lennox (38), of Stanford-le-Hope, Essex (the couple had split up, and Patricia had moved in with Graham), Graham's son Mark Lennox (13), and Emma's boyfriend Paul Dowman (22). All six victims had been travelling on tokens from the *Sun* newspaper.

Evidence was also given on the following victims – Stephen Redman (30) and his girlfriend, Loranda Massey (25); and Stephen Wren (32) and his wife Betty (32), who were all travelling together.

Survivor Gary Milton gave evidence of the last moments of his co-driver, John Millgate (26) of Dover. They had boarded early, had their evening meal and had both gone down to the bar for a drink:

> There came a point when I realised it was going right over and I turned to John and told him to follow me. I started to make my way towards the rear doors but I fell down to the opposite side of the bar area. I did not see John for a while. As I fell, the contents of the duty-free shop and perfume shop above me collapsed. The emergency lights came on and over to my left I saw John. He was still standing almost upright about 10–15ft away from me. When the emergency lights went off I lost John. That was the last time I saw him.

The inquest heard from east Kent pathologist, Dr Noel Padley, that John Millgate died of drowning and hypothermia due to head injuries. He had suffered a blow to the top of his head, enough to render him unconscious. It is not unreasonable to assume that John was struck by a bottle from the duty-free shop and was knocked out before falling into the water. Other survivors in that area below the duty-free shop spoke of being hit by bottles falling through the air.

William Jefferson (40) and his wife, Patricia Jefferson (38), of Portslade, East Sussex, had been on board with their two sons. They both died.

Mark Smith, of Wembley, gave evidence on his housemates, all travelling on *Sun* tokens – Melanie Wilson (23); Rosemary Smith (25); and Lynda Cockram (24). He saw two of them sliding away from him during the capsize and never saw any of them again.

On Thursday, 10 September 1987, the fourth day of the inquest, the coroner and jury were taken to the *Herald*'s sister ship, *Spirit of Free Enterprise*, to better understand the evidence that was being given about the layout of the ferry and where certain events had occurred. Sturt, his secretary and Marshall Lt Col George McEwan (former coroner to the Royal Household) went by car, while the jury went to Eastern Docks by coach.

The coroner and jury made separate visits to the *Spirit*. The coroner had also warned TV cameramen and photographers that the jury could not be filmed or photographed, as this would identify them and that would be a breach of the law, and could result in stopped proceedings and evidence being heard all over again. Arrangements were made to keep the coroner and jury apart during the visit. This worked so well that Sturt had to ask if they'd actually been, 'I didn't see them at all.'

Evidence was given on the following family – Brian Delafield (47) of Maidstone, his wife Carol (43), Brian's daughter Sharon Delafield (17); and Carol's son Andrew Fox (11). All of them had travelled using the *Sun*'s tokens.

Sonia Saunders of Wigmore, Gillingham, Kent, gave evidence about the last moments of her husband, Michael Saunders (47). They had been in the bar when the ferry capsized. Michael stood up but then fell flat on his face and slid into the water. She held onto chairs and eventually climbed up to be hauled out on a rope. She looked down and saw her husband floating face down, sure he was dead.

On 11 September, prosecutor David Jeffreys outlined his case to the court:

> The company … gave no thought to the possibility of there being any risk or, having recognized there was some risk, went on to take it and behaved with gross negligence. … You don't have to be a maritime expert to see what it meant to sail with those bow doors open. The … case is that the capsize was avoidable.

On the same day, 11 September, it was revealed that P&O planned to eradicate the name 'Enterprise' from its entire Dover-based fleet. The timing in the middle of the inquest could not have come at a worse time for the families of the victims, who already believed that P&O wanted them to just go away. Townsend Thoresen's headquarters at Enterprise House was to be renamed Channel House, in Channel View Road, Dover.

The changeover date was set for 22 October, in an attempt to distance themselves from the bad image of the *Herald* disaster. Newspapers and television across the world had splashed pictures of the capsized ferry. Since the early days of the company, the tag 'Free Enterprise' had reflected the 'thrustful' image of the Townsend Company.

The first ferry to bear the new P&O livery was likely to be the freighter *Empire Clearway* when she returned from refit. P&O kept the name. The *Free Enterprise IV*, which started service in 1969, was to be sold when the new ferry *Pride of Calais* entered service in late 1987.

George Lamy testified of the search for four members of his family, 'but I soon realised I was wasting my time'. He lost his wife, mother, daughter and grandson in the disaster.

David Gudgeon of Runwell, Essex, told the inquest how he tried to save his wife Eileen from drowning. They were on board with their daughter, Josephine Murphy, and her husband, Robert. He wept as he gave evidence. Water had cascaded in over them as they sat together and David began to climb up the seats. One big man scrambled over him, shouting and swearing. He said he saw two men standing on the end of a table and asked if they could help his wife and daughter, 'Sorry mate, there's no room up here.' His wife Eileen helped their daughter out of the water and then hung onto some seats. Eileen said she couldn't hang on much longer, so David tried to pull her up by her jumper. David became unconscious and was lifted out, taken to hospital and transferred to intensive care.

David told Sturt, 'I just felt I should have done something else to save her. I should have made more effort.'

Sturt replied, 'You have no need to reproach yourself, you made heroic efforts to save her.'

David simply said, 'But I failed.'

Miss Dolvis 'Dolly' Wellington-Fray (28) was a social worker from West Norwood, south London. She had three children and was on board with her friend, secretary Patricia Fox. Patricia saw Dolly thrown through the air during the capsize, somersault, and crash down on her head, breaking her neck. Half an hour later, both were rescued on ropes. A rope was put around her and she managed to hold on. Dolly died of injuries two months later in a London hospital of deep vein thrombosis (DVT) caused by her injuries.

Lorry driver Christopher Glendenning (41) of Morehall Avenue, Cheriton, left home on 2 March with a long-distance removal firm on a job to Luxembourg. On the day of the disaster, he phoned his wife, Pauline, to say he was on standby for the 1900hrs sailing. Dr Noel Padley told the inquest that Christopher had suffered a severe blow to his face and was knocked out. He died of asphyxia while unconscious. Christopher was identified by colleague, Gary Down, who had known him for ten years.

Peter Martin was a former Metropolitan policeman and former grenadier Guardsman, 6ft 9in tall and a marshal at Lancing College, West Sussex. He was on board with his wife, Kay, and their friends, Richard and Georgina Davies. They had been in the main lounge on C-deck and were contemplating going to the restaurant. Richard Davies, giving evidence, said:

A chap walking past us slipped and fell towards the two women. He regained his feet, apologised and started walking away. Then he came back down towards us, feet first. Then I was down on the port side, having been thrown out of my chair, down to the bottom. I had no idea where Peter was. I was in the water and I saw my wife and Kay perched on the seats where they had been sitting. My wife shouted that Peter was in the water just away from me. I called out to him and he put his hand out towards me, looking dazed, but it was impossible. There seemed to be a chap hanging onto him.

I saw one man fall the entire width of the vessel, through a port hole or plate glass window. I could hear explosions as the port holes gave way. I saw a man holding a boy of 10 in the water. A woman was shouting to the man not to let go of their son. The man said he couldn't do it. His arms were going. The woman started screaming. I tried to hold him out of the water and get a lifejacket on him. It was difficult to get a lifejacket on someone with a limp head, because you have to get his head through. We somehow got it on him. There was a young woman nearby who couldn't swim. Her boyfriend was about 2 or 3 yards from her and couldn't reach her. He was asking other people to keep hold of her. It was difficult to hold anyone else because you were desperately holding on yourself. My wife and Kay tried to keep his girl calm and above the water.

Three men above me were trying to break the windows. It seemed a long while and all the time, more and more bodies were coming to the surface. A female crew member told me to put my arm out and see if I could get a lifejacket. She shouted, 'for God's sake, put this on!' but I would not let go of the one thing I was holding onto. You would rip your ears off trying to get the lifejacket over your head. The most ridiculous knotted rope was lowered. There was no way a woman could have got up that rope. A big fat man climbed half way up and then seemed to freeze. He fell back into the water and I never saw him again.

Kay Martin and Georgina Davies were unable to put lifejackets on. Kay said the knotted ropes were 'pathetic'. Kay and Richard gave evidence of how it was impossible to help others because they were so weak, cold and helpless. They were clinging on for their own lives in the darkness with more and more bodies appearing in the water below them.

A two-part ladder was then lowered, but the bottom half fell into the water. Kay Martin managed to grab the rope ladder 2ft away. She was climbing up when her strength faltered. 'A man put my feet on the next rung and then another man pulled me up.' By this time, Kay had to take off the lifejacket she was wearing to get through the porthole.

Lorry driver Peter Hood (51) of Dover, was married to Pauline, and had two sons and one daughter. He was asked to go on a sudden trip to Belgium by his employers two days before the disaster, and was only able to leave a note for his wife, saying that he would be returning on 7 March. He rang her later, saying he was returning a day earlier than expected, on the 1900hrs sailing on 6 March. He died of drowning associated with head injuries.

The body of a man was recovered, carrying a Jersey passport and birth certificate in the name of Cecil Naftel. David West, who ran the EastEnders bar in Zeebrugge, knew the man as Cecil and that he had been given a lift by a lorry driver on the night of the disaster. Police discovered that the passport was false and Interpol were called. The mystery man was identified as 61-year-old Derek Wilson, of Sheffield. It turned out he had three names, two wives and seven children in England and Holland.

His common-law wife, Jean, said they had been together for twenty-eight years and had six children aged between 14 and 27. The family hadn't seen him for seventeen months. 'He was a man in a suitcase', she said. 'He couldn't stay in the same place for very long.' Derek's second wife, Elizabeth, was found in Amsterdam along with another daughter, born in 1953.

Derek had also been married before, and had two children in Sheffield, and may have had another wife and child in Malta – because of his many lives, he was the last victim to be identified.

Mark Glover of Sutton, Surrey, had been on board with friend Richard Higgins (20) of Wallington, Surrey. Both had been in the duty-free shop. Mark saw Richard fall from the shop to the other side of the ship. Richard Higgins may have been the man who Richard Davies saw fall through a window, and his death may also have been witnessed by David Gudgeon, who was with his wife and friends at the duty-free shop, buying a birthday present. The two men from Surrey were walking towards him, when they saw one of the men falling right across the ship straight through a window. Mark Glover was holding onto a metal bar when he saw a girl starting to fall and quickly grabbed her. He held her until they were both rescued.

Pamela Smith, of Gillingham, Kent, had been on board with her husband Richard (33), and family friends Irene Dowie (65) of Chatham, and Irene's daughter Carol (32). They were on the trip to buy cheap drinks for Frank Dowie's 65th birthday party the following week. It was also a birthday trip for Richard Smith, whose birthday was four days before the disaster. Pamela said that she, Irene and Carol were in the bar, and Richard had gone to the duty-free shop. 'I saw Richard flying through the air and under glass windows. He was lying on top of a number of people. He appeared to be reaching out for me. The next moment he was gone.' Then Pamela was swept away and can only remember being too numb to climb the rope ladder. She woke up in the intensive care unit in hospital.

The oldest victim was 78-year-old Austrian-born Julius Gutwurcel of Croydon, Surrey. He was travelling back from Austria with his friend, Major James Stanyer (48), of Farnborough. They were bringing back a new BMW that Julius had bought. Julius had told his wife that they expected to be gone just a couple of days, but there had been a problem with the car radio that needed to be fixed and they had been delayed. They both died.

Survivor Lynette Carvley (37) told the inquest, 'I don't normally have a newspaper because I find them depressing. But I bought the *Sun* specially to save up the tokens.

It was my birthday the following week and it was the first time any of us had been on a cross-Channel ferry. We went for the experience of crossing the Channel.' She saw her mother try to stop a woman rolling away in a wheelchair, and both had crashed through a window. Her mother Sheila McKenny (53) was killed.

David Woodhouse of Thundersley, Essex, fell into the water and came across a woman holding a man. She wouldn't let him go. The man was apparently dead. He and another man held the woman out of water but could not persuade her to let go of the dead man, even when a hose pipe was lowered down to them. Eventually David realised that the woman too had also died. 'I gradually let her go and she slipped away into the water.' He had forty stitches to a head wound. Earlier, he had seen his mother, Nora, confined to a wheelchair, fall over. His father, Derek, tried to grab the chair as did Sheila McKenny, but the momentum was too great and all three were swept away. Witnesses saw the two women sucked through a smashed window into the sea.

Mildred Martin (61) had been aboard with her daughter Susan Hinton (36), and son-in-law Simon (32), all of Basingstoke. The trip had been arranged as a pick-me-up for Susan, who had been ill. Her mother Mildred was with them at the last minute, as others had been unable to go and had dropped out. Mildred's husband, Norman, couldn't go as he'd just started a new job and had been asked to go into work instead. All three died. Mildred's body was found washed up on a Dutch beach on 23 March, seventeen days after the disaster. She was identified because her name was stamped on her dentures.

Coroner Sturt commented on this, 'It is quite an interesting point that if everybody had their names on their dentures it would make identification at this sort of disaster much easier.' Dental expert Derek Clark, who performed port-mortem examinations on victims' teeth for identification purposes, agreed with the coroner that marking dentures with the wearers' names would make the task easier. Clark added that it was a legal requirement in other countries.

Dr Noel Padley answered questions from the jury after Sheila Perkins, of Hastings, gave evidence. She survived more than an hour in the water, while two of her slimly built sons and daughter in law all drowned. Padley said that there were great individual variations as to how long people survived in cold water, depending on their build, amount of activity and type of clothing worn. The chief feature is that people with more fat survive longer. This is why women, because of their build, survived but men didn't. Most clothing, when immersed in water, loses its ability to insulate the body, but some clothing does trap water and retain its insulation qualities. Sheila Perkins said her son Simon (18) floated past her, conscious but dazed, apparently suffering from the cold. She and lorry driver John Wickham tried to put a lifejacket on him, but couldn't get it over his head. Simon was drowned. Sheila gave up after seeing Simon drown, but John pulled her to safety.

Christopher Moy (29) of Cheriton, Folkestone, had been on a day trip with his brother Stephen Smith (33), a London fireman, of Herne Bay, and Steve's wife, Julie.

Chris's wife, Janet, who wasn't on the trip because she suffered from seasickness, said her husband was a keen sportsman and was into weight training, badminton, football and swimming.

Julie was the only survivor. She gave evidence of the last moments of her husband and brother-in-law. Julie saw Chris fall 15ft into the debris of the Blue Riband restaurant. She saw that he had a gash on his forehead but he replied that he was all right. Julie and Steve held onto each other, with her husband telling her, 'whatever happens, hold onto me.' The force of the water crashing through the windows pulled them apart and stripped Julie of all but her underwear. Then she lost sight of Steve and Chris, and thought she was going to die. She resurfaced, but she thought that she had only delayed death by minutes. Chris was identified by his sister, Wendy Golding of Walmer.

Norman and Irene Blanchard, their daughter Sharon Horton, and 25-day old granddaughter, Rebecca, were in the Blue Riband restaurant. Sharon's husband, Maurice, was in a corridor on his way to book a cabin for his family when the *Herald* capsized. Maurice testified that, after grabbing a handrail and climbing to safety, he helped pull other people out. His mother-in-law, Irene, thought that she had been knocked out, but remembered holding onto a table. She felt a hand on her head and a man named Gary pulled her to safety through a window. The rest of her family were all found together in the restaurant when the ferry was righted. Husband Norman drowned, their daughter, Sharon, also drowned, but a blood clot found on her brain suggested that she had been unconscious when she went under water. Baby Rebecca had been knocked unconscious and also drowned. She was identified by her clothing – she had been wearing pink dungarees with Mickey Mouse on the front.

The father of Jonathan Reynolds gave evidence of his son. Alan Reynolds said that Jonathan was a keen sportsman, including weight lifting and judo. 'If anyone was going to get off the ferry, I would have thought he would have done it.' Dr Noel Padley explained that even proficient swimmers would have drowned in a couple of minutes, as the water temperature was only 4°C. Experiments carried out with water at that temperature in a swimming pool showed that some people got into difficulties and sank within one or two minutes.

Common-law husband and wife, Anderson McCameron and Mrs Bettina Picinco of Darlington, Cleveland, had heard the last message broadcast on the tannoy calling for the ship's carpenter to report to the bridge. Having lost his wife, Anderson was convinced that if there had been a message to warn the passengers of what was happening, many lives could have been saved. However, Anthony Cooper, counsel for Townsend Thoresen, said that the call for the carpenter was not a coded message.

Major Edward Crofton (52) of River, had been travelling alone, returning home on leave from 26th Regiment, Royal Engineers, based in Germany. He was married to June for eighteen years. He had phoned her the day before to say he was coming home. Edwards had been in Germany since 1985. He had previously made a visit home at Christmas 1986. His wife said he was very fit and active and was a marathon runner.

On 1 October, Army Corporal Peter Williamson (26) described how he had spent two hours saving passengers inside the *Herald*. He added that he had hung onto tables above the water and hauled passengers up. They had to be encouraged, cajoled and shouted at to get them to climb the rope to safety. He massaged the limbs of a child, man and a woman too cold to move, before they climbed to rescuers above. Williamson said that knotted ropes lowered from windows fell short of the water, and that people did not have enough strength to reach and grab them. He said that proper rope ladders were needed and after a time, one such rope ladder was sent down. Williamson also complained that the lifejackets were too bulky and the straps too difficult for a man's fingers to tie up. He also talked of the lack of light.

He gave evidence that a man started to climb a rescue ladder but then froze. For ten minutes Williamson shouted at him and encouraged him to move, but the man would or could not. Four other witnesses said that more than twenty people tried to get the man off the ladder until Williamson ordered him to be knocked off. The man fell into the water and was never seen again. His identity remains unknown. Coroner's officer, PC Bill Maddocks said, 'Everyone was shouting to get him off the ladder and shaking it. We don't know who the man on the ladder was, or whether he survived. No one knows who was instrumental in pushing him but at least twenty people could have been.'

Crew members

G-deck

Motorman Dean Hayward (27) of Deal, was the first crew member mentioned at the inquest and also the last to be accounted for. His sister, Susan, said that he had suffered from asthma since childhood. He had joined the *Herald* in 1983. His common-law wife, Yvonne Trice, said he took her to work on the morning of the disaster. 'He said he would see me the following day. I didn't see or hear from him again.'

Hayward was last seen in his cabin, off duty, by his colleague Keith Brown, who was on his way to his own cabin to get changed before going for a meal, and they chatted for a while. Hayward would never have a meal on board, and therefore there would be no need for him to change out of his overalls.

Hayward's body was found two months after the disaster, dressed in orange overalls, under wrecked vehicles on the G-deck car deck. Professor Jacques Timperman, pathologist at the University of Ghent, gave the cause of death as drowning and that his body had been crushed. Hayward could have been the 'orange man' that Chief Officer Leslie Sabel saw and assumed to be Mark Stanley, opposite the bow door controls. Coroner's officer, PC Bill Maddocks, gave evidence. He said that a photograph of Hayward looked similar to Stanley. But lawyer Christopher Ewing said the pathologist's description at the post-mortem was not similar. Why was Hayward on

G-deck for twenty minutes after the *Herald* left Zeebrugge with the doors open? Maddocks said that the position of his body made it unlikely that Hayward had moved since the capsize. 'If he was there, he would have been passing through and not hovering by the doors.'

Engine Room

Second Engineer Nick Ray, of Deal, gave evidence in the deaths of two colleagues in the *Herald*'s engine room. Upon sailing, Ray had been on the top car deck repairing a hydraulic air leak. He returned to the engine room which overlooked the engines. With him on the starboard side were Electrical Officer Graham Evans (43), and Motorman Ernest Rodgers (52). Third Engineer Mick Mordue was on the port side. When the ferry began to heel over, Evans called out that the ferry was going over and they should all get out quickly. The three men on the starboard side got out through the watertight doors into the alleyway leading to the main deck stairs. At this point, the *Herald* was listing between 50° and 60°. Rodgers then fell steeply, and slid away into the engine workshop.

Ray said, 'I heard him calling as we were on the stairway, but there was no way we could get back to him. There was nothing we could do.' Ray and Evans managed to get to the stairway, with the ferry tilting at 80°, and onto the car deck. As the lights went out, Evans fell and broke some ribs. They thought it would be better to go back to the stairway and keep out of the way of falling vehicles. Once they were inside, the engine room was in complete darkness. Injured, Evans stayed by the stairs while Ray went to the engine room escape door. There was a loud metallic crash and Ray called out for Evans but there was no reply. 'There was no cry, no shout or anything.' Ray assumed that Evans had ventured along the stairway and fallen off the end of the stairs. In fact, Evans had fallen 50–60ft into the engine workshop, suffering the same fate as Rodgers.

Graham Evans, of St Margaret's, was married and had three children. He was a part-time fireman. His body was recovered on 27 April, when the water had been pumped out by salvage teams, with severe head injuries and broken legs. His injuries meant that he died instantly.

Ernest Rodgers, of Aycliffe, had been married for twelve years and had children from a previous marriage. His wife's statement said that he had been 'fit and strong.' His body was found in the No. 1 engine room on 27 April, with bruising, fractured ribs and a fractured wrist. He died of multiple injuries and drowning.

The coroner asked Ray how he got out. Ray replied, 'With all respect, it's a very long and involved story and I would rather not go into it.'

B-deck, Petty Officers' Mess

Quartermaster Dick Barnard (38) of Tormore Park, Deal, had been at London Road fire station applying to be a retained fireman on the day before the disaster. Fireman

Dave Dadd had been talking to him the night before. 'He was straight down the line. He was a good bloke.' He had been married to Sandra for thirteen years and had children. He was a former third team captain of Betteshanger Rugby Club. Dick often went running, did weight lifting, was a good swimmer and often cycled to work. He had joined the Royal Navy at 16, for six years, and became a TV engineer for Radio Rentals and Rediffusion. He joined Townsend Thoresen in 1979 as a full-time seaman and he joined the *Herald* in September 1986. On the day of the disaster he had given a lift to his colleague, fellow Quartermaster Tom Wilson, also of Deal. Dick was last seen having a meal in the petty officers' mess. He had suffered a head injury, become dazed, vomited and inhaled fluid into his lungs. His body was recovered when the ferry was righted.

Steward David Santer (48) of Folkestone, was married to June for twenty-six years. She said he was very fit and healthy and had just passed a medical. He had all sorts of jobs before joining Townsend Thoresen. He was last seen in the B-deck petty officers' mess having a meal.

Assistant Purser David Disbury (37) of Dover, had been married to Vivienne since 1982, and they had two children. He had worked for the company for fourteen years and was last seen in the petty officers' mess on B-deck before the capsize.

Cafeteria supervisor Daniel Burthe (42) of Folkestone, was married to Mary, a teacher, who said he was fit and healthy and was a good swimmer. On the morning of the disaster, he had taken his children to their grandmother's because they had chickenpox. He worked for seven years on the *Herald* and was last seen in the petty officers' mess. His body was found on A-deck.

Chief Petty Officer Motorman Stanley Darby (57) of Hawkinge, had also been having a meal in the petty officers' mess. His body was recovered a month after the disaster.

B-deck, Galley

Edward Oldfield (54) of Dover, had separated from his wife of twenty-four years, before they divorced. He had two daughters. He spent most of his time off visiting his children and grandchildren in Southampton. He had been with the army in the Suez. He had worked for Cunard and P&O, and was with Townsend Thoresen for eighteen months leading up to the disaster. Edward had served aboard two merchant navy ships during the Falklands War. He was last seen in the *Herald*'s plate house shortly before the capsize.

Steve Helkvist (24) of Victoria Park, Dover, was a cook on board. Cardiff-born, he lived with Townsend Thoresen stewardess, Pauline Mercer, his partner of four years. He had transferred from the *Panther* in July 1986. Steve was last seen by Danny Wyman, sitting against the plate machine in the plate house next to the B-deck galley.

Cook Geoffrey Haney (31) of Dover, was originally from Manchester. He had left school at 16, and joined a liner as a galley boy. In 1977, he met and married a Filipino but they had separated, and his wife and child remained in the Philippines. He called his sister, Susan, to say he would be home on leave soon because the *Herald* was going in for a refit. He choked to death after inhaling his own vomit.

Cook Gerard Brazil (43) of Dover, was born in Sheffield. He had been married to Jill for nineteen years. Described as being in good health, he had just passed a medical and, as a keen angler, he was the junior secretary of the Dover Sea Angling Association. He had worked for British Rail and P&O, and had joined the *Herald* when she first came to Dover. Brazil had been in the B-deck galley at the time of the capsize. His body was found on the same deck. He died of drowning and head injuries, with extensive bruising to his face. The injuries would have knocked him out immediately.

Steward Kevin Worsley-Smith (25), lived in Dover. His mother June Worsley-Smith said her son was a happy and healthy man. He had worked for Townsend Thoresen for one year and three months on the *Herald*. Kevin was last seen in the plate house in the B-deck galley before the capsize, where his body was found. He had drowned. There was confusion at the inquest, after his family queried the post-mortem evidence of the pathologist, Professor James Cameron. When Cameron gave evidence on the colour of his hair, Sturt assured the family that his hair colour, which was dark, would have changed in the four weeks it had been in the water. This followed other detailed information about the body, including his teeth, clothing and valuables. His belongings included a key that fitted his parents' front door. Kevin's body was found with ginger hair, but RAF Wing Commander Ian Hill explained that dark hair would be made lighter and vice versa.

Cook Angus MacKay (43) of Deal, was last seen by his wife, Maureen, when she went to take the dog for a walk. 'I saw him standing on the corner of Foreland Square, waiting for his lift. We chatted for a few minutes and then Percy Calder arrived in his car.' His last words to her were, 'See you tomorrow, love. Don't eat breakfast 'til I get home.' MacKay was last seen in the B-deck galley. His body was recovered a month later. He had drowned. He left his wife and son, also Angus, aged 21.

Catering Steward Percy Calder (45) of Sholdon, had been married to Freda for twenty-six years, and they had three children – Deborah, Vincent and Ashley. He had worked for the company for seven years. Calder was last seen in the same galley as MacKay but his body was found one deck below.

Cook Barry Allen (49) of Folkestone, was married to Patricia. He had spent twenty-two years in the army catering corps, before joining Townsend Thoresen in 1978. Allen was last seen in the galley and had drowned.

Survivor Danny Wyman (17) was on his sixth trip, and was the only one to survive from the B-deck galley. He testified at the inquest that he had been talking to Chief Cook Ivor Moat (36), of Canterbury, when the ferry capsized. Moat told him to hold onto something, and grabbed a railing by the oven. Wyman noticed that the oven was bolted to the floor so he moved along and put his feet on it. Moat had been holding onto a shelf but he fell.

Wyman shouted for help. Another cook told him to stay where he was, and they would come and get him out. He heard a crew member ask Moat if he was OK when he was lying on the floor. 'I didn't hear what he said but he moaned something.' Wyman was swept away when water came in, through the serving hatch into the crews mess, hitting his head several times on the way. Wyman opened his eyes, saw the escape door above him but couldn't reach the glass door containing the key. He escaped when other crew moved the door. Sturt praised him for his bravery and presence of mind.

B-deck, Blue Riband Restaurant

Clayton Dyer (18) of Beauxfield, Whitfield, had joined Townsend Thoresen in 1984, training at Gravesend before going straight to the *Herald*. He lived with his parents. Clayton was last seen in the B-deck Blue Riband restaurant before the disaster. He had multiple small bruises and cuts but not sufficient to cause death. He died of drowning and hypothermia. He was identified by Captain John Kirby. The coroner discounted a report that Clayton Dyer was rescued alive and died in a helicopter. There were no signs of resuscitation attempts, said Dr Noel Padley.

Steward Barry Head (25), of St Margaret's Bay, had been with the *Herald* since its maiden voyage. He was last seen working in the Blue Riband restaurant. His wife gave birth to a son, two months after the disaster, who was named after his father.

On 16 September, evidence was given on the death of head waiter Michael Skippen (29) of Canterbury. He was last seen by Assistant Purser Charles Smith in the Blue Riband restaurant. Skippen had stayed in the restaurant, trying to calm passengers down and help them escape. Andrew Bentley, representing the National Union of Seamen (NUS) testified to Skippen's behaviour. Skippen died of drowning and hypothermia. He left a widow, Lynda.

Steward Nicholas Gough (19) of Aylesham, had been married to Donna for less than a year, and had one daughter, Rebecca. He was last seen in the Blue Riband restaurant. His body was found in the C-deck galley, where he had drowned.

Cashier Merna 'Marie' Richards (31) of Canterbury, had been in the Blue Riband restaurant during the capsize. When her body was recovered a month after the disaster, she was repatriated to her native Mauritius. She had a private memorial service at Canterbury Cathedral.

B-deck, Officers' Mess

Chief Officer Leslie Sabel, of Canterbury, gave evidence at the inquest about several of his colleagues. He had helped to load the vehicle deck before going to the officer's mess, on B-deck port side, and ordering a meal. Second Engineer Chris Thumwood (30) was also there, with third engineer Keith Brown (23), and Senior Storeman Lee Birtles (38). When the *Herald* began to capsize, Sabel rushed to the bridge. Brown fell into the room, and Thumwood went out of the door. A rush of water carried him out of the room and he found himself in a cross-alleyway. That was the last time that Brown saw Thumwood. They had travelled into work together that day.

Chris Thumwood, of Broadstairs, was found drowned in the chief engineer's cabin on A-deck. He was identified by Townsend Thoresen's electrical engineer officer, Kenneth Ellis, who had known Thumwood for ten years. Ellis had identified several members of the crew and was praised by the coroner for his brave and valuable help.

Lee Birtles (38) of Dover, was married to Monica, and had a daughter, Jane. He joined the company in 1973. He had been with the *Herald* since its launch.

Bridge

When Sabel reached the bridge, the ferry was heeling heavily to port. Captain David Lewry was standing at the central control and Richard Hobbs was at the helm. Sabel had just got into the wheelhouse when the ferry capsized. He lost his footing and fell to the port side. He fractured his spine and had rib injuries. Water then came in over his head in pitch darkness, and he pulled free and came to surface. He checked to see who was there – Lewry and Second Officer Paul Morter. A search was made for Hobbs but he couldn't be found. Hobbs had been engulfed by muddy water. Other crew members lowered ropes down and Sabel tied it round himself before they were pulled out in this order – Paul Morter, Leslie Sabel and then David Lewry.

Helmsman Richard Hobbs (23) of Aylesham, left a partner, Rita Wood, and a young daughter. He had died of drowning and hypothermia due to head injuries. He was identified by his brother-in-law, Dover fireman Dennis McCaughan.

Radio Officer Robert Mantle (38) of Deal, was married to Christine for sixteen years. He had worked for the company since 1979. He was fit, but he couldn't swim. Paul Morter was the last person to see him alive, hanging onto the handrail in the alleyway behind the bridge after the capsize. 'This is the last time I ever saw him.' said Paul Morter, who was hanging onto the door handle and cupboards inside the bridge. He died of drowning and hypothermia and was identified by his brother, Brian.

A-deck, Officers' Accommodation

Senior Chief Engineer Robert Crone (38) of St Margaret's, was married for eight years to Gillian, and had two sons and one daughter. Crone, along with Graham Evans, was a retained fireman at St Margaret's. He had worked for the company for twenty-one years. He had drowned. Crone's body was found in his cabin, port side on the top A-deck, in the officers' accommodation near the bow. Earlier evidence said that his body was reported to have been found near the duty-free shop. The inquest was attended by his widow, who sat next to Janet Eades, widow of Brian Eades.

Senior purser Brian Eades (47) of St Margaret's, was married to Janet in 1964, and had two children, Rachel (20) and Matthew (18). He had worked for the company for fifteen years. Charles Smith last saw Eades in the purser's office before the capsize. His body was found there, near the officers' accommodation. Eades had died of drowning associated with head injuries. Both Crone and Eades were identified by Kenneth Ellis.

C-deck, Perfume Shop

Stewardess Lynda Burt (38) of Dover, left a partner and son. Kim Burt said his wife was active, healthy and a strong swimmer. Having worked for Townsend Thoresen for three years, she was last seen outside the information office on C-deck, near the perfume shop where she worked. She died from drowning and hypothermia. She was identified by her son.

C-deck, Duty-free Shop

Duty-free kiosk steward Anthony 'Tony' Spink (41) of Newlands, Whitfield, had been married to wife Janet since 1968. They had one daughter, Nicola (12). Janet last saw Tony when she took him tea in bed, and they said they would see each other the next morning. Tony had previously worked for P&O, British Rail and British Transport Port Police, before joining Townsend Thoresen on the *Free Enterprise III*. He had been with the *Herald* since its launch. He was last seen working in the kiosk. His body was found nearby. He had drowned.

C-deck, Cafeteria

Steward Glen Butler (25) of Folkestone, was married. His wife said he could swim, and he had just passed a medical for life insurance for a mortgage. Glen used to work as an import/export clerk and had been transferred full time to the *Herald* after working summer seasons. He was last seen shortly before the capsize carrying a rubbish bag in the cafeteria on C-deck. Assistant Purser Stephen Homewood then gave evidence about his colleague and friend Glen, who was in the water below him, 'I asked him if he was all right. He said he was. He drifted off. He was dead before he was pulled out of the water. I was so numb with shock I didn't feel the cold.' Butler died of drowning and hypothermia.

Steward Steven Ewell (23) of Folkestone, had met and married Heather in 1982 when he joined the *Herald*. Heather was working as a stewardess on the ferry, but was not on duty that night. He played football for the ship's team and did weight training, and had gold medals for lifesaving. He had completed a survival at sea course in October 1986. Ewell had suffered a head injury and had been knocked out before drowning.

Steward Ian Lawson (24) of Dover, had been married to Sallie since 1984, who described him as a 'very fit, healthy and happy man'. He had played football for Rowley's in the Dover Sunday League. He was last seen at 'harbour stations', at the counter of the cafeteria by Assistant Purser Charles Smith. Lawson's body was found on A-deck near the crew's quarters.

Catering assistant Stephen Sprules (17) of Priory Hill, Dover, was the youngest crew victim. He had attended Astor Secondary School, became a dock runner at Eastern Docks and attended the sea school at Gravesend. Steve started as a catering rating in February 1987, only a month before the disaster. He suffered a head injury that would have knocked him out before he drowned. His body was found on A-deck near the electrician's store. He was last seen in one of the restaurants ten minutes before the capsize.

C-deck, Bar

Steward Alan Medhurst (25) of Dover, left a girlfriend and one child. He had been a keen sportsman and was a good swimmer. Medhurst was last seen serving behind the bar on C-deck. His body was found on the same deck. The pathologist told the inquest that Medhurst had a large bruise on his forehead and could have been knocked out. He drowned.

Steward Egerton Quested (39) of Eythorne, and his wife Sandra had known each other since he was five years old. They had been married for sixteen years. She said he was very healthy. Charles Smith last saw him serving behind the C-deck bar. His body was found on A-deck. Quested had drowned. A bruise on his scalp may have knocked him out.

Senior barman Terry Frame (34) of Deal, had been married to Pauline for three years. He had worked for the company for nine years, and had been on the *Herald* since the maiden voyage. He was last seen by Charles Smith serving behind the C-deck bar.

Barman John Warwick (29) of Folkestone, had been married to Catherine since 1984. He had also worked on the *Herald* since the maiden voyage. He had been serving customers behind the bar on C-deck when the ferry capsized. His body was found nearby.

Assistant Purser Stephen Homewood also gave evidence:

> It was a weird sensation, like a submarine ready to submerge as it ploughed in. It was very quick. I recall seeing a wheelchair going by with a lady. People were screaming and shouting. It was so awful it was something of a relief when the lights went out. It was something I will never forget and it will be embedded in my mind for the rest of my life, especially seeing people at the mortuary afterwards. It makes me appreciate life now. For the rest of your life you have got to live every moment.

Homewood added that a lot of people had drunk alcohol, but only one or two were the worse for wear. He said he was surprised that the emergency lighting had failed after only a few seconds. 'I had always been led to believe that the emergency lighting comes on and stays on for up to two hours. People were still screaming and praying to their faith and looking for a way out.' He also spoke of flickering lights guiding some survivors to a stairway. These were people probably carrying cigarette lighters.

Homewood continued:

I went around giving what help I could. I got hold of a pilot ladder and got it into the
C deck lounges. Mark Stanley and one or two others managed to lower it down in
sections. The main problems the divers had was that there was a sea of yellow lifejackets. The straps had become tangled around the legs and arms of some people.

Homewood was helping a diver hold someone's head above water:

There was someone else in more difficulties so I was holding his head and helping
hold a torch and holding onto a ladder. My foot slipped and I fell into the water.
I didn't realise how cold it was until I was in there myself. I was only in there for
a short time. One or two people were holding onto me, seeing me as between life
and death and I felt myself being pulled under. I had to secure myself to the ladder
to pull myself out.

Commander, and Townsend Thoresen director, Anthony Barnett gave evidence of
previous 'open door' incidents which had been reported:

1983 The *Pride of Free Enterprise* left No. 5 berth at Dover Eastern Docks with
the bow and stern doors open. The assistant bosun had failed to close them. They
were eventually closed before the ferry left the harbour. The assistant bosun was
disciplined.
1984 Two occasions were referred to when, again, the *Pride*, on the Zeebrugge
run, sailed with the bow or stern doors open. This was probably caused by job
changes from the Calais run.
1985 Townsend Thoresen Deputy Chief Superintendent John Alcindor was looking out of his company office windows when he saw the ferry *Tiger* leaving the
Eastern Docks with the stern doors open. The ferry was just outside the harbour
when Alcindor used a radio to call the captain, who said he was already aware. The
captain blamed a mechanical problem.
1986 The chief officer saw the assistant bosun at the door control panel and went
to check the cargo. He helped some disabled passengers into a lift when he looked
back and saw the inner doors were closed. The assistant bosun was gone. A passing
sister ship radioed to say the outer doors were still open. The chief officer checked
and found that the assistant bosun had returned to the outer doors after making an
'urgent call of nature.'
A month before the disaster, in February 1987 Alcindor saw the *Free Enterprise VI*
leaving Eastern Docks with the stern doors open, on its way for refit. He again
radioed the captain and then saw the doors starting to close. Barnett said the *Pride*
had no indicator lights but the *Tiger* and *Free Enterprise VI* did.

At the inquest on 8 October, it was announced by Sturt that it would be a criminal offence for passenger ferries to leave their berths with their bow or stern doors open. The new regulations would come into effect from 27 November.

Townsend Director Anthony Barrett, also commodore in the royal naval reserve, and chairman of the ferry section of the General Council of British Shipping, confirmed that alterations had been made to berths at Dover and Calais. This allowed ferries to shut their doors immediately. He further added that all Townsend ferries now have indicator lights on the bridge, and a positive reporting system had been implemented for communications between vehicle deck and bridge regarding the closing of the doors.

Under cross-examination, Barrett confirmed that the deck loading officer would wait to see that the doors were closed by the crew member given the responsibility. Barrett further testified that he would be passing on ferry safety suggestions made by Wing Commander Ian Hill, such as the redesign of lifebelts which many survivors had criticised. These suggestions would be forwarded through the Shipping Council to the Department of Transport.

WPC Maxine Smythe gave evidence about the identification forms police used. Forms were filled, in the UK, with information and descriptions of the missing given by the relatives. These were then compared with forms filled in by the authorities in Belgium, who had recovered the bodies. Some forms were designed so that by placing one UK form on top of a Belgian form, it would become immediately obvious whether they were the same person.

Herald crew member, Kenneth Ellis, of Whitfield, gave evidence at the inquest about the identification of many of the crew victims, and had viewed bodies that had been in the water for one month. Sturt thanked him, 'I know how distressing it was for you and your colleagues who carried out visual identifications. I am extremely grateful to you … I am sorry to have caused you so much anguish.'

Professor Jacques Timperman, pathologist at the University of Ghent, performed more than 120 post-mortems. He gave evidence at the inquest, while his wife sat with him. Sturt told Timperman, 'We are immensely indebted to you, as are the people of Kent to all your people.'

Coroner Richard Sturt explained that RAF pathologist, Wing Commander Ian Hill, would perform a detailed study of where everyone was on the *Herald* when it capsized, to determine the safest place to be if an incident happened again – where they were sitting or standing, which direction they were facing and where they last saw those who died. At one stage, one witness said that she was on the starboard side, but her statement indicated she was on the port side. Later, she said that she was on the side which went up in the air so her evidence was changed to the starboard side again.

Rescue workers were critical of the lack of equipment available to them on the night of the disaster. Elias Van Maren, the chief officer of the dredger *Sanderus*, the first vessel on the scene, and Captain Malcolm Shakesby, chief officer of the freight ferry *Duke of Anglia*, gave evidence. Shakesby said, 'One of the crew members told me that one of the ferries had capsized. At that time there was disbelief.' He ordered his crew to dress warmly and report to the bridge as lookouts. Shakesby then led some of his crew in a lifeboat to look for survivors. At one stage, he tried to manoeuvre the lifeboat into one of the flooded vehicle decks. He and his crew helped to provide blankets for survivors, before they were transferred from the *Herald* to the rescue tugs. Shakesby said, 'The first thing I can readily remember, which I thought was commendable, was that most of the *Herald*'s deck crew members were still assisting getting people out.'

More than four hours later, Shakesby was asked to take over co-ordinating duties for the rescue operation. He called for plans of the *Herald* and more portable lighting. He also ordered a systematic deck search for the living. Many people were too cold or tired even to keep the rope loop under their arms. Some slipped back into the water. In one case, a young girl, believed to be Nicola Simpson, was being pulled up on a looped rope:

> We nearly had her up to the window and I almost had her head when she fell back in. It was only the prompt action of one of the divers who jumped in immediately that got her out. I think she would have drowned had it not been for the diver's prompt action.

People also slipped out of straps that were attached to helicopter winch lines. Eventually the last two *Herald* crew members, Stephen Homewood and Tom Wilson, were told to go ashore. 'Mr Homewood was reluctant to go.' Shakesby said he felt that some divers were milling round. 'At one stage we had so many divers we did not know what to do with them. A lot of them were arriving without underwater torches.' He said more first aid and medical staff were needed to tend to survivors. 'It was impossible for us to state if they were alive or dead.' Two rescuers spent half an hour trying to resuscitate a man who was already dead.

After the last survivors – the three lorry drivers – were found, Shakesby and his team left, as the situation inside the ferry was getting too dangerous for them to continue. One of the team, Paul Gilbert, of Bearsted, said his crew were an inspiration. 'We were warm but most of them had had a thorough soaking and had been on there for a long time and were in shock. We looked at them and saw them working in such a selfless way.'

Another of the *Duke of Anglia* crew, Clifford Thoroughgood of Hawkinge, said sometimes the helicopters caused danger to rescuers and survivors on the *Herald*'s side. 'They were so low you had to lie down flat to stop being blown over. There was no communication between the ferry and the 'copters.' He agreed that many of the divers seemed happy to stand back and let ill-equipped seamen get on with the job. Thoroughgood told of one tragic incident in which a man was pulled out of one broken window, badly shaken but alive. 'In the darkness he stepped back and fell through another window. I don't think he survived.'

Alexander Black, bosun of the *European Trader*, at Zeebrugge, said the ferry was discharging freight vehicles at Zeebrugge. Upon hearing about the capsize, the ferry put to sea immediately to help and, once at the wreck, a lifeboat was launched. He and Second Officer Nigel Shepherd, who knew the layout of the *Herald*, later went aboard to help search decks. At the inquest, they called for lighting that would stay on, no matter what happened. They testified that ships needed to be better equipped for rescue, and more training at ports was needed to deal with such emergencies, along with better co-ordination.

On 3 October 1987, Coroner Richard Sturt began to sum up. He told the jury that potentially defective decisions (standing orders, indicator lights etc.), or non-decisions were 'too remote' to be considered to lead to an 'unlawful killing' verdict. 'You may want to make a verdict which undoubtedly implies that somebody has been guilty of one of the most serious criminal offences in the whole spectrum! But you must not name anybody. That is the rule.'

He outlined the verdicts available to the jury:

You can probably ignore 'murder' in all but one of the cases, [referring to Corporal Peter Williamson, who knocked a man off a ladder who'd blocked everyone's escape for ten minutes]. We now have further evidence that there were dozens of people who were trying to get him off the ladder. They were all pushing and shaking. They succeeded in getting him off the ladder but we do not know who he was or if he survived. This is all far too speculative for you to consider 'unlawful', failing in respect of 'murder'. Killing as an act of self-preservation or for the procreation of other lives is not necessarily murder at all and it may be said to have been a natural and probable consequence of what happened in the first place – the capsize.

Natural causes might be considered in the case of a girl (Dolvis Wellington-Fray) who died in hospital in London, in May 1987, from Deep Vein Thrombosis (DVT) after breaking her neck. 'I think natural causes are improbable.'

In the case of 'accidental death', the jury had to be satisfied that it was 'more probable than not' that death was caused unintentionally.

The jury needed to be sure of the facts, and of the ingredients needed for an 'unlawful killing' verdict.

There is a distinct difference in the amounts of certainty that are involved. For 'unlawful killing' you must be sure that the death results from an act, or omission, of any individual or several individuals who had a duty to act. The act, or omission, must be a substantial cause of the death. There must be no aggregation of several acts by different individuals. They must not be too remote from the actual death.

Even then, you are still only able to bring in a verdict of 'unlawful killing' if you are satisfied that there was gross negligence or recklessness. Carelessness is not sufficient. There must be an obvious risk and the person must have ignored the risk.

Sturt also spoke of 'open' verdicts, but he said that, in his opinion, a 'lack of care' verdict was not appropriate. He also advised them not to return 'accidental' verdicts on some, and 'misadventure' on others. 'The law you must accept from me, and the facts are entirely a matter for you. You have to give separate consideration to each death.'

The Zeebrugge Inquest costs at the time were thought to be around £60,000 – at least half going towards jurors and witnesses. Another £30,000 was spent on hiring Dover Town Hall, specialist recording and phone equipment, and the temporary appointment of specialist and typing staff. The cost was borne by Kent County Council and was due to be discussed by Kent's Fire and Public Protection Committee on 6 October.

On 7 October 1987, company counsellors met to discuss the proposed funding of the *Herald* Assistance Unit, which had already visited over 140 families. At that point, the unit was expected to close in mid-1988, by which time costs were expected to be £300,000. Already operational for six months, the unit had been divided into two teams, one based in east Kent, and the other covering everywhere else.

That same day, Sturt strongly criticised Second Officer Paul Morter during his summing up, for failing to answer the most simple of questions while giving evidence. This caused Sturt 'disquiet', telling the jury, 'I was disappointed, and I dare say you were.' Several hundred witnesses had all been willing to talk about their horrifying experiences but Morter was not. This gave the impression that he had something to hide.

Before the jury retired to the hotel, Sturt said that the roles of only three of the crew were to be considered if the jury was deciding on 'unlawful killing' as their verdict – Lewry, Sabel and Stanley. He told them to disregard the role of Kirby and Develin, as they were far too remote from the capsize. Sturt told them that in order to return verdicts of 'unlawful killing', the jury must be sure that an individual committed a crime due to gross negligence.

During the Zeebrugge Inquest, 800 witnesses were called and 430 statements were read. 348 witnesses gave oral evidence. Sturt said told the jury:

I hope the burden on you listening to this has not been unsustainable, and the therapeutic effect of humour has been of assistance. We feel desperately sorry for the bereaved. You may feel that Townsends should be held responsible and made to pay. You must understand these feelings and then put them away. We must be totally objective. Ours is a fact-finding tribunal. You would have needed hearts of stone not to be moved by the stories you have heard and the cumulative effect on you must have been hard for you to cope with. A case as big as this one has a way of setting precedents. The fact it happened abroad brought about a whole host of problems.

Sturt said that the inquest was unique, not only for size but its nightmare quality and almost unbearable grief:

> This is a matter of undoubted international interest and it is important that the press and media are given accurate information. The problems I have encountered have brought into focus the differences of the law relating to coroners. The greatest difficulty and responsibility for me has been in selecting the amount of scope of the evidence I put before you. I hope you will agree with me that we have presented to you a clear account of what happened. Consider only the relevant evidence, and nothing else. The witnesses you have heard are the ones I have decided you should hear. Do not consider what you have read or heard elsewhere.

Referring to the Zeebrugge formal investigation which opened seven weeks after the disaster, Sturt said that the Sheen Report was full of material that could not be relevant to the inquest. He referred to the 'daily catalogue of anguish'. He asked how many of the bereaved had showed signs of release when they'd finished giving evidence. Most had said that being there and telling their stories was therapeutic.

Sturt then referred to the crew survivors:

> You may have feelings of guilt, as I did, that we were putting on parade a group of more or less broken men and making them go through it all again. You may feel nothing but sympathy for the crew, particularly those who may be held responsible. But again, you have to put that out of your mind. Their anguish must be every bit as great as that of the bereaved.

The jury heard eighteen days of evidence, recorded on ninety cassette tapes and transferred by coroner's secretaries to more than 2,000 pages of transcript. Once verdicts were returned, each jury member and the coroner would have to sign 188 inquisition forms. He told the jury, 'You have coped absolutely marvellously. I am proud of you.'

On Thursday 8 October 1987, Sturt praised Kent Police for their help in the aftermath. A team of police officers was headed by Detective Inspector Alan Scott. In liaison with the authorities in Zeebrugge, they managed to produce an accurate and 'guaranteed' list of survivors to assist relatives – previous lists had proved wholly inaccurate, and some families had been told their loved ones were safe only to learn later that they were officially missing. He said that there were difficulties finding out who had died or survived because lists had been issued by seven different agencies. The lists were examined and calculated until a guaranteed list was produced.

Sturt told Scott, 'Nobody could have served the police force or the public more than you and your officers did. I am extremely grateful.' Alan Scott's team had helped with identification procedures, comforting grieving relatives and escorting all of the recovered bodies back to Dover.

Scott in turn gave praise to four Townsend Thoresen crew members, who had taken on the task of identifying the bodies of their colleagues – Ken Ellis, Barry Wick, David Thomasson and Richard Toptalo. 'They were introduced into an environment that was completely alien to them and they were deeply distressed. They are still deeply affected by it. No praise is too high for them.'

Also thanked by the inquest were the chief officer of the RORO ferry *Duke of Anglia*, Malcolm Shakesby, and his crew, who raced to the scene. After arriving, Shakesby took charge of co-ordinating rescue efforts on board the *Herald*. He oversaw many rescues, including the three trapped lorry drivers on H-deck. Shakesby praised Townsend officers Bill Tate and Nigel Forbes for their assistance during the search.

Two crewmen aboard the Townsend freighter *European Trader* had gone aboard the *Herald* to search for survivors. Bosun Alex Black and Second Officer Nigel Shepherd were also recognised at the inquest for their efforts.

Sturt told the jury that he'd run great risk of invalidating the whole inquest. 'I must not be guilty of an insufficiency of evidence, and if I admit irrelevant evidence your verdict might be quashed. This is a very serious risk.'

On Wednesday 7 October, Kent County Council met to discuss the proposed funding of the *Herald* Assistance Unit, which was expected to be wound up in mid-1988, after visiting more than 140 families who were directly affected by the disaster. The previous day, the expected costs of £60,000 for the inquest had been discussed by Kent County Council's Fire and Public Protection Committee.

The Verdict

On 8 October 1987, verdicts of 'unlawful killing' were returned on the 188 victims.

Most of them died quickly from drowning and hypothermia in sea water that was only 4°C. No deaths were due to toxic substances.

The verdict opened the possibility of a criminal prosecution by the Director of Public Prosecutions (DPP). Sturt said that the verdicts could be returned only if the jury believed a criminal act had been committed, and there had been gross negligence. Sturt had stressed that the inquest was to establish the facts and not apportion blame, but insisted that only the acts of three crewmen could have led to the deaths. Sturt did not comment after the verdicts were returned, but said that papers would be sent to the Prime Minister and Minister for Transport as well as the DPP. Families' solicitor Michael Napier said 'relatives will be hoping the director will take this as seriously as one would expect him to'.

Transport Secretary Paul Channon said that no one was immune from prosecution, but any decision was the DPP's alone. Earlier that week, with the Zeebrugge inquest verdicts looming, the Divisional Court had judged that future prosecutions for 'corporate manslaughter' might be feasible. The decision was embargoed until the verdicts were returned so as to not influence the jury.

Sturt referred to two disputes between relatives about the disposal of bodies. Sturt was called to rule, 'They were not among my happiest memories'.

Sturt congratulated coroner's officer, PC Bill Maddocks and his Dover based colleagues, Inspector Bob Fautley and PC Mick Kearney, who had worked flat out since the night of the disaster to prepare evidence for the inquest. The team had prepared 1,500 statements, involving pathology and background evidence, more than 500 witness notifications, and informed more than 100 solicitors firms of the dates that their parties were being called to the inquest. They had all liaised with the pathologists, dental experts and the *Herald* welfare groups and support teams. The three policemen had set up the incident room in Dover. Between that incident room and another one set up at Police HQ in Maidstone, they dealt with more than 7,500 calls in the first forty-eight hours. Each of the 188 files for individual victims contained at least sixteen pages of evidence, numbering a total of more than 15,000 pages.

Assistant Bosun Mark Stanley, the man responsible for closing the bow doors, was said to be 'totally shocked'.

Trial

In October 1987, the Zeebrugge Disaster Inquest had returned verdicts of 'unlawful killing' on 188 victims. The 189th victim was returned to Germany, and the bodies of four people were never found. The verdicts prompted hopes amongst the victims' families and survivors that there would be a trial of the men who had been identified in the inquiry as being responsible for the disaster.

On 11 September 1988, a year later and with no trial in sight, Peter Spooner of the *Herald* Families Association said that the families were considering a private prosecution of two P&O boards of directors.

On 23 November 1989, much to the dismay of many of the relatives of the victims of the ferry disaster, Belgian judge Arthur D'Hoest in Bruges ruled that Belgium would not hold a trial over the *Herald of Free Enterprise* disaster, because the ship and all of its victims were British. The judge had been working on the case for two years, but said that thousands of pages of evidence would be handed over to British officials. Spokesman, Filip Van Belle added that the decision was based on a 1961 international treaty stipulating that trials in such disasters should be held in the country of the ship's flag. He also said that two trials would be too confusing and a waste of time.

On 18 December 1989, P&O and seven defendants appeared at No. 4 court-room at Highbury Corner Magistrate's Court for committal proceedings. All of the defendants elected to opt for an 'old-style' committal with evidence and exhibits, and witnesses being called. Sabel and Stanley were released on unconditional bail until 29 December by chief metropolitan magistrate Sir David Hopkin.

The *Herald*'s chief officer and assistant bosun were told that they would have to return to court when evidence against the other defendants had been completed, and would be committed for trial if there was sufficient evidence to go before a jury.

If found guilty, P&O would be subjected to an unlimited fine. Individuals could face life imprisonment. There were no pleas. The summonses accused them of the manslaughter of four victims – Alison Gaillard, Martin Spooner, Richard Barnard and Maria Richards. Alison was the daughter of the *Herald* Families' Association (HFA) chairman Maurice de Rohan, and Martin was the son of Peter Spooner, the HFA's secretary.

Stanley and Sabel had been content to accept committal where no witnesses were to be called, but the others were not happy to accept this. P&O said it did not intend to contest committal.

On Monday, 10 September 1990, the Zeebrugge disaster trial began at the Old Bailey, and was expected to last for five months. The eight defendants, appearing before Mr Justice Sir Michael John Turner and a jury of ten men and two women, were:

P&O European Ferries (formerly Townsend Thoresen)
The system in operation for the *Herald* 'was inherently unsafe'.

Mark Stanley (Assistant Bosun)
It was his job on the day to close the *Herald*'s bow doors. He didn't because he was asleep in his cabin.

Leslie Sabel (Chief Officer)
It was his job on the day to supervise the closing of the bow doors, but he didn't and the doors were not closed.

David Lewry (Master)
He was on the bridge in charge of the *Herald* when she sailed out of Zeebrugge with her bow doors open.

John Kirby (Senior Master)
Senior master of the *Herald* (not on duty). He was responsible for co-ordination, for orders, instructions and the safe operation of the ship which went to sea with her bow doors open.

John Alcindor (Deputy Chief Marine Superintendent)
He received certain suggestions regarding lights on the bridge to indicate the state of doors. He did nothing to implement the changes.

Jeffrey Develin (Chief Marine Superintendent)
He failed to prevent excessive pressure from the operations department on masters and chief officers, that the ship should sail on or ahead of schedule, jeopardising the loading officers' duty. He also failed to require masters to report 'open door' incidents, and failed to provide clear, workable and safe instructions as to the closing of the bow doors. He was also accused of failing to order bridge indicator lights to be installed.

Wallace Ayres (Technical Director of the 'Think Tank' Department) (took early retirement three weeks after disaster). He failed to respond to requests for lights to be fitted. He failed to fit indicator lights to vessels in the fleet and, in particular, failed to respond to two requests for indicator lights on the bridge of ships.

They were represented by:

P&O	Sir Jonathan Caplan (later, by Sydney Kentridge QC)
Mark Stanley	Stephen Miller
Leslie Sabel	Christian Du Cann
David Lewry	Philip Hackett
John Kirby	Alan Mainds
John Alcindor	George Carman QC
Jeffrey Develin	Anthony Scrivener QC
Wallace Ayres	Richard Du Cann QC

All of the defendants pleaded innocent in the trial, which was largely considered a test case. Relatives had fought for more than three years to bring only the second case of 'corporate manslaughter' against a British company. The first, against a construction company in 1965, ended in acquittal.

The twelve-page indictment focused on the 'obvious and serious risk' of setting sail with the doors open, and the reasons why the doors were left open. To keep the case simple, the eight accused faced charges of unlawfully killing one passenger, 27-year-old Alison Gaillard.

On day three of the trial (12 September) all eight defendants denied a charge of gross negligence and breach of duty by P&O. They all denied killing passenger Alison Gaillard, who was the subject of eight sample counts of manslaughter.

The Old Bailey heard that there were 454 passengers and eighty crew members aboard the ferry. It was alleged that an 'obvious and serious risk' existed and that the ship sailed with its bow doors open and 'being trimmed by the head, capsized and

caused death – as in fact occurred'. The accused either 'gave no thought to the possibility of there being any risk or, having recognised there was some risk, went on to
take it and behaved with gross negligence.'

David Jeffreys, prosecuting, said the most obvious reason for the capsize was the
doors issue, but there were other contributing factors.

On the eighth day (19 September), Bosun Terry Ayling told the Old Bailey how
Lewry and Sabel had to be 'forcibly thrown off the *Herald*' because they refused to
leave their posts on the bridge.

Stephen Solley QC asked Ayling if he had saved his client's life (Lewry). Ayling
assured, 'along with others, yes'.

The court then heard about Lewry's injuries. Ayling spoke of Lewry:

> He couldn't stand properly and he had to have one of the able seamen standing
> with him to prop him up. When I came back to him he still stood there refusing to
> go. He was in a shocking state and I had to get a couple of ABs to carry him along
> and put him on one of the tugs. He was an excellent skipper, and a captain through
> and through.

Ayling also told court that the normal practice upon leaving Zeebrugge was that the
bow doors were closed by the assistant bosun before the ship reached the open sea,
but that it was not necessary as soon as the ferry had left the berth.

Able Seaman Leigh Cornelius, who was later awarded the Queen's Medal and was
now working as a lorry driver, testified that he was about to leave the crew's mess
when the ferry capsized and the ship plunged into darkness.

Cornelius was cross-examined by the defence counsel, Gilbert Gray QC.
Cornelius stayed in the icy water with his foot wedged in a locker to form the base
of a human ladder. Brian Kendal stood on his shoulders to form an escape route.
Mark Squire than climbed on Kendal's shoulders and both he and Kendal escaped. 'I
stayed put and the water was rising to my chest'.

'You were the ladder and the bridge over and upon which many people made
their escape?'

Cornelius explained that he had stayed in position until the icy water meant that
he started to lose the feeling in his legs. 'I did what I could for an unconscious woman
and when I could do no more, I got myself out onto the starboard side of the ship'.
He was then pulled up on a rope and smashed windows and hauled passengers up.
Gray praised Cornelius for his 'undoubted valour' and Judge Justice Turner thanked
him for taking his mind back to the event. 'It must have been very painful for you.'

As 'a favour' to Stanley, Cornelius revealed that he had closed the bow doors on
occasions to save Stanley from doing so, if the lower G-deck was loaded first.

Terry Ayling was questioned by the defence counsel, Alun Jones QC, 'What would
happen if Stanley was too tired to be at his harbour stations and shut the doors?'

Ayling replied, 'I just can't imagine Mark doing it.'

Ayling was then questioned about the capsize. 'At first, it was just normal, then it just didn't stop. When she first started going over I heard glass go in the carpenter's cabin, and then everything started to go off the cabin table. I was thrown into the alleyway but the ship still carried on going over.'

Gail Cook hung onto a fixed seat above him, and he screamed at her to let go and get out. He started to drag Gail (who had a badly injured ankle) along a corridor, using the wall as the floor. They came to a bend in the alleyway and were faced with a wall. He was unable to lift Gail over it, but then was helped by Michael Tracy, pulling her up. 'Then the bulkheads started to collapse around us'. They crawled through a 2ft wide space, and spotted a wooden door above their heads. They were joined by Mark Stanley. 'Between the three of us we managed to get Gail up and through the door.'

Ayling went on to rescue Lewry, Sabel and Morter. He spent the next two hours rescuing passengers. He left Townsend Thoresen at the end of 1987, and was now employed by HM Customs and Excise. Asked if Stanley was a reliable assistant bosun, Ayling replied, 'He was the best I've ever worked with.'

On the trial's eleventh day, the court heard about events on the bridge. Present were Lewry, Wilson, Hobbs and Ayling. Hobbs was on the port wing. The first sign of trouble was the sound of a fire alarm. Quartermaster Wilson was investigating this when the ferry capsized. Lewry tried to force *Herald* into reverse.

'The captain pulled the combinator handles back from the forward position to go astern. He shouted "what's happening?" and called for someone to close the internal watertight doors. Water came onto the bridge quite quickly, and I had no idea at the time what had happened'. Wilson denied that Hobbs was having trouble steering. Wilson was one of four crew awarded the Queen's Gallantry Medal.

On the twelfth day of the trial, Gail Cook's written statement was read out to court. She had visited Mark Stanley, who was staying in the same hospital, the next morning (after the disaster), 'He was in a dreadful state, crying. He sat on the side of the bed and said to me, "It is my fault, I did not close the doors".' She went on to explain how she got off the ferry, being taken onto E-deck, and walked across the vessel onto a tug. 'I led passengers onto the tug. Les Sabel was already on it, and appeared to be in shock. He was completely numbed and did not speak.'

Others crew members gave evidence – Stephen Greenaway and Billy Walker (both aft mooring gang), Mark Squire and Tony Down (forward mooring gang) and Keith Brown (engineer).

Passenger Rosina Summerfield told the court how she returned to the car deck after the ferry had left. 'There was no one else on the car deck, and I was down there for about five to seven minutes'. She was with friend, Julie Clark, on the second flight of stairs back up when the ship started to capsize.

Assistant Purser Stephen Homewood also testified that, when he had come across Mark Stanley on the upturned hull, Stanley had admitted leaving the doors open.

On the thirteenth day, evidence was heard from Colin Chandler, now a training manager. He was a loading officer with Townsend Car Ferries from 1978 until January 1989. He considered it his job to ensure the decks were secure before sailing. In October 1983, Chandler had to close the doors on the *Pride of Free Enterprise* as it left Dover for Calais, because Assistant Bosun Richard Samuels hadn't turned up on the vehicle deck. Samuels had been brought before the master and given a formal warning.

Townsend Thoresen whistle-blowers, on board freighter ferry *European Trader* had seen the *Free Enterprise VII* leaving Dover at about midnight, three weeks before the disaster. Relief Quartermaster John Byrne, now an exercise instructor, had been on the bridge and was waiting 3 miles outside Dover for clearance to harbour. 'As she started to come out through the pier heads there was an unusual amount of light from the bow section. I thought, first off, that somebody had been working on the port side of the ship when it was in port. Then I saw the outer bow doors were wide open.' P&O counsel, Sydney Kentridge QC, suggested that the doors were only open 2ft but Byrne was adamant that his eyes had not deceived him. 'When I looked they were wide open.' Byrne's claim was backed up by Quartermaster Alan Randall, 'It looked as though the inner doors were open as well, there was that much light.'

Day fourteen brought a warning from Mr Justice Turner – he told the jury not to make any private visits to see, at first hand, cross-Channel ferry operations. He said any juror who took such a trip should not draw on the experience for the purposes of analysing the evidence given at the trial.

On day fifteen, Graham Hartwell, former master of the *Pride*, who retired in 1988 for health reasons after fifteen years, told the Old Bailey how he strongly supported the idea of bow and stern door indicator lights to be fitted on the bridge, but that the idea was rejected by management. He had recommended lights.

The *Pride*'s maintenance master, Captain Anthony de Ste Croix, had also supported the fitting of lights:

> I had strong feelings that they would overcome the problem of the doors being left open and stop it happening again. I did regard it to be of importance because of the sequence of events that could follow, on previous 'open door incidents'. It was something that was against normal practice and instruction and something that had to be stopped.

The recommendation memo was sent from Ste Croix in October 1986 to Ron King (senior electrician with P&O European Ferries, then Townsend Car ferries). This memo was then passed to Deputy Chief Marine Superintendent John Alcindor. Alcindor responded that the idea was a 'no-go'. He said that if the doors were not closed, it should be a disciplinary matter. He said that full use should be made of an alarm which sounded if the outer bow doors were open but could not be seen from the vehicle deck because the inner watertight doors were closed. Graham Hartwell told the court that he was not aware that such an alarm even existed.

The court heard that Lewry had asked fellow master, Alan Rutherford, to consider switching duties on 6 March 1987 so he could attend a social engagement but Rutherford had to decline because he had a social engagement too. In view of what happened that night, '… it was one of the most significant social events I had ever attended.'

Philip Hackett, Lewry's counsel, suggested to the prosecution witness, and former master, Graham Hartwell, that Lewry was ignorant of previous incidents of 'open door' sailings. Hartwell said that he assumed all such incidents would automatically be reported to the company's shore-based marine department, who in turn informed masters on other vessels. 'The marine department's role was to inform the fleet when matters arose.' Hartwell revealed that during 'turn around' times in port, ship's officers and crew had to 'extend themselves to the maximum' during peak season, in order to stay on or close to sailing schedules.

On day sixteen, the court heard how Alan Rutherford had served as the *Herald's* master for virtually all of its seven years in service. He was responsible for the on-board safety and training of the 400 or so crew of the vessel.

Rutherford played a leading role in helping the crew survivors and bereaved. He told the jury of his 'complete and total surprise' when the *Herald* left port with its bow doors open. 'I just could not believe that it had happened. I thought the system was a safe one.' He said he was only told of the other 'open door' incidents four days after the disaster. He said, given good weather and calm seas, it would be possible to safely sail a ferry like the *Herald* with the bow doors open, that nothing more than spray would come onto the car deck. He said that he could still do this if the vessel was ballasted at the bow, or trimmed by the head (as the *Herald* was on the night of the disaster). Rutherford also said there were no problems with the visual bow door closing operations, where the chief officer sighted the assistant bosun at or near the controls. The three *Spirit* vessels completed 60,000 cross-Channel trips, 5,000 of them between Dover and Zeebrugge.

Cross-examined by George Carman QC, representing Alcindor, Rutherford agreed the disaster was a 'freak constellation of unhappy coincidences'. When asked if the company had sacrificed safety for profit, he said, 'It was quite the reverse.'

'Positive reporting' is when the master is told by the loading officer that the bow/stern doors on the vehicle deck were safely closed before sailing (as opposed to 'negative reporting' where the master is only informed if there is a problem). Hartwell said that there was no system of positive reporting in operation before the *Herald* disaster, and said he would only have demanded a verbal report from the crewman responsible for loading (usually the chief officer) in relation to any cargo being secure (and then only in rough weather). Hartwell said that he and his colleagues had never given any thought to the idea of positive reporting in relation to the doors. He said he and other masters had jurisdiction to introduce such a system on board. 'I know it sounds amazing after the event but we just did not think about it.' He added that indicator lights would have solved the problems of open-door incidents.

On day eighteen, Rutherford told the Old Bailey that the *Herald* had more life vests and lifeboat accommodation than was necessary, as laid down by the Department of Transport requirements. He also said the ferry was fitted with emergency chutes, similar to those used on aircraft.

Defendant Wallace Ayres told the court of his functions. He was instrumental in the decision to fit chutes, known as the Marine Escape System, to *Spirit* class ships.

On 19 October, Judge Sir Michael John Turner told the jury to acquit P&O European Ferries (Dover) Ltd, three former directors and two crewmen. The case against two other crewmen was dropped, after the prosecution said it would drop their case against them, '… evidence already called is such that you, properly directed, could not properly convict the company and the five most senior defendants.'

On 24 October 1990, the Zeebrugge disaster trial collapsed when all eight defendants were directed to be acquitted by Mr Justice Turner at the Old Bailey. The prosecution had failed to prove its case that they were guilty of 'manslaughter'. There had been several days of legal arguments in the absence of the jury. It raised doubts about the viability of ever prosecuting a company for 'corporate manslaughter'. The only other case brought against a company for corporate manslaughter in 1965 also resulted in acquittal. The trial had been expected to last five months. It took only twenty-seven days.

P&O chairman, Sir Jeffrey Sterling, sent a message to the company's staff worldwide:

> I take no pleasure in saying that those directly involved in the cause of the accident have and will suffer for the rest of their lives, and I strongly believe no good purpose will be served by prosecuting anybody who was at Zeebrugge or directly involved in the aftermath of the tragedy, as I was. [We] will never forget its awful toll of grief. The reputation of this company has been built up over one hundred and fifty years on trust – our responsibility is maintaining that trust.

Former defendant, Wallace Ayres, speaking to the *Independent* for a twenty-fifth anniversary story, said:

> It was, as far as I'm concerned, a monstrous injustice and a monstrous waste of money, the fact that I was on trial. It's in the past, but it's still in the present. The *Herald of Free Enterprise* was well built and it was misused. It was just one of those tragic accidents.

6

LEGACY

Advancement

In 1989 the UK's Marine Accident Investigation Branch (MAIB) was formed, as a direct result of the *Herald of Free Enterprise* disaster. The MAIB is part of the Department of Transport and can investigate any accident occurring in UK waters, regardless of the nationality of the vessel(s) involved, and accidents involving UK registered ships worldwide. Their empowering body is the Merchant Shipping Act 1995 and, like their older counterparts, the Air Accident Investigation Branch, they report to the Secretary of State for Transport. The MAIB website states:

> The role of the MAIB is to contribute to safety at sea by determining the causes and circumstances of marine accidents and working with others to reduce the likelihood of such accidents recurring in the future. Accident investigations are conducted solely in the interest of future safety. The Branch does not apportion blame and it does not establish liability, enforce laws or carry out prosecutions.

The MAIB, based in Southampton, consists of four teams of experienced accident investigators, comprising a principal inspector and three inspectors from the nautical, engineering, naval architecture and fishing sectors.

The Zeebrugge trial paved the way for the Corporate Manslaughter Act (in England, Wales and Northern Ireland) and the Corporate Homicide Act (in Scotland) 2007. Given royal assent on 26 July that year, it finally came into force on 6 April 2008, almost exactly twenty-one years after the *Herald* disaster. Although there were numerous disasters and workplace deaths throughout that time, it is widely acknowledged that it was the Zeebrugge Disaster that highlighted the need for a change in the law. The government's Health and Safety Executive (HSE) states:

Companies and organisations that take their obligations under health and safety law seriously are not likely to be in breach of the new provisions. Nonetheless, companies and organisations should keep their health and safety management systems under review, in particular, the way in which their activities are managed or organised by senior management.

The 'corporate manslaughter' case concerning the Zeebrugge Disaster failed because the various acts of negligence could not be attributed to any individual who was a 'controlling mind'. The HSE further states:

Prosecutions will be of the corporate body and not individuals, but the liability of directors, board members or other individuals under health and safety law or general criminal law, will be unaffected. And the corporate body itself and individuals can still be prosecuted for separate health and safety offences.

Finally it seems that nobody in the body corporate is immune from prosecution. However, the legislation does not apply to armed forces operations, including peacekeeping and counter-terror work, or to essential hazardous training related to police operations.

The IMO realised that to impose new legislation as a 'one size fits all' policy on the maritime industry every time a tragic incident occurred was not viable, so they developed an international standard of maritime safe working practice and management to regulate themselves. In 1989, two years after the *Herald* disaster, the IMO put forward Resolution A647, which was adopted by the IMO in 1993. The resolution became the *International Management Code for the Safe Operation of Ships and for Pollution Prevention*, known as the ISM Code.

Five years later, the code became mandatory. Essentially, the code addresses ship safety, requiring each vessel to have a procedures manual, and provides for regular internal and external audits to check that procedures are being followed. Based around the Safety Management System (SMS), the document includes instructions and procedures to ensure safe operation of ships; defined levels of authority and lines of communication amongst shore and shipboard personnel; procedures for reporting accidents and non-conformities; procedures to respond to emergencies; and procedures for internal audits and management reviews.

In the wake of the *Herald* disaster, several amendments were made to the SOLAS 1974, which had been in existence since the 1974 Convention in London, attended by representatives from seventy-one countries. Adopted on 21 April 1988, the first amendments came into force on 22 October 1989.

The UK had proposed a series of emergency measures, many based on the findings of the inquiry, designed to prevent a recurrence. They included new regulations, 23-2 and 42-1 of Chapter II-1, intended to improve hull and superstructure damage prevention, indicator monitoring of doors and cargo areas, and on the bridge, CCTV monitoring of the vehicle deck, and to improve supplementary emergency lighting.

Further amendments, adopted on 28 October 1988, came into force on 29 April 1990. They included details of how the stability of damaged passenger ships should be determined, and a requirement for all cargo loading doors to be locked before a ship leaves the berth and to remain closed until the ship has arrived at its next berth. A lightweight (hull, machinery, crew and fittings without fuel and stores) survey was also made compulsory every five years for passenger ships, to ensure their stability is not adversely affected by extra weight or any alterations to the superstructure.

Amendments for the stability of ships in a damaged condition were being prepared before the *Herald* disaster, but were brought forward because fears had been realised. Other amendments concerning the stability of passenger ships in the damaged condition were also adopted. These regulations had been in preparation before the *Herald of Free Enterprise* incident, and their adoption was brought forward due to its relevance to RORO safety.

Despite further adoptions to SOLAS, and amendments to existing regulations being made for the future of ferry safety, several high-profile disasters with heavy loss of life still occurred after the *Herald*.

In 1993, the Polish ferry, *Jan Heweluisz*, capsized and sank in the Baltic Sea, killing fifty-five people.

The deadliest maritime disaster in peacetime Europe happened in 1994, when the MS *Estonia* capsized and sank in heavy seas, after the bow door visor was ripped off by a huge wave. 852 people, and possibly as many as 912, died in the disaster. Urgent revisions to SOLAS 90 were rushed through to address the disaster findings. They included adaptions for a ferry to stay afloat with 50cm (20in) of water on a car deck, new life raft regulations, and new evacuation procedures.

In 2006, the Egyptian RORO ferry MS *al-Salam Boccaccio 98* caught fire in the Red Sea. Water from fighting the fire gathered in the hold and vehicle deck of the ship after the drainage system failed, and the ferry capsized and sank. An estimated 1,020 passengers and crew were killed. The ferry was erroneously reported to be the former Townsend Thoresen ferry *Free Enterprise IV* – it is true that most ferries that had been operated in European waters, and subsequently deemed to be unsafe to do so, were sold off to the Third World.

SOLAS, as of 2013, was still to develop in all of Africa, Mexico, Central America, parts of South America, eastern countries of the Mediterranean (including Greece, Turkey and Cyprus) and all of Asia, except China, Japan, India, Taiwan, South Korea and Hong Kong. Incidentally, the countries that are not yet part of SOLAS are also the poorest, and often where ferry accidents are more prolific.

Clive Garner, head of International Travel Litigation at Irwin Mitchell, represented dozens of victims from the *Costa Concordia* cruise liner disaster off Italy in 2012. Garner said:

All of these disasters could and should have been avoided. As well as financial settlements for the victims, the investigations into each of these tragedies lead to calls for better regulation, and important safety improvements for the design and management of vessels have been made as a result. But rather than reacting after an accident has occurred we want the regulators, including the IMO, to be more proactive in improving safety to avoid deaths and serious injuries rather than merely learning lessons after disasters like these have occurred.

Presently, the Belgian DVI team will be ready to leave for a disaster area in Belgium within six hours. If a disaster involving Belgians occurs abroad, 'Plan *Simonet*' is put into action, backed up by the air force. Members of the Department of Health, the Red Cross, Civil Defence and DVI Teams are sent to the scene. Known as the 'polyvalent' team, it is their job to collect as much information as possible, in co-operation with local authorities, to inform the authorities in Belgium whether further help is required.

Fateful

Speaking in 2013, Philippe Barremaecker had been a 20-year-old conscript working at a desk at Zeebrugge's naval base on the day of the disaster. The next morning, Philippe was called in for disaster duty and remained there until the day the *Herald* was towed away. He recalled being sprayed by spilled fuel as he stood guard at the naval base, watching the helicopters carrying salvage workers and divers leave for the *Herald* wreck site:

> Almost all of our duties were practical jobs from helping to sort out personal belongings and bringing ashore cargo and car wrecks. Sorting out children's clothing was particularly difficult; bringing in the personal belongings to the hangar full of coffins or body bags … you can't imagine what is going on until you see all those victims together. Some of the images will stay with me forever. Let's say that everything happens for a reason, even if this means losing friends or relatives. This may sound a bit odd, but it helps to go on and accept. So, enjoy life while you can and be grateful for what you are and have … we will have learned something and the loss of all these people will not go into history as an 'accident' and be meaningless.

Mike Marten, who was one of seven Royal Navy divers who recovered bodies from the wreck of the *Herald* after she had been raised, was sent to the South of France as part of a NATO exercise with the Fleet Clearance Diving Team in the summer of 1987. He decided to go water skiing while he was off-duty, when he was involved in an accident. Mike broke his neck and was paralysed from the chest down. He spent months in hospital and is now confined to a wheelchair. But he lives a full life, watching his beloved Arsenal at every opportunity and is often involved in wheelchair marathon sponsored events to raise money for people with injuries similar to his own. It wasn't until ten years after he was on board the *Herald* that he realised suddenly what the survivors and victims had gone through. Mike was at the cinema watching James Cameron's *Titanic*, when the scenes of people being trapped and drowning took him back to the ferry capsize. It was only at that moment he fully appreciated the horror of the *Herald of Free Enterprise*.

Jane Hind, who lost her mother, sister and uncle in the disaster, says the loss of her loved ones has brought her immediate family, brother, sister and niece, very close together but has left them all mentally scarred. 'We all look fine from the outside, but have a lot going on inside.'

Remembering the people that they have lost, she says:

I have a picture of them in my mind constantly; my memories of them are as if it were yesterday. I love nothing more than being able to talk about my mum. I don't think there is many a day where I, my brother and sister do not think about them, and we always talk about them when we are together.

I have spent twenty-five years wishing that day had never happened, feeling so guilty, as it should have been me on that ferry, not my sister. At least that way I would have been with my mum at the most terrifying time of her life. She couldn't swim, and I couldn't think of a worse way for her to die. I have spent all these years achieving things and wanting to turn to my mum or phone her to get acceptance. My whole ambition in life has been to become 50 per cent of the woman she was … not easy footsteps to follow in. I have always tried to be strong, when inside I am in turmoil. I can still be driving home sometimes and just feel the tears rolling down my face. I cannot put into words how much I miss them, and life without my mum has been a very hard one. I never had children, but am sure had my mum been here that would have been different. A mum's support is such a big loss. I have always tried to do my best in life, for her. I just wanted her to be proud of me. How do you get over something like that? But I am a great believer that there are so many people out there that are worse off. I try hard to be a good person, but for the first time I can say that I think it affected me more than I would have ever let on to anyone. I have always tried to be strong for everyone around me.

'So how do you cope with something so big and terrible?' asks Tracy Lamy-Edwards. Tracy lost her mother, grandmother, sister and baby nephew on the *Herald*. Tracy campaigned with others to get new legislation for lights on ferry bow doors, the registration of vehicles and cars when sailing by ferry and advocating travel by Eurotunnel. Her militant action for safety enabled her to campaign for seatbelts on school minibuses and coaches, as well as other campaigns to promote safety.

I still get goose bumps and a horrible sensation when I see a picture, or the ferry is mentioned. The orange hull and white boat haunt me in my memories and on occasions, my dreams. But it is a big part of my history, my life and my destiny. It shaped me into being a militant campaigner and an advocate for justice. It moulded me into being a counsellor and having an empathy with people that have also lost. After all this time, it affects the survivors and families on regular occurrences and when people find out, it still shocks. I am proud to be Mrs Lamy-Edwards, as I have the names of both the men I love most in the world, my husband and father.

Writing in 2013, survivor Jan Willis reflected on her life since the disaster:

For me Zeebrugge, whilst a dreadful event, was so life changing, and probably what made me as a person. It brought out the caring, proactive side that had been suppressed through feeling inadequate in my childhood.

Jan joined the Metropolitan Police in the summer of 1988, and served as a detective there and in Cambridgeshire for most of her eleven years with the force. She worked mostly for the Criminal Investigation Department (CID) on murder and trauma type cases:

Since then I have always tried to save the world, probably failing but choosing work that involved child in care advocacy, youth offending, an advocate in secure children's homes and I am a qualified counsellor and family mediator.

Although Jan did not receive any after the disaster, she had counselling over the years whilst training to be a counsellor herself, which included Cruse bereavement care. 'I am excellent in a crisis now, I started practicing early.'

Now married to an airline pilot, Jan moved to Rugby, near Coventry, in 2010 to be near her husband's work, and has two children aged 10 and 13:

Funnily enough, along with mediating in Coventry, I have a job at Rugby College offering pastoral care to BTEC business students, the same course I was doing at the time of the ferry.

I always say that everyone has their 'Zeebrugge' in life, just mine was a pretty big one. Life is a rollercoaster and the fact none of my friends died makes it so different to those who were less fortunate. I think that Zeebrugge has made me live my life to an ultimate full. I have had a career, travelled the world and have a wonderful husband and two beautiful children. That is not to say emotionally I am not damaged by the few hours [during the disaster] and how everyone treated me afterwards.

Jan loves to travel and experience everything – 'as my kids say, mum's done everything! I have travelled many times on ferries, though I will obviously never forget. It has become easier. I have had a very full and interesting life, probably thanks to that day.'

Army Corporal Peter Williamson, who testified about having to force a man off a ladder as he was blocking the escape route for survivors in the water, was killed in a motorcycle crash on 10 July 1989.

Lorry driver Joseph Kay, who had been resting in the cab of his lorry on the vehicle deck and had leapt to safety, lived with the memories of those cries of the desperate people around him who he could not help. It was rumoured that, in 1990, after three years of stress and depression, he jumped from a bridge above the M62 motorway and was killed.

Crewman Nick Delo, died on 28 February 2005, aged 55. He had helped, with other crew members, to pull survivors out of the wrecked ferry.

Steward Ken 'Kiki' Hollingsbee took over the 'Coach and Horses' pub in Canterbury, Kent, in 1991, renaming it the 'Fools and Horses'. He reunited with his childhood sweetheart, Lyn Walker, and after suffering a heart attack in 1992, they moved into the 'Royal Oak' pub in Broad Oak. He had a triple heart bypass in November 2003, but was plagued with chest pains and breathing problems, and died in Ashford in May 2005. Ken saw his eldest son Dylan reach No. 3 in the UK charts only a month before with his partnership group, Bodyrockers, and the song 'I Like The Way (You Move)'.

Richard McKenny had lost his wife Sheila in the disaster. He was persuaded to go to a bereavement support group near to where he lived in St Leonards. He met June, and soon afterwards they married. Richard and June had a very happy and full life, with Richard taking up painting, amongst other hobbies. June recalled fondly one visit to Bruges when she and Richard had stopped to watch a busker who was singing in the street. Richard felt compelled to join the busker and they stood side by side for a few minutes, singing together. Richard died in 2006, aged 83.

Richard's step-daughter, Lynette Carvley, and Lynette's daughter, Becky, were both diagnosed with PTSD later in 1987. They used their compensation money to buy a house together in Hastings. It was a fresh start for both of them. Soon afterwards, Becky fell in love with Jim, the boy next door, and they married in August 1991. Becky now has three children of her own and still lives in Hastings.

Years after the disaster, Lynette suffers nightmares and flashbacks. 'My outlook has changed. Nothing in life seems important except for life itself. Jobs, bills, money have little meaning. Being alive is all important.' Lynnette remarried and moved to Manchester in her native north-west.

Becky fell out with her mother Lynette after the disaster. 'I put a lot of the family trauma down to the disaster. I could have had a better relationship with my mother, and a career, but at least I survived.'

David English's last memory of his mother, Ann, was when he was stood on a chair in the kitchen of their home looking through the window at the snow outside.

She was telling him to be careful. He was only 4 years old when she died aboard the *Herald*. David was brought up by his mother's partner, whom he called dad. At the age of 18, he blew all of his compensation money on drink and drugs, but has since turned his life around, has a young daughter and plans to marry his girlfriend.

Gillian Baddeley was 16 when she lost her mother, stepfather and uncle in the disaster. When she was 17, she met Richard, a friend of her brother's, and they married and had two sons. She insisted her children learned to swim at an early age, just like her mother had done for her, a factor which had helped save Gillian's life in the disaster. She works in a nursing home:

> It's hard not to feel angry. I feel I've been robbed of my loved ones. It wasn't a natural disaster, there were mistakes made. Mum should have seen me grow up, should have seen my boys become men. But being angry won't bring her back. I still talk to her most days, which is a great comfort. Looking back, I think surviving that day made me a stronger person. When I've had trials and tribulations I think, if I can get through that, I can get through anything.

Sara Helkvist lost her brother Steven, who was a cook aboard the *Herald*:

> The pain of losing my brother changed me forever. My mother has never been the same and suffers anxiety, especially about my welfare. Live life for today, enjoy yourself and don't worry about the future. It could all be gone tomorrow. My mother is the opposite, she's terrified of everything. I just want this horrible event to be remembered and the people that lost their lives never to be forgotten. The victims need to be seen as real people with real lives.

Lynne Hawkins will never forget her friend, Heidi Pinnells, who was lost in the disaster:

> I met Heidi in 1981 when we moved in a few doors down from the Pinnells family. We soon became best friends. Even though we went to different primary schools, we were inseparable. We went to St John's Ambulance once a week and had spent the evening laughing as we bandaged each other up, getting told off because we had arrived on our roller boots, knocking everyone over! My fondest memory of Heidi was when we were sitting in her bedroom listening to music and chatting. Heidi suddenly said she wanted to tell me that I was like a sister to her and we will never be apart; we made plans to travel when we were older. She was my best friend. In 1985 we had to move because of my dad's work. I remember all those things we said to each other on the day before we moved. That will stay with me forever. I miss you Heidi, I miss growing up with you and experiencing life together. I miss your laugh and the way you played the recorder terribly! Always in my heart forever. Your best friend.

Disaster Action was formed in 1991 by Maurice de Rohan, chairman of the *Herald* Families Association, who lost his daughter in the disaster. Based on the experiences of survivors and bereaved from twenty-seven disasters, mainly occurring in the UK but also involving British subjects internationally, the organisation aims to 'help create a health and safety culture in which disasters are less likely to occur, to offer guidance and support to others who find themselves similarly affected and to raise awareness of the needs of survivors and bereaved'. It was years of constant campaigning by Disaster Action that helped bring about the Corporate Manslaughter Act of 2008. The organisation is mainly funded by the Joseph Rowntree Charitable Trust.

The Patterson Donnelly Memorial Award was set up to commemorate two 'highly professional' LGV drivers lost on the *Herald*. Cavewood Transport, for whom Paul Donnelly and Neil Patterson worked, set up the award to assist community projects. One example of such a scheme was in 1995, 'How Could it Have Happened to Jock?', a play written and performed by the Momentum Theatre Company based at Little Chalfont. The play toured schools in Buckinghamshire teaching children the rules of road safety.

Survivor Brian Bunker's wife, Diane's funeral service was held in St Peter's Italian Church, Clerkenwell, in London, where the couple had married. Brian is half Italian and his Roman Catholic faith helped him through those harrowing times after the loss of his family. He was also helped by the British Army, in particular the mates who rallied round him. In those early days he particularly remembers Diane de Winter, a Belgian volunteer who was very helpful, in the immediate aftermath. He was also helped by the Rev. Michael Masterston of Leatherhead. Brian carried on with his military career and was sent to Hong Kong to learn Chinese for two years. He left the army in 1989, and chose not to talk about the disaster.

Brian does not believe that justice was done and still feels very bitter towards the ferry company. He decided to set up a fund to commemorate the memory of his wife and daughter lost in the disaster. He enlisted the help of family friends, the internationally renowned ballet dancer and actress Moira Shearer, who was married to the broadcaster Ludovic Kennedy, and their son Alastair, with whom he had served in the Gurkhas. Amongst those they approached was Sir Jeffrey Sterling, the chairman of P&O, who, after the company's derisory compensation offer, granted them a few thousand pounds.

The Diane and Nadine Bunker Trust was set up in December 1994 by Brian Bunker, in honour of the wife and daughter he lost in the disaster. It is a subsidiary of the Brigade of Gurkhas Education and Welfare Fund, and is controlled by the same trustees, but its funding and investments are separate. The trust's single objective is to provide relief for the sick, disabled, handicapped or infirm children of members of the Brigade of Gurkhas being resettled in Nepal. Currently the trust provides £5,000 annually in grants for medicines, provision of specialist treatment, home help and special needs such as speech therapy. Presently, the needs of fifteen children are closely monitored by the SSAFA nurse in Kathmandu. The Gurkhas are close to Brian's heart as he served with them for four years during his army career. His wife Diane would have approved of the trust.

Brian doesn't talk about the disaster as he still feels enormous guilt for not being with Diane and Nadine at the worst time of their lives. Every year, on his behalf, Father Carmello di Giovanni says Masses for Diane and Nadine at St Peter's Italian Church on Clerkenwell Road, London.

The disaster that befell the *Herald of Free Enterprise* outside Zeebrugge harbour on 6 March 1987 killed at least 193 people, all but seven of them British. At the time of writing (May 2014), the death toll on the *Herald* remains the worst British loss of life in a single incident since the Second World War.

SURNAME	TITLE	FIRST NAME	AGE	RESIDENCE	STATUS	NATIONALITY
ALLEN	Mr	Barry	48	Folkestone, Kent	Crew	British
BADDELEY	Mrs	Eileen	41	Wallasey, Merseyside	Passenger	British
BADDELEY	Mr	Keith	54	Wallasey, Merseyside	Passenger	British
BARNARD	Mr	Richard	38	Deal, Kent	Crew	British
BIRTLES	Mr	Lee	38	River, Kent	Crew	British
BLANCHARD	Mr	Norman	49	Hullbridge, Essex	Passenger	British
BOATWRIGHT	Mr	Robert	36	Feltham, Middlesex	Passenger	British
BONNER	Mrs	Daphne	41	Gravesend, Kent	Passenger	British
BONNER	Mr	Terence	42	Gravesend, Kent	Passenger	British
BRAGANZA	Miss	Jennifer	20	Enfield, north London	Passenger	British
BRAY	Master	Jody	7	Teynham, Kent	Passenger	British
BRAY	Mr	John	32	Teynham, Kent	Passenger	British
BRAZIL	Mr	Gerard	43	Dover, Kent	Crew	British
BUCKLEY	Mrs	Carole	37	Yeovil, Somerset	Passenger	British
BUCKLEY	Miss	Nichola	13	Yeovil, Somerset	Passenger	British
BUCKLEY	Mr	Patrick	44	Yeovil, Somerset	Passenger	British

BUNKER	Mrs	Diane	29	Enfield, London/ Bielefeld Germany	Passenger	British
BUNKER	Miss	Nadine	9 months	Enfield, London/ Bielefeld Germany	Passenger	British
BURT	Ms	Lynda	38	Dover, Kent	Crew	British
BURTHE	Mr	Daniel	42	Folkestone, Kent	Crew	British
BUSHAWAY	Miss	Laura	12	Milton Keynes, Buckinghamshire	Passenger	British
BUSHAWAY	Mr	Ronald	63	Milton Keynes, Buckinghamshire	Passenger	British
BUSHAWAY	Mrs	Rosina	59	Milton Keynes, Buckinghamshire	Passenger	British
BUTLER	Mr	Glen	25	Folkestone, Kent	Crew	British
CAIN	Mrs	Astrid	55	Feltham, Middlesex	Passenger	British
CAIN	Ms	Janice	32	Feltham, Middlesex	Passenger	British
CALDER	Mr	Percy	45	Sholden, Kent	Crew	British
COCKRAM	Miss	Linda	24	Wembley, NW London	Passenger	British
CROFTON	Major	Edward	52	River, Kent	Passenger	British
CRONE	Mr	Robert	48	St Margaret's, Kent	Crew	British
CROSS	Mrs	Margaret	42	Windsor, Berkshire	Passenger	British

DARBY	Mr	Stanley	57	Hawkinge, Kent	Crew	British
DAVIES	Mr	Wayne	25	Caerphilly, Glamorgan	Passenger	British
DELAFIELD	Mr	Brian	47	Maidstone, Kent	Passenger	British
DELAFIELD	Mrs	Carol	43	Maidstone, Kent	Passenger	British
DELAFIELD	Miss	Sharon	17	Maidstone, Kent	Passenger	British
DISBURY	Mr	David	37	Dover, Kent	Crew	British
DOCKRILL	Master	Andrew	8	Stanford-le-Hope, Essex	Passenger	British
DOCKRILL	Miss	Emma	17	Stanford-le-Hope, Essex	Passenger	British
DOCKRILL	Ms	Patricia	41	Stanford-le-Hope, Essex	Passenger	British
DONNELLY	Mr	Paul	24	Southampton	Passenger	British
DOWIE	Ms	Carol	32	Chatham, Kent	Passenger	British
DOWIE	Mrs	Irene	65	Chatham, Kent	Passenger	British
DOWNMAN	Mr	Paul	22	Stanford-le-Hope, Essex	Passenger	British
DYER	Mr	Clayton	18	Whitfield, Kent	Crew	British
EADES	Mr	Brian	47	St Margaret's, Kent	Crew	British
EDWARDS	Mrs	Maureen	48	Mansfield, Nottinghamshire	Passenger	British
ENGLISH	Ms	Ann	29	Strood, Kent	Passenger	British

EVANS	Mr	Graham	47	St Margaret's, Kent	Crew	British
EVERARD	Mr	Thomas	24	Co. Meath, Ireland	Passenger	Irish
EWELL	Mr	Steven	23	Folkestone, Kent	Crew	British
FINNEGAN	Miss	Louise	20	St Neots, Cambridgeshire	Passenger	British
FINNEGAN	Mr	Roy	41	Wood Green, north London	Passenger	British
FIRBANK	Mr	Alan	21	Doncaster, South Yorkshire	Passenger	British
FOX	Master	Andrew	11	Maidstone, Kent	Passenger	British
FRAME	Mr	Terence	34	Deal, Kent	Crew	British
GAILLARD	Mrs	Alison	27	St John's Wood, NW London	Passenger	Australian
GAILLARD	Mr	Francis	27	St John's Wood, NW London	Passenger	British
GAYLARD	Mr	John	36	St Alban's, Hertfordshire/Germany	Passenger	British
GLENDENNING	Mr	Christopher	41	Cheriton, Kent	Passenger	British
GOUGH	Mr	Nicholas	19	Aylesham, Kent	Crew	British
GUDGEON	Mrs	Eileen	48	Runwell, Essex	Passenger	British

Surname	Title	First name	Age	Location	Role	Nationality
GUTWURCEL	Mr	Julius	78	Sanderstead, Surrey	Passenger	Austrian
HANEY	Mr	Geoffrey	30	Chorley, Manchester / Deal, Kent	Crew	British
HARRIS	Mr	David	24	Plymouth, Devon / London	Passenger	British
HARRIS	Mrs	Lita	34	West Malling, Kent	Passenger	British
HARRIS	Mr	Nicholas	39	Gillingham, Kent	Passenger	British
HARTLEY	Mrs	Elsie	65	Cotmanhay, Derbyshire	Passenger	British
HARTLEY	Mrs	Hazel	38	Cotmanhay, Derbyshire	Passenger	British
HARTLEY	Mr	Joseph	65	Cotmanhay, Derbyshire	Passenger	British
HARTLEY	Mr	Richard	31	Cotmanhay, Derbyshire	Passenger	British
HAWLEY	Mrs	Patricia	40	Cotmanhay, Derbyshire	Passenger	British
HAYWARD	Mr	Dean	27	Deal, Kent	Crew	British
HEAD	Mr	Barry	25	St Mary's Bay, Kent	Crew	British
HEARD	Mr	Robert	36	Coventry, West Midlands	Passenger	British
HELKVIST	Mr	Stephen	24	Cardiff, Wales/Dover, Kent	Crew	British
HIGGINS	Mr	Richard	20	Wallington, Surrey	Crew	British
HILLING	Mr	Peter	47	Swindon, Wiltshire/Germany	Passenger	British

HINTON	Mr	Simon	32	Basingstoke, Hampshire	Passenger	British
HINTON	Mrs	Susan	36	Basingstoke, Hampshire	Passenger	British
HOBBS	Mr	Richard	23	Aylesham, Kent	Crew	British
HOOD	Mr	Peter	51	Dover, Kent	Passenger	British
HORTON	Miss	Rebecca	23 days	Canvey Island, Essex	Passenger	British
HORTON	Mrs	Sharon	28	Canvey Island, Essex	Passenger	British
HOWARD	Mrs	Anna	46	East Ham, east London	Passenger	Irish
HOWARD	Miss	Catherine	21	East Ham, east London	Passenger	British
HURLEY	Mr	Stuart	17	Yeovil, Somerset	Passenger	British
IBBOTSON-GALE	Mr	Maurice	36	Scunthorpe, Humberside	Passenger	British
JACKSON	Mrs	Ivy	66	Burton-on-Trent, Staffordshire	Passenger	British
JEFFERSON	Mrs	Patricia	38	Portslade, Sussex	Passenger	British
JEFFERSON	Mr	William	40	Portslade, Sussex	Passenger	British
JOHNSON	Mr	Edward	17	Milton Keynes, Buckinghamshire	Passenger	British
JOHNSON	Mrs	Kathleen	43	Milton Keynes, Buckinghamshire	Passenger	British

Surname	Title	First name	Age	Location	Passenger/Crew	Nationality
KENNY	Mr	Stephen	33	Gillingham, Kent	Passenger	British
LAMB	Ms	Brenda	31	Raynes Park, south London	Passenger	British
LAMY	Mrs	Frances	42	Bow, east London	Passenger	British
LAMY	Miss	Kim	20	Bow, east London	Passenger	British
LAMY	Master	Steven	11 months	Bow, east London	Passenger	British
LAMY	Mrs	Victoria Maud	75	Bow, east London	Passenger	British
LAWRENCE	Mr	Christopher	49	Lancashire	Passenger	British
LAWSON	Mr	Ian	24	Dover, Kent	Crew	British
LENNOX	Mr	Graham	38	Stanford-le-Hope, Essex	Passenger	British
LENNOX	Master	Mark	13	Stanford-le-Hope, Essex	Passenger	British
LLOYD	Mr	Gary	19	Leicestershire	Passenger	British
LOPEZ	Ms	Shirley	40	Caterham, Surrey	Passenger	British
MACKAY	Mr	Angus	43	Deal, Kent	Crew	British
MALONEY	Mr	Terence	55	Hitchin, Hertfordshire	Passenger	British
MANTLE	Mr	Robert	40	Deal, Kent	Crew	British
MARSHALL	Mr	Paul	34	Rochester, Kent	Passenger	British
MARTIN	Ms	Mildred	61	Basingstoke, Hampshire	Passenger	British

MARTIN	Mr	Peter	53	Lancing, west Sussex	Passenger	British
MASON	Mrs	Catherine	28	Golborne, Lancashire/ Germany	Passenger	British
MASSEY	Miss	Loranda	25	Feltham, Middlesex	Passenger	British
McKENNY	Mrs	Sheila	54	Hastings, East Sussex	Passenger	British
MEDHURST	Mr	Alan	25	Dover, Kent	Crew	British
MILLGATE	Mr	John	26	Dover, Kent	Passenger	British
MOAT	Mr	Ivor	36	Canterbury, Kent	Crew	British
MOY	Mr	Christopher	29	Cheriton, Kent	Passenger	British
OLDFIELD	Mr	Edward	54	Dover, Kent (of Southampton)	Crew	British
PARSONS	Mrs	Kiran	28	Mansfield, Nottinghamshire	Passenger	British
PASHLEY	Mr	Hugh	37	Farnborough, Hampshire	Passenger	British
PATTERSON	Mr	Neil	47	Chesham, Buckinghamshire	Passenger	British
PAYNE	Miss	Nicola	20	Hastings, East Sussex	Passenger	British
PEACH	Mr	Thomas	42	Rugeley, Staffordshire	Passenger	British
PELLING	Mrs	Margaret	58	Beckenham, Kent	Passenger	British

Surname	Title	First name	Age	Location	Role	Nationality
PENNICARD	Miss	Lea	18	Essex	Passenger	British
PERKINS	Mr	Darren	21	Hastings, East Sussex	Passenger	British
PERKINS	Mr	Simon	18	Hastings, East Sussex	Passenger	British
PICINCO	Ms	Betina	49	Cleveland, Co. Durham	Passenger	British
PIERCE	Miss	Emily	4	Sittingbourne, Kent	Passenger	British
PINNELLS	Miss	Fiona	20	Leighton Buzzard, Bedfordshire	Passenger	British
PINNELLS	Miss	Heidi	13	Leighton Buzzard, Bedfordshire	Passenger	British
QUESTED	Mr	Egerton	39	Eythorne, Kent	Crew	British
RAY	Miss	Karen	22	Wembley Park, NW London	Passenger	British
REDMAN	Mr	Stephen	30	Feltham, Middlesex	Passenger	British
REEDER	Miss	Jacqueline	16	Dunstable, Bedfordshire	Passenger	British
REYNOLDS	Mr	Jonathan	19	Addersbury, Oxfordshire	Passenger	British
RICHARDS	Mrs	Marie/Merna	31	Canterbury, Kent	Crew	Mauritian
RODGERS	Mr	Ernest	52	Dover, Kent	Crew	British
SANTER	Mr	David	48	Folkestone, Kent	Crew	British
SAUNDERS	Mr	Michael	41	Gillingham, Kent	Passenger	British

Surname	Title	First name	Age	Location	Status	Nationality
SAXBY	Mr	David	44	Luton, Bedfordshire	Passenger	British
SCHMIDT	Mr	Wilhelm	34	Raynes Park, south London	Passenger	British
SCOTT	Mr	David	20	Cheshire	Passenger	British
SCULTHORPE	Mr	Wayne	19	Leicestershire	Passenger	British
SEELY	Mr	John	62	Swanley, Kent	Passenger	British
SEELY	Mrs	Joyce	61	Swanley, Kent	Passenger	British
SHERRATT	Mr	Norman	40	Woodchurch, Kent	Passenger	British
SIMPSON	Mrs	Patricia	39	Welwyn Garden City, Hertfordshire	Passenger	British
SINGHAL	Mr	Sadersham Lal	57	Nottinghamshire	Passenger	British
SKIPPEN	Mr	Michael	29	Canterbury, Kent	Crew	British
SMITH	L. Cpl	Brian	29	Manchester/Germany	Passenger	British
SMITH	Mrs	Donna–Marie	27	Manchester/Germany	Passenger	British
SMITH	Mrs	Mary	44	Essex	Passenger	British
SMITH	Master	Michael	4	Germany	Passenger	British
SMITH	Mr	Richard	33	Gillingham, Kent	Passenger	British
SMITH	Ms	Rosemary	25	Wembley, NW London	Passenger	British

Surname	Title	First name	Age	Location	Role	Nationality
SMITH	Master	Sean	21 months	Manchester/Germany	Passenger	British
SMITH	Mr	Stephen	33	Herne Bay, Kent	Passenger	British
SOPP	Mr	Barry	39	Bedfordshire	Passenger	British
SPINK	Mr	Anthony	41	Whitfield, Kent	Crew	British
SPOONER	Mr	Martin	31	Enfield, north London	Passenger	British
SPOONER	Mr	Neil	37	Essex	Passenger	British
SPRULES	Mr	Stephen	17	Dover, Kent	Crew	British
STANYER	Major	James	48	Farnborough, Hampshire	Passenger	British
STEDMAN	Cpl	Alan	31	Germany	Passenger	British
SWIETOCHOWSKI	Mr	Pitek	33	Ealing, west London	Crew	Polish
TAYLOR	Miss	Beverley	36	Swindon, Wiltshire/Germany	Passenger	British
TAYLOR	Mrs	Carol	30	South-east London	Passenger	British
TAYLOR	Mr	Stephen	34	South-east London	Passenger	British
THIRKETTLE	Mr	Donald	57	Enfield, north London	Passenger	British
THOMAS	L. Cpl	Gary	24	Huyton, Merseyside	Passenger	British
THUMWOOD	Mr	Christopher	30	Broadstairs, Kent	Crew	British

Surname	Title	First name	Age	Location	Status	Nationality
TURNER	Mrs	Janet	30	Meopham, Kent	Passenger	British
TURNER	Mr	Steven	38	Meopham, Kent	Passenger	British
VIRTUE	Mr	Colin	46	Bromley, Kent	Passenger	British
VIRTUE	Mrs	Jacqueline	44	Bromley, Kent	Passenger	British
WARWICK	Mr	John	29	Folkestone, Kent	Crew	British
WATERS	Mr	Alan	61	Windsor, Berkshire	Passenger	British
WATERS	Mrs	Molly	56	Windsor, Berkshire	Passenger	British
WELLINGTON-FRAY	Miss	Dolvis	28	West Norwood, south London	Passenger	British
WHITWORTH	Mr	David	38	Maghull, Merseyside	Passenger	British
WIELICZKO	Miss	Malgosia	22	South London	Passenger	Polish
WILSON	Mr	Derek	61	Sheffield, South Yorkshire	Passenger	British
WILSON	Miss	Melanie	23	Wembley, NW London	Passenger	British
WOODALL	Mr	Alan	24	Luton, Bedfordshire	Passenger	British
WOODHOUSE	Mr	Derek	62	Dagenham, Essex	Passenger	British
WOODHOUSE	Mrs	Nora	54	Dagenham, Essex	Passenger	British
WORSLEY-SMITH	Mr	Kevin	25	Dover, Kent	Crew	British

WREN	Mrs	Betty	32	Twickenham, Middlesex	Passenger	British
WREN	Mr	Stephen	32	Twickenham, Middlesex	Passenger	British
WYATT	Miss	Jacqueline	24	London (of Plymouth, Devon)	Passenger	British
YOUNG	Ms	Christine	32	Sittingbourne, Kent	Passenger	British

GLOSSARY AND ABBREVIATIONS

AB	Able Seaman
Aft	At or near the stern (rear)
Athens Convention	Adopted 1974, settling liability for damage suffered by passengers and their luggage carried in a seagoing vessel
Ballast	Heavy material used to stablise a vessel
BAOR	British Army of the Rhine
Bonn Agreements	Mechanism by which North Sea states and the European community work together in combating pollution in the North Sea
Bow	At or near the front
Bow spade	Lip on the front of a vessel that reduces drag by cutting through waves
Bridge	Control room from where a vessel is steered
Bulkhead	Vertical partition or wall in a vessel
Cable (measure)	$\frac{1}{10}$ of a nautical mile or 185m long
CEPO	County Emergency Planning Officer
CHU	Centre Hospitalier Regional Universitaire
Combinators	Mechanism controlling proper combination of pitch and shaft speed of propellers
DPP	Director of Public Prosecutions
Draught	Depth of a vessel's keel below surface (especially when loaded)
Draught reading	Reading of the keel depth of a vessel
DVI	Disaster Victim Identification team
EF/L	European Ferries/Limited
Fore	Front part of a vessel
Free liquid effect	Tendency of liquids to slosh about or to move in response to the shift of a vessel
Freeboard	Vertical distance between the sea and top edges of the deck

Galley	Where food is prepared and cooked
Harbour stations	Call for on-duty crew members to report to their respective posts
HAU	Herald Assistance Unit
Helm	Steering mechanism for a vessel
Herald Link	Quarterly booklet published by the HAU to connect survivors and relatives
HFA	Herald Families Association
HSE	Health and Safety Executive
Hull	Frame or body of a vessel; the superstructure
IMCO	International Maritime Consultative Organisation
IMO	International Maritime Organisation
Knot	Speed over water of 1 nautical mile per hour
Link span	Vehicle ramp used to drive onto ferry
List	Tilt to one side
MAIB	Marine Accident Investigation Branch
Manifest	Customs document listing passenger and cargo aboard vessel
MCDO	Mine Warfare and Clearance Diving Officer, Royal Navy
MES	Marine Escape System
Mess	Usually dining room where off-duty crew members eat and relax
Midships	At or near the centre of a vessel
MRT	Medical Rescue Team
Nautical mile	Equal to 1.151 statute (land) miles; 6076.1ft or 1.852km
NUMAST	National Union of Marine, Aviation and Shipping Transport officers
NUS	National Union of Seaman
Pitch	Motion of a vessel, causing fore and aft ends to rise and fall
Port	Left-hand side of a vessel when facing forward
PTSD	Post Traumatic Stress Disorder
Rampplan	Belgium's disaster plan
Ramptoerist	'Disaster tourist', known in Britain as 'rubber-necker'
RHA	Road Haulage Association
RNLI	Royal National Lifeboat Institution
RORO	Roll-On, Roll-Off; applicable to ferries where vehicles drive on one end and exit the other
SAR	Search and Rescue
SMS	Safety Management System
SOLAS	Safety of Life At Sea
Starboard	Right-hand side of a vessel when facing forward
Stern	Rear part of a vessel
TGWU	Transport and General Workers' Union
Trim	Relationship of ship's hull to the waterline
TSSA	Transport Salaried Staff's Association

URS   Unie Van Redding en Sleepdienst; leading towage and salvage
                 company for all Dutch and Belgian ports on the River Scheldt
VHF   Very High Frequency; radio frequency
Watertight   Doors and bulkheads designed to keep water in or out
Weathertight   Applies to doors and bulkheads designed to prevent ingress of
                 water from sides exposed to the weather
WINTEX   NATO exercise that was held every two years to test how prepared
                 their administration was for attack from the Soviet Union during
                 the Cold War. The last exercise was in 1987, at the time of the
                 Herald disaster, as the Berlin Wall fell two years later

BIBLIOGRAPHY

Newspapers

Birmingham Daily News
Daily Express
Daily Mail
Daily Telegraph
East Kent Mercury
Express and Star
Glasgow Herald
Independent
Irish Independent
London Daily News
Mail on Sunday
Melton Times
News of the World

New York Times
Northants Evening Telegraph
People
Southern Evening Echo
Sun
Sunday Independent
Sunday Mirror
Sunday Times
Sunday Today
The Times
Today
Yorkshire Evening Post
Yorkshire Post

Periodicals & Magazines

Civil Protection, No. 3, summer 1987
Cycling Weekly, 12 March 1987
Health Services International, No. 2, April 1988
Ja, No. 12, 10 March 1987
Paris Match, 20 March 1987
Pick Me Up, no date
Trucking International, May 1988
Tug, No. 45, Smit International 1987
Woman's Own, no date

Websites

Disaster Action, www.disasteraction.org.uk
Dover Ferry Photos, www.doverferryphotosforums.co.uk
Kent Online, www.kentonline.co.uk
Shipbreaking (Robin des Bois), www.robindebois.org/english/shipbreaking
TruckNet, roundtable.truck.net

Booklets & Newsletters

Debate in Parliament (Hansard, 9 March 1987)
Herald Link (Herald Assistance Unit)
Report of Court no. 8074, Department of Transport Formal Investigation
Sea Breezes (Mannin Media Group)
The Crew's Story (National Union of Seamen, April 1987)

Books

Homewood, S., *Zeebrugge: A Hero's Story* (Bloomsbury, 1989)
Vandenbussche, F., *Raise the Herald* (Aksis, 1988)

INDEX